T0380628

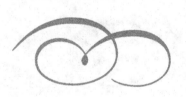

SAF
Simplified
Self
Awareness
Formulas

The Rosetta Stone for humans translates our *Symptoms*

Kathy M. Scogna & Joseph R. Scogna, Jr.

BALBOA
PRESS
A DIVISION OF HAY HOUSE

Copyright © 2019 by Kathy M. Scogna

All rights reserved. No part of this book may be used or reproduced by any means, graphic, electronic, or mechanical, including photocopying, recording, taping or by any information storage retrieval system without the written permission of the author except in the case of brief quotations embodied in critical articles and reviews.

This book contains portions of research, manuscripts, and computer programs from the Scogna Library files and is being presented anew, so that new generations might comprehend the importance and share the vision of this life-affirming research and body of knowledge.

SAF® is a registered trademark. Its use signifies this is the authorized version of Scogna research and work.

For information on other books, on training practitioners, and on upcoming workshops, write: kathy@scogna.com

Balboa Press books may be ordered through booksellers or by contacting:

Balboa Press
A Division of Hay House
1663 Liberty Drive
Bloomington, IN 47403
www.balboapress.com
1 (877) 407-4847

Because of the dynamic nature of the Internet, any web addresses or links contained in this book may have changed since publication and may no longer be valid. The views expressed in this work are solely those of the author and do not necessarily reflect the views of the publisher, and the publisher hereby disclaims any responsibility for them.

Print information available on the last page.

ISBN: 978-1-9822-0573-7 (sc)
ISBN: 978-1-9822-0574-4 (e)

Library of Congress Control Number: 2018906676

Balboa Press rev. date: 07/12/2019

TO THE READER: The purpose of this book is to educate. The information within these pages reflects the work of Joseph R. Scogna, Jr., which includes published and unpublished books and manuscripts, audio and videotapes of seminars, plus the SAF and the Life Energy computing programs and interpretations for chain deciphering.

The author and the publisher are not liable for the misconception or misuse of any information provided. The author and publisher have neither liability nor responsibility to any person or entity with respect to any loss, damage, or injury, caused or alleged to be caused, directly or indirectly, by the educational information in this book.

THIS BOOK is not a medical manual nor should it be used to diagnose disease or to prescribe drugs. The information is presented here for those who want to enlighten themselves and help others to understand their life more fully. It is educational in nature, in order to help the Reader make informed holistic decisions about healthy living.

REMEMBER, our health, wellness and lifestyle choices are and have always been our own responsibility. The Reader is urged to evaluate his or her own health status and unique set of circumstances before using any of the information in this book. If disease, chronic illness, or continuing symptoms of any sort are present, the Reader is urged to seek the proper medical or health care practitioner before beginning any health, nutritional or spiritual quest.

Contents

Preface

For at least the last 5,000 years of recorded history, medicine and spirituality were aligned in natural philosophy, which was used and followed in all cultures around the world. While many Asians followed the tenets of Lao Tzu, who wrote down the ancient teachings into the *I Ching*, the Greeks followed the study of the humors, the progression a disease takes as experienced by symptomatology. In these early natural philosophies, illness was not considered a specific disease but rather a collection of symptoms brought on by an imbalance. Once the imbalance was corrected, harmony would be restored; that was the purpose of healing in those times.

With the invention of the microscope in Europe in the late 1500s, the formerly invisible became visible, and a new world opened up, causing a schism to occur within natural philosophy. Medicine and science took a sharp turn on the path to address only what was visible (1% of reality) leaving philosophy and spirituality to grapple with the invisible.

Our base of knowledge is greater today than in the past, but are we smarter than the ancients? Of the writings that remain, it would appear we have lost something dynamic - our will to know ourselves as a composite of body, mind, and spirit, fully ensconced in the visible and the invisible realms.

While the microscope has been justly heralded for its benefits to mankind, it has also led to our downfall as perceptual beings. No longer are we allowed to intuitively know and understand life or explore our spiritual selves with our vast but invisible abilities. Knowledge must now be *seen* for it to be true, and that duty of seeing and diagnosing has been relegated to the doctor and lab technician with the microscope. We have lost our capacity to understand the invisible, which makes up 99% of existence! Instead, we have become patients, waiting for the doctor to give a title to our ailment and then bombard us with the latest drugs and coal tar-derived medicines. We never hear a word about balance. Anyone who even whispers the word "balance" is dismissed as a quack and is perhaps driven out.

Joseph R. Scogna, Jr. was not one to accept the status quo. He was able to peer down the time track of humanity looking for energetic solutions to the troubles of humans, their symptoms, and their imbalances. On this mental trek, Joseph took with him his vast understanding of cosmic and atomic energy. He applied this to the studies of the past, specifically symptomatology as found in the humors of the Greeks, in homeopathy, and in the balance of the *I Ching*. He used philosophical reflection and various modern machines to define the electroplasmic field (EPF) around living beings - the human energy field, Life Energy, the chi that we all possess. He was able to codify the metabolic connections of body, mind, and spirit. He dismissed the word "patient," brought back the word "balance," and has given humankind a modern day natural philosophy that incorporates the visible and the invisible. With SAF, Joe Scogna reignited the role of balance and harmony in the healing endeavor, and created a new language in the process.

SAF (the Self Awareness Formulas) is the result of Joseph Scogna's research into symptomatology and our metabolic connections. We can learn to speak this ancient-future language, built into our DNA. We can listen in to our symptoms and their chatter, which tell a story of traits and behavior patterns, and when these began. It is enlightening! The reader is encouraged to discover and then increase his or her awareness level, for it is through self knowledge that we grow and evolve. It is through self awareness that we can bring about balance in our lives. It must begin with us! The balance and harmony we create in our own lives is much like the butterfly effect; as small as we may think that process is, this personal work will create a ripple, which will eventually affect all mankind.

-- Kathy M. Scogna

A Quick Tour on How to Use this Book

This book has been designed to help you discover for yourself what the Self Awareness Formulas have to offer. SAF is the practical use of the theories and writings of Joseph R. Scogna Jr., who was a pioneer in this field.

Our health and well being have always been our responsibility. But what are we to do if we cannot see the cause of our problems? The SAF method is a tool we can use to better understand ourselves and our loved ones. We can now see and grasp the Cause and Effect in our daily life, which brings us back into the balance we all seek.

Our symptoms do mean something. These are expressions of the body, and are trying to tell us something. The question is: Are we listening?

With this method, you will discover a new language, an ancient-future speak as our symptom chatter, a sophisticated communication link, is translated from 23 organ and gland systems. You will learn how to listen in, find what your symptoms mean, and most importantly, you'll learn how to dissolve old patterns and make positive changes in your life. In SAF, we like to say you'll learn to face your dragons, those unknown causes of a situation you are in today. By utilizing specific techniques, each of us can overcome emotional traumatic stumbling blocks, and at the same time greatly enhance our own telepathic powers.

SAF will present an opportunity for you to see your situation in a new light, and then, something magical can happen. A spark of understanding occurs – you will have an AH-HA moment. When this occurs, energy is released, and the path for you opens– it is transformative!

Whatever problem areas you have can be addressed with self awareness and self knowledge. If you have any problem *in* your life, this means it is *in* your system. Doesn't it make sense that the solution would be found *inside* your system, too? The trick has always been: how do I find my answers?

Throughout this book and with this new language of translated symptom chatter, you'll learn how the mind works, and how unresolved traumas from the past are still influencing you in the present time. You'll learn how and why this particular self awareness program is so personal and why its solutions are so effective.

It is recommended that you read *SAF Simplified* completely to get a working understanding of the theory behind SAF, why and how it works. If you are adventurous, you may certainly work on a chain sequence yourself; Chapter 6 will give you some tips for doing so. However, keep in mind the interpretation you first complete will be on an introductory level, such as "Spot ran home."

It would be far better and wiser to seek out an SAF trained professional who is versed in the nuances of SAF chain reading, in its language, and in the techniques we use for emotional release. Certified practitioners have access to many different interpretations through their own SAF training, protocols, and studies. Or, perhaps you would consider become trained yourself, see page 225 for details.

SAF personal work can be easy and fun; and it is always interesting! But more importantly, it will help you change your life.

We are excited you've picked up this book. You are about to depart on an amazing and interesting excursion, one of self-discovery and adventure. When you're ready to depart on this fascinating journey, simply turn the page and begin reading.

> "You cannot teach a man anything – you can only help him to find it within himself."
> --Galileo

Chapter 1

SAF: A Light in the Darkness

What Is SAF?

SAF stands for Self Awareness Formulas. It refers to a precise formula, an algorithm, for increasing self-knowledge about our life, our business, our health, our emotions, our past, and the role our past is still playing in our lives today. The idea is to improve our life, to move through any blocks we may find so that we can create the lives we envision. When we are lost, and this does happen to us from time to time in life, SAF is the road map we need to follow to find our way back.

The SAF formulas are part of the collective work written by Joseph R. Scogna Jr., a brilliant researcher and prolific writer. He was able to take a step back and observe the workings of the greater universe and our human place in it; the macro and the micro, which can be written thus: as above, so below. In his published and unpublished manuscripts, books, articles, audio and videotaped teaching seminars, and training materials, Scogna touched on and cross-connected bioenergetics; psychology; Western medicine; sound, color and vibration; traditional Chinese and Asian medicine; acupuncture; nutrition and naturopathy; quantum physics; herbs; and homeopathy, to name a few. He was so far ahead of his time that his holistic health evaluations, questionnaires, and various computer and computing programs have no comparison to what is out there for us, even today.

He created the science of SAF. This is truly the science of healing for future humanity. The purpose of SAF is to increase the awareness of every man, woman, and child on many levels, always encompassing the body, the mind, and the spirit. This is accomplished through symptom awareness, whether physical, mental, emotional, spiritual, or related to business and family issues.

In the Beginning

At the very first seminar on SAF in 1980, those in attendance were absolutely floored by the information gleaned from a simple questionnaire. Even Scogna, who created it - mostly to help himself - was surprised. He was heard to mutter under his breath, "Gee, I didn't think it could do it *this* quickly for so many."

What Did SAF Do?

The first thing SAF did was to take the mystery out of symptoms by unmasking them. After the simple questionnaire had been completed and the answers decoded, much to the surprise of those in attendance, Scogna was able to tell each person

A - What conditions were manifesting in the present day (the Effect)

B - What situations had occurred before the present day condition (the Cause), and

C - Based on mathematical probability and the assumption that no action was taken, what conditions were likely to appear in the future

The second thing SAF did was establish a sequence to help steer each person to the correct order in which he or she should proceed to work to make right the problems and imbalances. For example, if one person had eight symptoms, the SAF protocol pointed out the preferred order for addressing these.

The third thing SAF did was prioritize what remedies could be used to bring about necessary changes, such as personal reflection, vitamins, minerals, enzymes, glandular preparations, herbs, homeopathic remedies, exercise, and many more.

But probably the most exciting thing SAF did in that first seminar was give the attendees a tool to measure themselves against higher, more intelligent beings.

Man vs. Superman

The idea of man and superman had been posited by philosophers, including Friedrich Nietzsche in his 1883 book *Thus Spoke Zarathustra*. Superman, or a superhuman, was called "Übermensch" in German, his native tongue. Nietzsche's idea was of a free spirit who disciplined himself to wholeness.

Philosopher Carl Jung followed suit and wrote in the early twentieth century about the archetype of a hero. He explained that inner balance, a state of wholeness and completeness, could be achieved by uniting the opposites in us, the man and the superman. He considered the journey of the hero to be a movement toward self-integration; it consisted of the struggles and conflicts in our lives, the dichotomies that provide inspiration and creativity.

In vogue in the mid to late 1800s before Jung, were various theories propounding the origination of the human species, the most prominent being Darwinism. While Charles Darwin touted how much monkeys and apes resembled human beings in looks and emotional makeup, Jung and others were later to expound on how much people were like God. Neither theory ever produced a realistic modern-day scale, but differences in human behavior were regularly compared to actions of God and primate alike.

When SAF appeared on the scene, it froze forever in a cryogenic display case the archaic foibles of those sciences, for now SAF could cause a real distinction between a person who is God-like and one who behaves more like a primate.

A Scale to Measure Progress

With Carl Jung's philosophy in mind, Joe Scogna drew the SAF Scale of Unified Existence in order to measure progress. At the bottom of this chart is 0, listed as "nonexistence" (not death; death is about 2.5 on this scale). At the top is 1000; in our SAF work, this is what we call Unchained Spirit; this is the Übermensch or superman of Nietzsche and Jung.

We humans desperately try to move up the scale when we want to flourish or down if we want to succumb. Of course, very few of us consciously want to be vaporized! There is definitely movement on this chart; we humans move up and down it on a daily basis. But how do we consistently move up this scale? How do we attain health and healing?

Seminars conducted with various groups netted these answers:

Astrologer: "Observe proper astral cycles of behavior."

Buddhist: "All living beings owe their present state of health to their own karma."

Chiropractor: "Eliminate nerve blockages to depleted organs with spinal adjustments."

Macrobiotic: "Balance yin and yang foods: five parts whole grain, three parts vegetable, grown and consumed in season. Cook these in proper utensils with a peaceful mind; consume well-chewed food with a spirit of gratitude."

Massage therapist: "Restore electromagnetic balance and polarity to the body, mind, and spirit with daily massages."

Medical doctor: "Destroy all foreign organisms in the body with the healthy use of antibiotics and other chemicals."

Naturopath: "Correct errant biochemistry with herbs, digestive enzymes, and proper nutrition."

Nutritionist: "Organic whole foods, quality juices, and mega dosing supplements of vitamins, minerals, and enzymes are essential for optimum functioning."

Shiatsu therapist: "Apply pressure, stretching and holding human skin with fingers, thumbs, and palms along key channels to correct internal malfunctions and maintain health."

Shinto practitioner: "Foster a spirit that regards both good and evil as blessings, and the body spontaneously becomes healthy."

Spiritual people: "Eliminate negative thoughts through daily prayer, meditation, and positive affirmations."

Taoist: "Pursue a middle course. This will help you keep a healthy body and mind."

Yoga practitioner: "Yoga is a meditative way to focus on a goal, overcome dysfunctional perceptions, achieve release from suffering, and gain inner peace and salvation."

These answers show the movement of a person away from annihilation and up the chart of existence toward Unchained Spirit.

Which method is right?

All are, and none are. The bottom line seems to be that what works for some doesn't work all the time, not for everyone. So people move from practice to practice, modality to modality, in a quest to attain the status of Unchained Spirit.

But how would you know you were an Unchained Spirit if you became one? Is there a common denominator?

Immunity Is the Answer

The word *immunity* refers to various barriers of protection, from the cell on up to the holistic human being; it can exist on any level. It is a state whereby a person is protected; he or she is exempt from the obligation of having to fight a war against another entity.

Immunity has been spoken of so many times by orthodox practitioners and in medical journals; could it be that SAF and orthodox medicine have something in common?

In a way, yes. However, those schooled in SAF wonder how a person can gain immunity by always making war and not peace. The very word *antibiotic* carries a belligerent attitude. *Anti* (against) *biotic* (life) means to war on life. By taking antibiotics, we aren't building immunity; we are making war. The war is against microorganisms, to be sure, but the microorganisms are bothering us because we're not immune (not at peace) with them. So orthodox theory says, "I'll fix those blankety-blank bugs. I'll incinerate them with my new squadron of Erythromycin."

The only problem is after a good deal of these skirmishes within the boundaries of the body, the patient looks and feels like a war zone during a major offensive.

As contrary as it may sound, immunity is gained by *making peace*. Super immunity, the kind an Unchained Spirit possesses, is gained by a vast ability to make peace with all entities on Earth. There are people who have ongoing wars with common substances such as chocolate, wheat, milk, and corn, to name a few. A person who nips at a piece of chocolate and falls over in anaphylactic shock is certainly a long way from 1000 on the SAF Scale of Unified Existence. He or she is more likely at 3 or 4, very close to death, which is 2.5 on the chart.

Someone who has achieved the capabilities of an Unchained Spirit is in total harmony and absolute serenity with the environment. Such a person has total immunity.

Is Achieving Unchained Spirit A Pipe Dream?

It takes intention, dedication, and hard work, but certainly total immunity is a state we can strive toward. Most readers of this text are floating between 3 and 15 on the scale. Their immunities are low. They have ongoing wars with the atmosphere, pollutants, water, foods, emotions, philosophies, and other people.

Split each of these categories up into finer and finer parts, and we have in front of us an immense amount of travail. As an example, someone may be afraid of the dark; we could say that the dark wars on him. When it gets dark, the soldiers of emptiness invade his mind spaces and surround him. So he needs to gain immunity; make peace with the dark.

All manner of entity, shape and form can make war on us. Some examples could be a barking dog, the face of an ex-lover, ice cream, the smell of woods, certain sounds, a car, air-conditioning vapors, angry words sent our way, and even specific locations.

In other words, to have total immunity (on body, mind, and spirit levels) there can be no fear, no stress, and no anguish. A superman, with total immunity, has *no allergies*. If a highly evolved person with many such abilities were shot with a bullet, his body would just spit the lead out because he is immune to bullets. Not only is he immune to bullets, but he is immune to the hate and negative emotions that caused the bullet to be fired toward him in the first place.

Even Superman of the comics and movies had allergies. Remember Kryptonite and how superman was affected by it? It caused him to become weak, almost death-like, without the energy to do anything; he could not fly or save humanity as he had been doing.

Can Superman, or a slight facsimile of this, be had for humankind? SAF is where you will begin your journey of self discovery with that goal and intention in mind.

Does SAF Use A Personality Test?

No, the Stress-120 Questionnaire is not a psychological evaluation or an IQ test. SAF is not like anything you've ever experienced before. The evaluation is precise, and yet this process will not provide a cookie-cutter solution. Because it is a subjective evaluation about you and your own issues, there are no right or wrong answers. It is designed so you can learn more about you and your stresses, and to help you make positive changes and choices.

For our purposes in this book, we use the Stess-120 Questionnaire for input. The personal solutions (the output), the interpretations and remedies for the chain sequence vary greatly. These solutions are chain specific; these will fit the owner of the chain, as we would expect. This has all been calculated into the SAF protocol.

Why Would I Want More Self Awareness?

This very title, Self Awareness Formulas, signifies that it is used to increase your awareness … about yourself.

This method will teach you about the interconnections between the body, mind, and spirit in order to improve your life. Through self-knowledge, we can learn to understand, experience, and break down barriers in order to get to the next higher level of understanding. Greater self awareness allows us to integrate more knowledge. Then, as we continually move upscale, we can assume greater responsibility for the creation, co-creation, and sustenance of our own energy (power) and health.

Who Would Want to Use SAF?

Because it is about increasing *self* awareness, the reasons for working with SAF are as varied as there are people on the planet. SAF is for those who want to seize the day and make a difference in their lives and the lives of their loved ones. For some, there may be traumas from long ago that are haunting and affecting them, or perhaps they are not satisfied with simply existing. Still others may have sensitivities and allergies, or have ongoing wars with emotions, foods, people, alcohol, drugs, or locations. Others might just be curious at what this method will find for them.

SAF Can Find The Root Cause

People use SAF as a realigning tool, in order to find root causes, to help dissolve old behavior patterns, and to bring about resolution to situations that they want to change.

If given the choice, we each have a trouble or two in our lives that we could do without. It might be a physical symptom (an ache or a pain), or an emotional issue (lost love, upsets with the boss), or a vexing situation with our spouse, children, neighbors, or parents.

But the fact is we DO have a choice. In fact, we make choices every day. But somehow, either we make the wrong choice and our lives never improve, or the same old problems creep up on us again and again. After awhile, we come to the conclusion that life is too complicated to understand or to fully manage.

Why Is Life So Complicated Sometimes?

The reason why things seem so complicated is because the answers to important questions remain unknown. We might think we have the solution but then it doesn't always hold true. Or something does change in our lives but then it seems we are right back where we started.

Can Life Be Made Simpler?

Yes. Simplicity is the opposite of difficulty. It is accomplished by applying known information to any complex situation to make the complex situation more easily understood. This process is the most basic learning routine, best exemplified by how a baby learns. When babies are born into the world, everything is foreign and complicated. However, by using a step-by-step process of association, children can ultimately learn about their environment. They use the learning technique that has been handed down through the generations since the beginning of time: children learn by *experience*.

This learning routine - experience - is based on "feelings." When something "feels good," then it is thought to be right. When something "feels bad," then it is believed to be wrong. As adults, we continue to learn by experience in this same way.

We call right feelings "happiness." We all want to find ways to increase our quotient of happiness. When we have much happiness, we call this well being.

The word used for wrong feelings is "sadness." A good deal of sadness is known as disease.

> We learn "good" from "bad" through a tried and true learning technique: we learn by experience.

How Does SAF View Disease?

A disease is a complication too severe or too large to comprehend at once. It means that we have a problem, any kind of problem that we cannot solve. We use the word "insoluble" to denote a problem that cannot be broken down into its finer parts. Our mechanism for breaking down our problem becomes inhibited and therefore causes distress or discomfort. This type of distress is the SAF definition of disease; sometimes it is written as dis-ease, meaning "not at ease," or "off the resting point." Disease is an "out of balance condition."

How Can I Make Myself Feel Better?

To feel better is as simple as solving a problem. The problem might be a puzzling or a difficult circumstance; there is some heaviness and pressure. It implies the notion of impenetrable mass.

So, to solve a problem, we must dissolve it, break it down so that it will have less mass, less pressure. We do this primarily by breaking it down into smaller bits so it is easier to understand. It is difficult for us to solve a great problem without first taking it apart. Once the problem is dissected, it can be understood more easily.

As an example, if you were to attend a university to study physics, chemistry, or medicine, you couldn't understand all the ramifications of these sciences in a single one-hour long class, or even throughout one school year. You must become a student and analyze these bodies of knowledge, one piece at a time. You must learn the language of the subject; you must feel your way through the various courses until you know the subject from the inside out. Anyone who has ever said he could learn a whole science by just glancing at one textbook is fooling himself. It takes concentration and effort, and necessitates splitting the subject into smaller pieces.

When we have a problem, we must provide remedies to solve the problem and, of course, the remedy must match the problem.

How Do Remedies Really Work?

When the remedy matches the problem, this right remedy *always* solves the problem! We can find examples with our own bodies to prove this. For example, when we're hungry, we're presented with the problem of having a particular uncomfortable sensation in our stomach and a gradual loss of energy. The remedy, of course, would be to provide our body with food. That would be the right remedy.

Or, let's say that our friend has a cut. The immediate problem would be the body signaling there is a tear in the skin, with the common symptoms of bleeding, pain and swelling. If the friend wanted to solve this problem, then he or she would provide a clamp or Band-Aid that could close up the cut, or perhaps they would need to get it stitched up.

In another example, if you miss someone very badly, then your body will receive signals through your mind and viewpoint by providing an aching feeling in the heart. We each have our own way of signaling when we miss someone, but generally there is a feeling of disconnection. The remedy for this particular problem is to supply the missing person and relieve the pain of separation, if possible.

In some cases, however, we miss someone who cannot be replaced, and therefore a very specific remedy is needed, in order to adjust our viewpoint.

The proof as to whether or not this program has been successful would be the symptoms that alerted us about the problem in the first place. Are the symptoms of disconnection or aching heart still present?

When the symptoms are removed, we feel better, and when we feel better, we feel "right" about our existence.

Can Any of Us Feel Better And Stay Better?

Theoretically, if symptoms were taken away, we would always feel good. We could logically conclude that the reason for our disaffection for disease is the fact that we must bear the symptoms. But we cannot simply take symptoms away and not eliminate their causes, because the symptoms (the effects), would just keep reappearing in our life.

Why find Cause and Effect? Because this is how we can make changes in our life. We are sitting *in* the effect now, but what was the cause? Do we dare look?

We can't change the events in the past, or delete them. Those events happened. It doesn't help to try and tune them out, or whistle a happy tune, or try to ignore the loud symptoms we are hearing and feeling. By processing with SAF techniques, the images become clearer, not less so. We are *more* conscious to them, not less so.

But by finding the Cause and its Effect (the before and the after) we can see the bigger picture. How is this done?

Once we have defined the Effect (symptoms), using this innovative method we work backward through the emotions to pinpoint the Cause. With that understanding, we then experience a change of attitude about those past events, and suddenly, without much effort on our part, we just *want* to accept what was, and let it go. And so we do.

Almost all disease and physical ailments are caused by mental or spiritual distress. The answer to getting better and staying better is to consistently upgrade our awareness of the causes and the effects of mental, physical, emotional, and spiritual symptoms.

As you can see, *symptom awareness is crucial when we want to change and transform.*

> SAF is not medical diagnosis. Physical diseases have underlying emotional causes – some may be very deep indeed, so it is this aspect of the human being that we address in the science of SAF.　　　　　　　　　　　–Joseph R. Scogna, Jr.

Humans, since the beginning of time, have tried to observe their relationship with the environment to learn more about themselves through many studies and philosophies (chemistry, biology, physics, medicine, religion and many more). But the most important subject of all is the study of human beings themselves.

What Is A Human Being?

In the simplest definition of a human being, we could say that he or she is composed of body, mind, and spirit. These are not divisions, per se, there is no way to actually divide or cut these three apart, and yet each one, if you will, has its own separate science and awareness. Today, medical science and physiology attempt to increase the awareness of the body and its processes; psychology and related sciences of the mind attempt to accumulate more information on mental capabilities; and religion and spirituality have always had the spirit in their area of influence.

Is There A Science That Deals With The Whole Person?

Yes. SAF is a universal tool for understanding the connections of body, mind, and spirit. It is a method that includes and uses all sciences. This book provides an in-depth study of this unique approach to health and well being. There are other Scogna-authored books on complementary areas of study, such as *The Promethion; Junk DNA; Nutrionics; Project ISIS; The Numbers of SAF;* and others that utilize the SAF interface. (See page 223 for a list and descriptions)

How Does SAF Use the Sciences?

SAF deals with the interrelationships of all sciences that affect the human person and our environment. Sixty-four dichotomies of these bodies of knowledge are explained in one book as these relate to the human being. In short, the science of SAF-can be applied to any body of knowledge to measure it.

How Can SAF Connect Sciences?

SAF connects sciences because it is based on the most fundamental knowledge there is – mathematics.

Do I Have To Know A Lot of Math To Use SAF?

No, there are no tabulations necessary. And don't worry; there is no new math or old math either. The questionnaires we use for input and the online process will do all the tabulating necessary.

Then How Is Mathematics Used In SAF?

In our everyday life, we use numbers to measure the magnitude and quantity of objects, places, and things. Any science that employs quantities or qualities must have numbers for its basic measurement. When you look into it, you'll find that all sciences and all conditions must yield to numbers. Galileo wrote: "The story of the entire universe is a grand book, written in the language of mathematics."

A mathematical matrix, an algorithm, is an integral part of the processes of SAF and so it is able to connect all sciences. Numbers comprise the language of SAF. Chapter 5 provides an in depth look at this special language.

Is SAF Numerology?

No, numerology is a study of numbers and their meanings much like astrology or a birth chart. We have a different use for numbers in our SAF work.

How Are Numbers Used?

A number is simply a symbol we use to represent a quantity or quality. A number has no feelings until it is assigned feelings; it has no energy until it is endowed with energy. SAF has assigned qualities, such as feelings, emotions, and energy to numbers. Using numbers fits in very handily with computer use.

How Can Numbers Tell the Way A Human Being Feels?

The numbers 1-24 are used in the science of SAF (see SAF Operative Chart 4, page 219).

Let's look at the number 6 as an example. In the assignment of the organs and glands of the human body, the number 6 has been assigned to the liver and gallbladder. In the breakdown of emotions, the number 6 is dubbed sadness, while the condition or function given for number 6 is transmutation. In each particular study listed with SAF programming (880 studies in all), there is a separate meaning for the number 6. This is not a statement to impress anyone with the enormity of the science of SAF, but merely to show that a number can mean different things in various bodies of knowledge.

In this book, each number we use will have four meanings, namely, the number, the organ/gland complex, the emotions, and the conditions or functions.

SAF is very logical. *The SAF chain contains chains of information that we can learn to read,* much like a grammatical sentence. As you read this book and become familiar with the process, the information will make more sense to you.

When the SAF chain sequence has been created, the number designations and their meanings have been prioritized. The numbers are put into a sequence of importance that has meaning for a particular person, the chain owner, and for that person alone. The only true meaning of existence comes in the way of a sequence.

What Do You Mean By A Sequence?

A sequence is a number of items following one another, a progression. In our SAF work, we follow the chain link of energy from which everything is made, and we create sequences of numbers to follow. Here on planet Earth, man has learned to live with his sequences and understand them to a certain extent. Philosophers and scientists who understand many sequences of energy have led the population out of its misunderstandings about life. These were learned men and women, such as Socrates, Lao Tzu, Hippocrates, Hahnemann, Einstein, Jung, Hawking, to name a few.

Each human being must learn the basic sequences of existence in order to survive. Any event that occurs on Earth must either precede or follow another event; we call this action *time*. The examples of time are many. Everything must take time, and for time, there are sequences.

An easy example of a sequence is the corn on the cob that was served at dinner, which was produced by events through time. The corn grew from a seed and that seed came from an earlier corncob. There is a complete series of events that takes place in order to produce an ear of corn. Each ear of corn must have a birth, then grow and mature into a ripened state, and then eventually decay until its final death or demise. We take the corn in its ripened state and eat it for nourishment. This sustenance helps us create sequences of energy in our own bodies.

In another example of a sequence, a human being is born and grows to an age at which he or she is fit to behave as a mature adult. Eventually we begin to grow older, decay, and then reach a point in our lives when we must face the finish of our existence as a human being - death. Again, this is a sequence of time. It is a succession of energy; it is a chain link of past and present events upon which we can speculate about the future.

As we grow older, we can look back on our earlier lives and see our own sequences. If we are in good shape and have good recall, the emotional cycles and patterns of our behavior are apparent and known to us.

It is the tracks of time that control human beings, and SAF tracks time. We create sequences of numbers to do this.

How Can SAF Tell How We Feel In Time?

SAF tracks time and intensity. Remember that we must assign significance to an event in this time sequence and assign it some feelings. The intensity for this significance comes from the chain owner.

Let's look at another example. If you want to go to the store for an ice cream cone, then you may assign significance to this event as being pleasant (Incident #1). However, if one day on the way back from the ice cream store, you are in a car accident, then you may award a very different kind of significance to this event. You may call this Incident #2 event unpleasant, and in unpleasant circumstances, we perceive intensity, pressure, and stress.

But Once That Sequence Is Over, We Should Get Better, Right? Doesn't Time Heal All Wounds?

Time can heal wounds, but only to a certain extent. We do have self-regeneration mechanisms that can help us heal, but the *intensity* of the event and the *strength* of our regeneration capabilities are the real factors, not time. If we were weak to begin with, we may never get over the trauma of the accident. Because each of us is a unique individual, different people recover from similar events in differing lengths of time. Post Traumatic Stress Disorder (PTSD) is an example of this, and is readily observable by any of us.

How Can a Past Event Haunt Us? Why Can't We Just Blot a Trauma Out of Our Memories?

Let's look at the two events again, pleasant and unpleasant. Your body and mind have the ability to record everything – the good, the bad, and the ugly so you can remember it for future reference. This is all part of the *we-learn-by-experience* discussed previously. These recordings are stored in our protein structures, in our DNA for our future reference and learning. In the ice cream cone-car accident event, the ice cream cone was retrieved (bringing pleasure) but you had to pay for it with some pressure and stress (the car accident).

The Graph of Emotions on page 13 shows the differences in energy as they are recorded in the body. In the pleasant event, the energy is light, airy and without stress. In the unpleasant event, the energy is compressed, angry, mean, and stressed. The memory of the event is power-packed with energy, and worse, the images have become so ensnarled in the pressure that the afflicted person cannot tell one event or sequence of events from the other.

Incident #1, the ice cream cone adventure may be easily recalled. Incident #2, the car accident, may not be remembered at all. This often happens with PTSD; the events could be cloudy and confused in the mind of the afflicted person.

In the case of a car accident, even a small fender-bender, those involved often don't remember what led up to the accident or what immediately followed, even though they were said to be fully conscious.

Remember there are certain amounts of intensity, stress, and pressure associated with a traumatic event, such as the car accident, Incident #2. With PTSD, the afflicted person often stays stuck in the unwanted event.

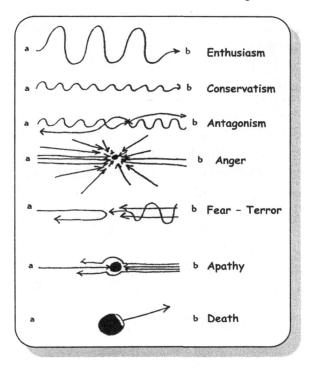

The Graph of Emotions

The differences of energy as recorded in the DNA protein structures. Incident #1, the idea of eating the ice cream cone would fall on the above graph at Enthusiasm; it is light, airy and without stress. On the other hand, Incident #2, the car accident would fall between Anger and Death; in this situation, the energy is compressed, mean, and stressed.

How Can This Kind of Pressure Affect My Health?

Your well being depends on your view of life. If your mind is happy and well adjusted to life and living and you have few stressors, life will seem to be good for you. On the other hand, if your mind is clouded by negative emotions such as hate, anger, resentment, fear, and mental stress, these hostile feelings will eventually affect you physically, as well.

How Can a Negative Emotion Affect Physical Well Being?

Remember that we learn by experience. Were your early experiences positive ones or negative in nature? Emotions are made of energy; they are the experience of life in the environment where we are living. Emotions are mental experiences, which have biochemical (physical) significance and tell your body how to be, how to feel.

A person's well being depends on his or her view of life. If the mind is happy, well-adjusted, and we are productive, we would say life is good. On the other hand, if the mind is clouded by negative emotions, such as anger, hate, resentment, and fear, then the physical state will suffer.

So, Is All Emotion Bad?

No, not at all. Emotions occur in a healthy human being. Emotions, when used in the proper circumstances, provide pleasure and enjoyment in life in a positive way. The word "emotion" in SAF terminology means expressed motion, or electrified motion.

Remember the ice cream cone sequence and how the mental images of it became ensnarled and confused with the car accident? It is the impact and intensity of experience that confused the expression of motion – the emotion - in the body.

Have you ever heard someone say, "I don't know how to feel"? It means the person's memory banks and experiences are so befuddled and balled up that any old feeling may come out at the wrong time.

The ice cream cone-car accident may present the following confusion of emotions (reminders).

Confusion of Expressed Motion (Emotion):

Ice cream	Fun and tasty
Driving	Exhilaration
Ice and snow	Pretty but be careful
Cold and wet	Uncomfortable
Slip on the ice	Fear, out of control
Metal hitting metal	Sound of impact, unconsciousness, pain, anger, hurt and bewilderment
Ambulance	Loud siren, spinning lights, flashing lights
Hospital	Scared and worried
Stitches	Pain and confusion
Drugs	Numb, confused, disoriented, vomiting

As you can see, there is a confusing disarray of emotions. Having all this under control in your mind and body is the ultimate secret weapon against confusion. After a car crash, you may be able to write a best-selling novel and become famous for it, but what if this event and others like it are lost inside your memory banks and never completely work their way out? What if this abnormal event cannot be controlled and therefore becomes confused in your normal processes of emotion?

In the science of SAF, traumas can exert their influence outside of your control and are beneath your awareness level, in the invisible realm.

It is through an examination of these traumas that we can learn more and gain greater awareness about ourselves. In our personal work with SAF, we view and sometimes *welcome* traumas as a part of our learning experience.

Down through the ages, dragons have been used by all cultures to represent the unseen and the unknown - definitely a force with which to be reckoned. These hidden trauma-dragons can present themselves in a number of unwanted ways, such as becoming mixed up with our everyday feelings, causing us to react unreasonably and illogically. Dragons and traumas, and the ensnarled confusing energy of emotions these create, are presented throughout this book. Please note that the dragons in this book are merely teaching mechanisms; these are not real creatures; they do not have a soul.

To go back to the ice cream cone-car accident, this is what could happen: any reminder of the ice cream cone-car accident in our sample can trigger a reaction. The key word here is *reminder*: it means to put *something* into the conscious mind again.

Any reminder of an event, whether we are conscious of it or not, can start the whole chain sequence of emotions and patterns of that former event (car accident) occurring once again. This means that we will actually feel the same sensations and pains as we did when we were in the accident. These expressions of electric motion can all occur on their own volition, *without* our control.

Now look again at the list of confusing emotions. These are the reminders. Remember, the mind has been squashed and one reminder is as good as the next. Any *one* of the feelings or actions in the event can be a reminder.

Have you ever had a bad experience and when someone later asked you about the incident, did you say "Please … don't remind me"?

On a hot summer day, you might be out at a party enjoying yourself when a friend asks if you would like to get some ice cream. Your mind and body become confused and take the reminder "ice cream" to signify *an impending disaster or a collision*. This is because the pleasure of eating ice cream has become mixed in with all the negative experiences of the accident. So instead of feeling good, you now feel bad at even the thought of ice cream, often for no reason known to you.

> The mention of "ice cream" stimulates the earlier "unhappy car accident" event; it presses on your consciousness without your consent, exerting its own control over you. You may be able to see only the ice cream cone but can feel the rest of the now-jumbled sequence.

These "bad feelings" occur to us all the time. These triggers can be just fleeting thoughts, a flashback, or they can flood in with or without understanding their origin, such as with *déjà vu* experiences. These can have a tremendous and disruptive influence in our life. We may find that we are acting out, or doing something inappropriately, something that we would not normally do. We may consciously know about the past events, and yet still be bummed out about them. It is another reason to get started with your personal SAF work so that you can shed light on the confusing stimulations.

Why Do We Feel Bad? The Accident Was in the Past. It Can't Hurt Us Now... Can It?

In our ice cream cone-car accident scenario, the reminders could come without our conscious permission or even recognition. Here are some possible reminders:

An ambulance speeding by

The sound of a siren in the distance

Feeling of exhilaration

Seeing crashed cars on the side of the road

Someone being angry or hurt

Slipping on ice

Sound of metal hitting metal

Something that tastes cold and sweet (like ice cream, but not)

Notice, in the above list, that simply a feeling of exhilaration or tasting something cold and sweet could remind the person, on a subconscious level, of the ice cream cone-car accident. The mind and the body are logical, but only when they are in *good working order*. Remember, we learn by our experiences, the automatic recording of these experiences in our DNA, and in this case, having fun and car accident is all jumbled together.

The mind and body have been programmed to avoid pain and death at all costs. This is why human beings seek pleasure and avoid uncomfortable situations that involve pain.

The DNA-RNA of all genes was programmed by your ancestral urges to *exist at all costs*. This command directive doesn't *ask* you to behave; it *demands* you to behave. The genes *command*. They say, "You are directed to protect and defend this unit at all costs, and if you do not, you will receive a punishment of pain and be riddled with chronic disease." You have inherited these genes and their directives, and ancestral traumas have also passed to you from your genetic family lines. Plus, you have acquired your own traumas and those directives or codes as a result of living on this planet and interacting with others.

It is natural to avoid accidents and hurt because these are against our primal directive in life. When you get into these experiences, you are, therefore, in the eyes of the genetic blueprint, *wrong*!

To be *right*, you must behave yourself. You must avoid having collisions with the environment that knock you into insensibility. You must not collide with objects that will then impact their energies against your body, mind, and spirit in a sense adding mass to mass, so as to confuse your ability to recall them.

Reminders

Following the DNA recording of an accident, any reminder, as listed above, will tell the mind and body, "Oh no, you're at it again!" The mind and body think you're going to do *it* again. They think that you're going to have the same accident again because the event, brought on by the reminders, is being replayed in the mind. And this occurs even if you consciously do not want it to. The mind and body think that you will get into trouble and will try to help you to get out of it. This is the basic fear reaction.

I'm sure you've heard of someone who is said to be "accident-prone." Such a person continually repeats the "bad" behavior. They don't want to have a repeat accident but they are stuck in a sequence, stuck in a trauma.

Why Do the Body and Mind Keep Reminding Us of the Same Confused Situation? Don't They Realize We Do Not Want To Get Into An Accident?

No one *consciously* gets into an accident. Accidents and bad times happen *unconsciously*, at times when you are less aware. And remember, you may be operating under the influence of ancestral traumas, as well. This does not mean that when someone ignores a stop sign and plows into a car, injuring those occupants that they are at fault. We are not blaming the victims but saying that the occupants may have been in some way, less than fully aware.

Pleasure is orienting to us. Pain is *disorienting*. In other words, pleasurable circumstances add to our awareness, while un-pleasurable, painful experiences do much to confuse and beguile us.

What Does SAF Have To Do With This?

The SAF program is constructed to read the status of your memory banks to see how much trouble you may have unwittingly caused yourself. SAF is like a searchlight in the cave of your mind. It helps you to see yourself better. It finds those places that harbor reminders of events and incidents that have traumatized you.

> "The sole purpose of human existence is to kindle a light in the darkness of mere being. Just as the unconscious affects us, so the increase in our consciousness affects the unconscious."
> —Carl Jung

How Does SAF Work?

This is the subject of many books and training materials, but suffice to say that SAF finds what organ systems are affected, tracks where the energy is stuck, and identifies the emotional component of the trauma. SAF helps areas of the unaware, unknown parts of your mind to become known again, and appreciated. Currently, we utilize two different methodologies for gathering information to create a chain link of numbers; special questionnaires and an infrared device.

The numbers that are presented in an SAF chain sequence are readouts of your memory banks and the intensity of the pressure.

The SAF chain can be read like a sentence of the particular chain owner's trauma. It is tailor-made with specific meaning for the person it depicts. The balance of this book explains the theory, the number system, and Chapter 6 will present an easy, though introductory, way to read SAF chains.

Your own SAF chain will only be significant to your particular trouble or complaint. Once finding your resistance and traumas, SAF allows you to approach these barriers repetitiously until they are totally understood and their impact over you is dissipated.

Keep in mind there will be not just one chain sequence for you to work on; you have many chains within your sphere of influence. The recordings in your DNA-RNA contain times of impact, lessened awareness, and upheaval. How many of these impacts does a human acquire in a life time? There will be chains for each time period or personal area of distress. So be forewarned; be prepared to roll up your sleeves and learn the tools necessary to work on yourself.

How Can I Learn What *MY* Numbers Are?

Once you have finished reading this book, you will have a better understanding of the theory of SAF and how to read a chain. Online, go to www.LifeEnergyResearch.com. Click on Questionnaires, and then you will see the Stress-120 Questionnaire for emotional issues. This is what readers of this book will use. It is an excellent method for creating a chain sequence of numbers. Chapter 1, Chapter 5, and Chapter 6 can then be used for a quick reference and refresher.

The Stress-120 Questionnaire is a subjective test, which means it works on the basis of input. It will present your viewpoint, your reality as you see it. This particular questionnaire is geared toward the emotional issues each of us faces in our everyday life, and the results will be a customized evaluation.

Your answers to the questionnaire will be put in an order of priority to heal, to understand. This is the SAF chain sequence, and will reveal the effects and the hidden, probable causes. It will take what you do know about yourself and help you learn what you don't know about the causes and earlier events that created the situation you find yourself in today.

Therapists say SAF helps them get to the main core issues in a few minutes, where it previously might have taken a year or more of talk therapy. SAF has been able to unmask symptoms and reveal some astounding information.

By completing the subjective questionnaire, *you* give the input. And *you* will learn to uncover the answers for yourself. Not only will you discover a new understanding and greater awareness of your traumas and barriers, but you will be able to get back self-determinism and a sense of self worth. In the process, you will free up energy that has been stuck in time, and you will *feel* this revitalization!

Our health and well being have always been our responsibility. Through the self awareness techniques in this book, it is possible to know yourself more completely. It is possible to find answers.

Once you have the understanding and the knowledge, it is easy to find the remedy and make the correct decisions.

A Quick Rundown On SAF:

- The SAF chain contains chains of information.
- Our chain sequence tells a tale of stressed organ and gland systems, with correlating emotions and conditions; these are connected through time.
- Using SAF, we can learn about our patterns – physical, mental, emotional, and spiritual.
- SAF can radiate energy into the unconscious to make it conscious.
- When the past is in perspective, the present time becomes synchronized.
- SAF defines radiational energy as any particle of energy, including emotional, that moves inward toward our core, our center.
- The hidden directive or code is held in the anchor, the emotion of the chain. This may have helped us survive when we were helpless children, but it may be detrimental to us now.
- Once we know the Effect, with SAF we can find the Cause and get some resolution.
- Drugs, and even over the counter (OTC) products put a drag on our energy and affect how well we can envision and understand what it is the lessons are presenting to us.
- SAF dissects problems into finer particles so we can understand them.
- Time does not heal all wounds. Instead, it is the *intensity* of the event, and our own *regenerative* capabilities that determine the healing outcome of the wounds.
- Unresolved traumas are still alive and take our energy.

> The goal of SAF is to move us in the direction of Unchained Spirit, to raise the awareness and consciousness level of every man, woman, and child. This is accomplished by raising our awareness of symptoms. Most physical diseases have underlying emotional and spiritual causes; some may be very deep indeed. So it is this aspect of the person that we address in SAF. In this way, the immunity level is increased.

With the Algorithms of SAF, We Can:

- Understand the hidden messages of body, mind, and spirit with SAF chain sequence work.
- Find our psychosomatic Effects and trace these back to their source, the Cause.
- Recognize and eliminate the devastating effects of traumas, dysfunctions, and disorders.
- Learn how acquired patterns from a past forgotten (and still unconscious) trauma can create emotional instability today, by making you act a certain way, as if you were *still in the past*, and
- Find practical ways to implement this new knowledge into your life.

When we make peace within ourselves, our immunity rises on three levels – body, mind, and spirit. As a result of our own work on ourselves, our family members will benefit, our business life will be more satisfying, and the community of mankind will be more harmonious.

> "By using my method of pinpointing psychosomatic causes and tracing this back to the source, we can now understand and eliminate the devastating effects of traumas, dysfunctions, and disorders."   --Joseph R. Scogna, Jr.

Thoughts and Study Questions in Chapter 1:

What is self awareness?

Using SAF, we can learn about our patterns – physical, mental, emotional, and spiritual.

SAF sheds light into the darkness so we can see better.

When the past is in perspective, the present time becomes synchronized.

With our SAF work, can we find the cause of and then dissolve old behavioral and emotional patterns?

Unresolved traumas are still alive and take our energy.

What is meant by immunity in the SAF sense?

How does SAF connect sciences?

Why doesn't time heal all wounds?

How can a past event haunt someone?

How are numbers used in SAF?

Is this a true statement: Our chain tells a tale of stressed organ and gland systems, with correlating emotions and conditions?

What is meant by the hidden directive, or a code that we still follow?

When should I create a chain sequence?

Chapter 2

Anatomy of a Disease and Rapid Aging

Loss Of Energy

We must make certain that we have enough power to offset the interference of a disease. The energy of all humans comes directly from a blueprint of the genetic matrix; this matrix contains the exact memory traces that induce power or energy. If these circuits become confused or interfered with in any way, our energy is cut to that degree.

In other words, we don't actually *use up* energy. We have an infinite amount of power and energy in our system. We might have the problem of not being able to *access* our energy banks, as when a disease process intercepts the corridors of energy normally used. This is a different view of a disease. Many people have the idea that energy is being drained out of them, when in actuality there is an agent, an entity or some causal effect interfering with our ability to reach down inside the cell and pull energy out of a vast warehouse of power.

> An individual must make certain he has enough power to offset the interference of a trauma or a disease.

We Are Loaded With Stored Energy Patterns

Stored energy patterns are facilitated by our ability to experience the digestion or absorption of energy patterns in the environment through food or through activity; this enables us to access those particular energy banks that are native to our genetic structure. It is only when a structure from the outside, such as a food or a toxin, becomes disharmonious with that energy pattern, that interference with our energy absorption results.

The actual blueprint of energy can be added to through experience. The genetic structure compiles coded symbols of actions within its memory banks so that we can access these banks and gain energy.

Energy Is Created By Patterns Of Experience

Many do not understand what energy is and therefore have a difficult time identifying how they "lost" it. Energy, as defined in Webster's dictionary, is "the ability to do work or perform functions." This definition, however, falls short. It doesn't help us understand the composition of energy. We can't get a better understanding of energy by this definition alone. We must look intrinsically at how energy is created.

As we study Life Energy and energy related to the spiritual aspects of an individual and the mental capabilities, we learn *that true energy is created by the pattern of experiences impressed upon the cells of the body, the mind, and the spirit.*

As an example, if you wanted to learn to fly an airplane, you would have to go through all the motions to learn all the patterns of flying. You must input these lessons into your memory banks so you would have the energy (the knowledge) to be a pilot. If you were suddenly thrust into the cockpit of a 747 without having learned these patterns, and were asked to fly that bird, your energy would most likely shut off. You would become terrified and frozen. You wouldn't be able to move. The energy would be completely drained from your body. If that airplane were to take off with you at the controls, the only way you could possibly escape death would be to access a memory bank that was similar to the airplane's function and this would permit you to get into action and fly it.

Now, do not run out and try this airplane experiment! There is a simpler, much safer test. Ask someone a question to which he or she doesn't know the answer, or ask that person to define an unknown word. The person's mind will draw a blank. He or she will try to fit the pattern of the word into similar words so he or she can go into action and come up with an answer. Or show someone Greek or Hebrew words that they have never seen. The mind will freeze at the sight of the strange characters, and if the person focuses on it long enough looking for answers, he or she will become tired, slightly less conscious than before.

This occurs because we cannot draw power or knowledge from what is unfamiliar to us, in this case, with unknown letters or words. *We draw our power from learned memory patterns, and the body draws its own power from learned memory patterns in the genes.* The only way to actually stop a person, to convince them that they are "out of energy" (which is impossible because energy cannot be destroyed), is to mix memory patterns with patterns they don't understand.

Energy Is Created From A Starting Point

Energy is always created from a starting point, so we must have a stable home base. If we don't have a stable base, we appear to lose energy. The energies in the environment can more easily interfere with our database if we are always on the go. As an example, when you are away from home you have probably noticed that your energy is less coordinated than when you are on a solid home base. This home base doesn't necessarily have to be where your family is located, or where you sleep at night, but it must be a nice, safe place from which to operate. It must be an area where you can allow your energies and your mental image patterns, which provide you with energy, to roam freely. If you have interference, such as the kind of opposition found in a crowded household or with familial tensions, you will lose power. In this case, it is very easy for you to gain back your energy. You simply need to withdraw from the offending energies that are moving into your system and interfering with your mechanism. This withdrawal allows you to reach into that endless pod of energy inside your mind and your genes. Many people can be saved tremendous hardships by just moving out of the environment that created an incredible phenomenon of energy starvation.

Energy Must Be Free Flowing

If energy is utilized improperly or out of sequence, it will break down. Even if we can access our memory patterns of energy, if we use these incorrectly, we may double back on our own power to make it interfere with itself, just the way a garden hose can be crimped or knotted, and thus, impede the flow of water.

An Endless And Timeless Power Pack

The greatest power that is given to us is our ability to absorb energy from our own system, an endless and timeless power pack. If we don't know the exact formulas for extracting energy from our memory banks, we will wind up with the primary phenomena of disease, which is loss of energy and loss of the ability to think. Our energy will move into a state of confusion. We must learn the formulas for sequentially extracting energy from our system, or we will remain obstructed, impeded, and suppressed.

The Mechanism Of Similars

One of the most important mechanisms to understand is the ability of the human system to translate one pattern from another. This is called the mechanism of similars; we can move very handily in a new situation if we can compare the new situation with similar ones in our memory banks.

To return to the airplane example mentioned previously, there was a well-publicized incidence of such a transition. It took place on a small plane. A passenger had his first flight lesson in the air when the pilot suffered a fatal heart attack. As the passenger sat in the cockpit looking at the lights, dials and strange controls, nothing looked familiar. A second pilot flew behind the distressed airplane and was able to talk the passenger successfully through the landing process. He did this by getting the passenger to look at the panel of the airplane as if it were a car dashboard, to see that the yoke was similar to a steering wheel and the brakes and other controls had similarities, as well. If the passenger/pilot had not been able to make that transition of similars, then his energy would have been frozen, blanked out, and missing. He and the other travelers in the plane would have perished. But because this passenger had the ability to translate energy into similar patterns, he was able to act appropriately in this terrifying situation.

Disease Entities Use Similars

The use of similar patterns can also be accomplished by disease entities when entering a person's system. In fact, any similar energy pattern can move into a person's body and disrupt his energy by confusing and beguiling his system.

One good example is the chelation of minerals. The human body has the capability of knowing every substance that belongs to it and this makes it very difficult for some people to absorb certain minerals. Manufacturers, in an effort to gain greater absorptive power for their products, disguise the metals in a chelated form; basically, metals are enclosed in a structure of protein so the body believes it is a protein and thus accepts it. By this method of creating a similar, the body is tricked into absorbing the metals.

Similarly, a disease entity can chelate itself and fool our protective mechanisms into letting it inside the body's sacred guarded areas. Many of the powerful diseases such as HIV, AIDS, polio, chicken pox, measles, shingles, and other contagious illnesses have this same mechanism; they trick the body into letting them inside by disguising themselves as friends.

Body, Mind, And Spirit Must Be Synchronized

A person can easily destroy his body with his mind. A greater percentage of illnesses are psychosomatically-caused rather than created by physical means. This occurs in the same ratio as airplane crashes; pilot error is more than 80% the cause of crashes while the actual physical structure of the airplane is much less often to blame.

In a similar way, the pilot of the human body - the mind and spirit - is more than 80% to blame for mishaps. The body itself is such a miraculous mechanism that it can extricate itself from almost any kind of danger or trouble. So, it is very important for those who seek increased energy, health, and well being to make certain that body, mind, and spirit are synchronized.

Unsynchronized Body, Mind, And Spirit Energy Creates Disease

If the energy patterns are not matching, there will be trouble. For example, if you are performing grueling mental work and you forget to eat, you may wind up "eating your body," or chewing through your energy stores. The mind, when learning and accepting a lot of information, is also programming these bits of data into the genetic structure. This action causes a depletion of energy because the mind's mechanisms are interfering with the old, known patterns of the body. The body must catch up, so to speak, and assimilate this information so that it can implement these actions.

For example, you can very easily learn the rules of basketball from a book, but when you first play the game, you will be very clumsy and sloppy. This is because the body has not been programmed with the messages the mind has learned from the book. It takes time for the new muscle groups to improve. The body must be inscribed with hard work, practice and exercise.

This is true also for those who want to improve at their own game of life. It takes much reading and learning, sheer mental practice, strong intention, and visualization.

The entire phenomenon of this connection between the mind, the spirit and the body is the basis for all upsets and diseases. When we are out of harmony with our own system (on body, mind, or spirit levels) we create more trouble for ourselves than any kind of offending substances in the environment ever could. The familiar saying "man is his own worst enemy" is very true. Once we learn how to harmonize our training with body, mind, and spirit, we are much more adept at being able to control invading forces from the outside.

Prevention of Aging

The human being's system must be protected at all costs. It must build a barrier against invading ideas that are not consciously understood by the body, mind, and/or spirit. In effect, if we wanted to exist forever, we must never let anything come in that is unknown. We must never let blackness enter our field of light, for this is unfamiliar information moving into the known system. It may interfere with our most precious energy sources, the wells of power that have been built up from generations of existence.

Origin of Life Energy

From where does energy come? From where does a human being take his Life Energy? These questions are asked frequently at lectures and seminars. Few people realize that energy is passed on from cell to cell, from one generation to the next; energy is part of a tremendous process that originated with the first inscription of our DNA on planet Earth. Humanity and all life have experienced this cellular engraving over and over again. It is a present our parents gave us at birth, but we must take care of this present and nurture it.

Genetic Code Must Be Learned For Infinite Power and Energy

If we don't learn the genetic mechanisms that have been bequeathed to us, they will *consume* rather than *give* us energy. As a result, the process of aging is programmed into mankind.

It is the ultimate goal of a person who is using sophisticated symptom and self-awareness programs (SAF) to understand the basic inscription of the genetic codes. Once we learn these inscriptions, we have an infinite source of energy. (For information on the inscriptions of the genetic codes, read: *Junk DNA: Unlocking the Hidden Secrets of Your DNA*)

Life is a blueprint and a mechanism, a genetic challenge that enables each of us to carry out our particular codes or program. If we don't heed our program, we will suffer from it, for it seems the genetic codes have allocated only a certain amount of time here on Earth, and only so many memories are allowed to escape the energy pod upon which we draw energy.

> Once we learn the genetic code inscriptions, we will have an infinite source of energy.

The Sun's Role in Life Energy

This genetic mechanism takes its cue from the sun, and so we have to obtain an understanding of the exact relationship of the sun to our body. If you believe that the sun is just a pretty orb that shines in the daytime to provide warmth, then you are far behind in your quest to know the human machine.

Earth's Resistance and Ohm's Law

Planet Earth has been endowed with the sun's light. More than likely, the Earth started as just a point in space. This particular solitary energy point resisted the sun. As the sun irradiated the Earth, there came a great energy struggle. This energy struggle produced the fire that molded the planet into position.

The most basic electric law on planet Earth provides an understanding of this resistance -- Ohm's Law. It states that "every energy in the environment will meet with an opposition or a resistance." This basic law, which must be obeyed, is programmed into every human being, into every cell, nucleus, fiber, and entity as well. (To understand more on electric laws that affect us, read: *Project Isis: Fundamentals of Human Electricity*.)

The Sun Clock and Genetic Timetable

The genetic structure, over eons of time, has programmed a human being to pay attention to the cycles of time. We are given only so many days and these days number close to 25,000 for a full lifetime. Each one of these days has a specific amount of radiation attached to it. It is one day of the sun - a sun-day - and as the planet rotates, the sun sprays its energy upon the inhabitants and each one of us is nourished by it. Each one of us receives one more push or step forward on our genetic program.

The genes respond in kind, for they are, according to Ohm's Law, a resistance. Each time the sun crosses the sky, another arbitrary "click" is triggered in the genetic structure, and another digit is added to the genetic timetable, which is the aging clock for a human being. As people age, they never realize that if they were to let go of the resistance, eliminate or vanquish the resistance, they would stop aging. Theoretically, they would never get old, they would be whatever they wanted to be; they wouldn't have to follow the preprogrammed timetable that has been provided for them.

However, the sun is a very formidable power. Its intense heat and tremendous energy create a subtle apathy. In one sense, people are certain they will be here every day. In another sense, they acknowledge their eventual fate in the same way they observe the growth and decay of vegetation.

A kernel of corn grows into a beautiful stalk and produces a ripe fruit, but as it is exposed to the sun over and over again, its own genetic program causes a treacherous-looking demise. The living corn wilts, decays, and loses its precious fluids.

Human beings follow the same actions. We will grow strong and reach maturity, only to wither and die. Mankind has reluctantly accepted this as fact. It has been programmed into our cells. In the course of a lifetime, human beings struggle against the program. We fight and kick by using drugs, poisons, herbs and all manner of psychic and physical remedies to get away from this blueprint, or to disassociate from it.

Deities, Saints, and Saviors: Breakers of the Genetic Code

No one has ever beaten the prime genetic blueprint except those considered deities, saints and saviors. Homage is paid to these individuals because somehow they have broken the genetic code; they have seen through it. The funny thing is, there is never a penalty for understanding the genetic law. As a matter of fact, there is a reward: eternal life. By understanding the genetic code, a person escapes dying in a feeble state of unconsciousness; he or she escapes from never really understanding from whence he came.

SAF- The Key to Unlocking Genesis

Today the SAF program of self-knowledge awards this genetic information, this ability for understanding the connections of body, mind, and spirit, to the population. Just as Prometheus took fire from heaven and gave it to mankind, the SAF program is bequeathing these genetic secrets to the human population. Because poisons are completely corroding this planet, and background radiation in the environment has increased at least ten fold in the last 60 years, it is imperative to use a tracking system that will detect radiant sources that push the organs and the human body into a more rapid status of decay. Humankind must learn more about their own systems. When it is our time to die, we can do so peacefully and more consciously. It is hoped that by learning this information, we won't have to leave this earth plane in misery, misery that comes primarily from misunderstanding or not knowing.

(Read: *Junk DNA: Unlocking the Hidden Secrets of Your DNA*)

All That Exists Was Once Sunlight

What causes aging and dying? Is it really just the sun? If this is so, then how can some people sit in the sun all day and be nourished?

The sun has a particular function in relation to our hormonal balance, and the irradiation of sunlight on the skin produces the much-needed vitamin D for healthy bones, teeth, and energy. It is actually the planet's hidden energy sources, which were once of the sun, that interferes with the human being.

We must recognize, first off, that everything that exists on this planet was once of the sun. Trees, animals, even the rocks were all, over time, fashioned out of sunlight. The relative density of each of these materials depends on the concentration of sunlight. The whole scale of life on this planet is essentially a variation of congealed sunlight. Any product that uses energy, especially electricity, is one that has broken up sunlight into its finer electronic parts.

Electricity: Sparks of the Sun

In ancient times, researchers discovered some amazing natural properties in minerals. Thales and Pliny both wrote that when petrified resin (amber) was rubbed with fur, this fossilized vegetation had a power to pull things to it. The physician of Queen Elizabeth I was the first to coin the word electric, after the Greek word *ēlektron*, which means amber.

Even earlier, Stone Age man had discovered that when he struck a flint rock, sparks were produced. The astute observers at the time noted that when this congealed energy of the sun (quartz) was broken apart, a tiny piece of the sun (a spark) split off from the rock.

In the same sense, the electrical energies that pervade our environment today (appliances, television, radio waves, microwaves, etc.) use tiny split-off sparks of the sun. When we are near electrical devices, these unseen energies can sneak into the body and interfere with the genetic blueprint, disrupting its power sources. Without knowing it, we can become contaminated with this radiation.

It is not enough just to say background radiation increases the daily tally of sunlight; it is the *kind* of electrical phenomenon and radiation (ionizing or non-ionizing) that can adversely affect the human being. These particular toxins and environmental contamination produce all manner of descriptive diseases and leave their own signature on us.

Aggressive Energies Do the Most Harm

Basically, it is the aggressive energies in the environment that we would never suspect that do the most harm, causing us to lose our ability to maintain energy and power.

It is very easy to create a scenario of hypoglycemia (low blood sugar), a condition manifested by tiredness, exhaustion and anxiety, by just giving someone a certain amount of x-rays. A much easier test would be to lie out in the sun for six hours straight and receive a severe sunburn. Along with the burn, the feelings that accompany this are exhaustion and weakness, or hypoglycemia. What happened in the second case is the poison of the sun, the excess radiation, has overridden the person's own energy mechanisms. From both x-rays and the sun, the person will remain in the low energy state, hypoglycemia, until he recuperates and gets his energy back.

Study and Track the Offenders

It is *vital* for us to study and learn all the possible contamination and radiation sources that exist, and then detoxify.

If we allow these toxins to sit in our system (often it is unbeknownst to us that we even have any toxins), then we are liable to encounter an energy starvation situation. In addition to the lack of vitality, by not detoxifying, you may seem to age more rapidly. Your hair may turn gray faster. Lines and wrinkles may appear. Your bones or muscles may ache or become weak. You may be susceptible to infections or simply have a very low energy status.

Poisons Are Inherited

The real sadness of this predicament is that if we keep specific poisons locked inside our system, they are passed on to the next generation. Part of the problem is that people refuse to look at the idea that such a transmittal is possible. Alcoholism, syphilis, and many other disease states are passed on from one generation to the next. Babies are born with the condemnation of being an alcoholic for the rest of their lives. While giving birth, women with active Herpes Simplex II can blind their newborn when the lesion rubs across the baby's eyes when in that very delicate state of balance. More harmful yet is the genetic miasma passed on to the baby.

Mental Negativity: The Most Potent Poison

It may be a more acceptable notion that physical diseases are passed on, but it is often the mental processes, which also lodge their poisons, that are not acknowledged or accepted as being able to be passed on to another generation. It is very important that we have that perfect harmony between the mental state of energy and the physically created state of energy in order to avert any excessive aging process.

No matter how many physical toxins are removed, a person who harbors bad or ill feelings, such as hatred, shame, regret, fear, and resentment, will be doomed to a rapid aging process. Even though we have cleansed our physical body, we will be subject to the same laws of decay, for the energy of the mind is an even more formidable sun-generated energy. It is the energy of sunlight that gives us the ability to create perfect mental energy pictures.

So, if you hold onto a mental image of an unpleasant circumstance from an argument, upset, or confusion with a family member, or if you have lost a loved one and cannot come to a resolution in this matter, then you will have dosages of mental radiation that will also adversely affect the body. Such diseases are said to be psychosomatic in origin. It is this aspect that we look for and address with the self-awareness techniques of SAF.

> If you hold onto a mental image of an unpleasant circumstance from an argument, upset, or confusion with a family member, or if you have lost a loved one and cannot come to a resolution in this matter, then you will have dosages of mental radiation that will adversely affect the body. These mental traumas and diseases are said to be psychosomatic in origin; it is this aspect that we look for and address in our SAF emotional release work.

Thoughts and Study Questions in Chapter 2:

How do patterns of experience create energy?

What is meant by the mechanism of similar?

Why must body, mind, and spirit be synchronized?

Theoretically, how could we prevent aging?

What is meant by the origin of Life Energy?

The genetic code must be learned, because ...

What is the sun's role in Life Energy?

Earth's resistance and Ohm's Law; what is this?

How can SAF be the key to unlocking genesis?

Is electricity really just a spark of the sun? How so?

How can or do aggressive energies cause the most harm?

How is mental negativity the most potent poison?

Chapter 3

Discomfort, Pain, and Sensation

Interference Detectors

A disease has its own survival plan. In order to complete its own cycle of birth, growth, maturity, decay and death, the disease has a natural tendency to interfere with the body. Fortunately, the genetic mechanism has already factored in a program to detect when another entity is encroaching on the space of the human body.

Not only does the body have this interference detector, it also has mechanisms to sense when anything is being taken away or stolen from the human body as well. These two detectors are pain and sensation.

Pain and Sensation

It will be noted that when we have continuous pressure on the same area of the system, it will produce pains of various sorts. These pains are descriptive, and depend upon the type of entity that produced it. The following is a list of descriptive pains common to humankind: stabbing pains, stinging pains, jabbing pains, searing pains, lancing pains, throbbing pains, dull pains, to name but a few.

The difference in the pain phenomena experiences of one person as opposed to those of another person comes directly from the geometric form of the intruder, the entity, and the chemical and physiological relationship of this material to the human being involved. For example, with jabbing pains, there may be some type of energy lodged in the system that is capable of producing a jab; something that has a knife-like quality to it can produce this type of pain. With a pulsating pain, on the other hand, there may be more of an impacted kind of pressure that is rounded on the surfaces. Each person feels pain differently. Pain is invisible to all of us, and so in addition to the descriptive adjectives, an intensity scale of 1 to 10 is usually elicited to further define the pain that is felt.

While pain is a building up of pressure, sensation is a loss of pressure or resistance. It is space or increasing space. The qualities of sensation include dizziness, cold, and feeling weak, or a weakness of some sort.

Programs Needed to Detect Pain and Sensation

To understand the mechanisms of pain and sensation, we have to contend with the encroachment of another entity and cope with this particular upset. Any diagnostic program developed for humans in pain, or one with power to free us from our disease state, must be able to detect when another entity, no matter how subtle, is impinging on any of our circuits. The equipment used to discover the origins of pain must be able to detect this not only on a physical basis, but on a mental and spiritual basis as well.

The program must be able to detect what chemicals, toxins, vermin, poisons or trauma entities may be interfering with the working mechanisms of the human being. It must also be able to uncover losses in the system, such as deficiencies of minerals, vitamins, or enzymes in the physical structure, deficiencies of mental capacity, and also deficiencies and losses of a spiritual nature, including those of attitude and consideration. These particular losses could come in the form of personal defeats, such as losing at love and relationships.

The actual detection of the pains and sensations from gains and losses of energy in the system can be easily detected by the build-up, or loss, of electrical resistance in the system. We experience these losses and increases of pressure and energy by way of symptoms.

It is important to note that each individual disease entity afflicts certain organs, putting heat and pressure on those glandular structures associated with its own genetic and DNA patterns. While pressure is put *on* specific organs and glands, pressure is *taken away* from others.

Diabetes, for example, will put pressure on organs such as the thymus, liver, adrenal glands, pancreas, and endocrine system. At the same time, it steals energy away from other organs, such as the colon. The diabetic entity is a very powerful one that has been handed down through generations of genetic codes. In other words, human beings have a receptor for this disease. It should be noted that all diseases have their own organ and gland affinities, or organ and gland receptor sites.

SAF has created several different modalities to address symptomatology, including various questionnaires and infrared detection. The subjective questionnaires rely on the awareness level of the client, while the infrared detector objectively measures the temperatures of venting sites. As heat and pressures build, pain is felt. As cold and loss of pressure is measured, sensations are felt.

In many ways the questionnaires are the preferred method for chain creation. Without an understanding of the SAF numbering system, and with little or no verbal exchange as the infrared operator scans the face, hands, feet, or other area, the use of infrared seems to work "like magic," without much input from the client. In these cases the operator seems to be the one in control, not the client. Although it might seem that this defeats the purpose of *self* awareness, by using the infrared device to create a chain sequence, the objectivity of the device allows for the bypassing of the client's defensive mechanisms, their ideas and their *think* on the subject or complaint being scanned.

As we mentioned previously, for those reading this book we suggest the use of the Stress 120 Questionnaire for chain creation purposes.

Again, SAF is a logical method. Remember that a thorough understanding of the SAF numbering system is the only thing that is essential for you to increase your self-knowledge.

Discomfort and Disease

Discomfort felt from a disease condition is merely an unseen trauma or an entity (sometimes called a "dragon" by practitioners and participants) encroaching on the human space and taking up root there, much like a parasite. When this happens, you may think you feel a loss of energy, but in fact it is the aggression, the attack of the entity that is interfering with your ability to reach your own energy pods.

> Discomfort from a disease condition is merely an unseen trauma or an entity encroaching on the human's space and putting down root, much like a parasite.

Structure of a Disease

The structure of a disease entity is very simplistic in nature. It is based on a binary system of pressure and space. Its pressures (pains) have specific affinities for specific organs and glands, and its spaces (sensations) are those organ areas that it doesn't attack.

The Disease Entity Can Change Form Rapidly and Easily

Because the entity changes form, it is impossible for drugs of any nature to cure a disease. There is no such thing as a curative drug for diabetes. There actually are not any curative drugs for any condition. The only "cures" that have any workability have been vaccinations, but even they have fallen short of the mark. This is because the disease mechanism has the innate ability to change itself and alter its ability to produce pain and sensation within the body. This characteristic must be traced and followed if humankind is ever to rid itself of disease and other such confusions.

> Disease mechanisms can alter themselves and change their ability to produce pain and sensation within the body. This characteristic must be traced and followed if humankind is ever to rid itself of disease and other such confusions.

Disease entities primarily use the nervous system to inflict pain and sensation on the human body. It is the electric character of disease organisms that gives them the ability to change and to aggress against the human state. This is why it is so incredibly difficult to eliminate a disease from the body. When a disease entity is attacked, it can simply change form and turn into another disease.

For example, a person can have a kidney problem or urinary tract infection and very easily, after treating this condition, have it migrate to his feet and cause what we call gout. There are many examples of this kind of phenomenon. Very few people are aware of this mutation process until they or someone they know has developed cancer and the metastasis is evident; the different areas that have become metastasized begin to fester, oxidize, and grow anew.

Disease Entities Are Mental in Nature

It must be understood at this stage of the game that disease entities are wholly mental in nature. Their electric potential is attitudinal only. Diseases themselves have no substance. The actual entity or vortex of a sickness or a trauma is absolutely invisible. In order to activate, diseases must already be buried in the human mind. The disease entity has no wish or will to do harm to the human body, it merely wishes to survive on its own. It sees the body as a feeding ground. It sees an area where it must take up root to survive. It is not stealing energy from the person; it is just interfering with the human's energy pods.

Diseases Have Their Own Genetic History

Disease entities gain most of their energy and power against humankind the same way that a human being acquires all of his energy. Disease entities have their own genetic history. *The longer and older the disease, the more formidable it is against humans.* Newer diseases are vanquished quite easily, while older ones take up root and, with their own genetic mechanisms, foment plans and programs that alter their structures and confuse people and scientists into thinking they are other diseases. For example, syphilis may have been stopped by the action of penicillin; however, it may have easily transmuted into another condition, HIV perhaps.

Mental Origin, Stored Trauma

The disease entity itself cannot muster enough energy to create itself in a single lifetime. This may be the most fantastic statement that has ever been made about a disease. It must have a predisposed receptor site for which certain environmental toxins have an affinity.

It may be the medical breakthrough of the millennia to realize that all diseases of present day origin have already been logged and catalogued by the genetic structures in the ancestry of the individual. It is a medical fact that a disease process cannot initiate without a person having the predisposition or the receptor sites within the body to generate such a process.

> All diseases of present day origin have already been logged and catalogued by the genetic structures in the ancestry of the individual.

There Is No Such Thing as a New Disease

Diseases are merely formations or re-formations of the same old characteristic illnesses. The main problem is that we have weaknesses in certain organ structures. These weak organ structures give rise to the characteristic formation of disease patterns. As mentioned earlier in the text, a diabetic will have degradations of the thymus, the liver, the adrenal glands, the endocrine structure and the pancreas. There may also be upsets and imbalances in the posterior pituitary that control the fluid balance of the body, but this varies depending upon the type of diabetes, which is generally an inability to process sugar-glucose properly. Glucose is the main food source (energy) essential to the body for all of its metabolic processes, so problems in this area spell real trouble.

How Does Weakness In the Organs Begin?

The answer to organ weakness can be found in traumatic experiences that were created in the environment long ago. The genetic mechanisms record everything: every trauma, every brush with danger in the environment, and every upset that may have some bearing on our general ability to survive. This is a necessary survival mechanism so that future generations can concoct systems and programs to avoid these same dangers.

The organs that are the weakest are frail because they have not been able to solve the riddles of concussion that occurred in the past. If we are born with weak kidneys, for example, then some trauma or some upset that happened to an ancestor remains unsolved. It then becomes the task for each of us, who are awake and aware in our present day environment, to solve the hand-me-down riddle of our genetic structure.

Weaknesses Are Caused By Past Confusions

It is the primary bewilderment of our present day body organism that causes us weakness in any zone of our body, mind, or spirit. In a sense, when you were born, you contracted to spend this lifetime trying to figure out the miasma of your ancestors. This is no errant rule or principle, and this is not a process that is mystical; it is an obvious day-to-day, clinically observable situation. A person who acquires Herpes Simplex II at birth will almost certainly deposit or relinquish his segment of this disease to his offspring. Fathers who are diabetic certainly increase the risk of diabetes in their children. Alcoholic mothers and/or fathers will give birth to babies who are alcoholic. These babies will have to contend with the added problem of fetal alcohol syndrome, especially if the mother also drank while pregnant.

How Is the Disease Stored as A Trauma?

From the most basic laws of electricity and the phenomenon of magnetism, we can begin to get an understanding of this genetic blueprint. *Energy, in collision with other energies, makes tracings the same way that light from any energy source in the environment can make a photographic print. Mankind has been able to duplicate this process into a startling effect—a photograph.* This tracing is the same mechanism used within the human body.

Metals in our system (especially silver, cadmium, zinc and heavy metals) have the propensity to be etched upon the memory banks in particular formations, enough to store the entire content of many of our dramatic life situations. (For more on the elements, read: *The Promethion*.)

Does SAF Always Focus on Pain?

The SAF system is able to trace *all* events, whether they contain pain or pleasure. Pleasurable events are stored in one memory bank while unpleasant events are stored in another memory bank. But all of these particular mental-origin recordings are there primarily for reference and energy. Remember that we draw all our energy from the genetic mental image banks. It is these energy patterns that give us our power to perform any action. Of course, at the same time, there are dramatic, traumatic mental images etched in the genetic structure that can alert us to danger in the environment or stop us altogether.

How Is A Past Trauma Recalled?

These mental images are stored in particular sequences, and they have their own ability to be called or recalled for examination. What give them the ability to be recalled are familiar circumstances in the environment around each of us. Any particular pattern, sound, or color that is present in the environment in the present time has the ability to call up or pull forward for examination images from past genetic stored mechanisms. This is how we obtain power. If our recall system is cued in to pleasant events, then our power will be great. If our recall system is cued in to negative, dramatic emotions and events, then our power will be diminished.

Remember the ice cream cone-car accident in Chapter 1? That would have been recorded by the genetic mechanism as a pleasant, happy event. But after getting the ice cream cone, there was a car accident, which would have been recorded as unpleasant, pain, confusion, etc. The pleasant and unpleasant emotions of those events became ensnarled so that *the mention of "ice cream" brought to mind the tasty cone, as well as all the darkness of the unpleasant accident. This happens to us on a daily basis, often just below our conscious level.*

Present Environment and Past Situation: The SAF Method Finds the Link

By selectively editing such situations, we can gain great power and energy. Otherwise, if we are cued in to an unhappy circumstance in our genetic memory banks (and don't know how to edit these), we will certainly lack the power or the energy to deal with situations in the present environment. If we are able to separate pleasant situations from negative ones, we will be able to operate more efficiently. The SAF method is not a shotgun system that would just spray out into the darkness hoping to hit something; it is not hunting in the dark. It is a program used primarily to seek and hunt down negative emotional and physical characteristics that haunt us.

The SAF method has the qualities of a screening mechanism. It can filter out the negative situations while leaving the positive ones alone. Some people doing the SAF formats will note that SAF is focusing primarily on negative emotional states; this is precisely why the system was created. Others ask the question, "Doesn't the SAF say anything positive?" The answer is yes, it does, in the sense that it will indicate when a negative is diminishing. But it doesn't focus on positive circumstances because these don't necessarily need to be corrected. The SAF program is indicated in situations where a person has negative emotional ties that are draining his or her energy in the present environment.

> The use of the SAF method is indicated in situations where a person has negative emotional ties that are draining energy in the present time.

Mental Attraction and Contagion

Throughout the history of mankind, disease entities have continually infected the human race. However, there is a specific law in the universe that states: *two particles cannot occupy the same space at the same time.* (Pauli Exclusion Principle.)

In other words, you will lose power if an entity moves into your space and tries to take up your location. Your power diminishes because the entity is interfering with your most basic energy function: to reach back into the genetic tracing banks and obtain power.

When an infection or virus is able to infiltrate its way into the actual DNA mechanism itself and reprogram it, then we will certainly suffer. Our bodies will begin to deteriorate rapidly because we have all but lost our defense mechanism. However, we shouldn't put all our attention on the disease as a process that needs to be eliminated. The defenses of someone with a disease were weakened long before he or she contracted the disease. That particular genetic line was interfered with over a period of eons, so the virus was able to invade. That particular riddle of defense had not been solved.

This situation is seen with many diseases, such as autoimmune diseases where some aspect of the body seems to be attacking itself. It is curious to note that some people who have close contact with those suffering from Acquired Immune-Deficiency Syndrome *(AIDS)*, have developed specific antibodies. Only time will tell whether these people themselves will be protected from this disease, or if they will develop the full-blown AIDS condition from the HIV virus (Human Immunedeficiency Virus).

This antibody-type process is effective in vaccination: usually a live substance from a particular virus is put within the body to tell the DNA-RNA genetic planning mechanisms the exact blueprinting structure of the offending organism. If we want to gain immunity from a certain disease, we must have those blueprints. If our defense system doesn't have the blueprints, any organism in the environment may be able to attack us.

Immunity Can Exist On Any Level: Physical, Mental or Spiritual

Immunity, in the perspective of SAF, can exist on any level; it doesn't have to be from viruses, bacteria, parasites or physical invaders. There can be immunity from emotional disturbances, addictions, thinking problems, confusions, or spiritual distress. The whole or holistic system— body, mind, and spirit—has protective mechanisms capable of thwarting or warding off potential invasions by any errant entity.

Contagion comes about because 99% of these disease energies and traumatic ensnarled energies are *invisible*. It is almost impossible to know whether the person next to you in the elevator or across the room harbors some type of gigantic entity, even if it is able to encompass an area of four city blocks! This is often referred to as the elephant in the room. Those who are aware can sometimes *sense* such an unbalanced person as soon as he or she enters the room. The poisons injected into the environment by those who harbor such incredible toxins make the world unsafe.

SAF Method Puts Light in the Darkness

A disease entity, in our particular sense, is a complex of energies that is able to cause a situation or condition in the body. It is unfortunate that many people believe "an entity" must have wings and a long, pointed tail, but this is not necessarily so. Entities, in the SAF way of thinking, are any mechanisms that have mobility and a pressured environment. In this sense, an entity could be a refrigerator, car, airplane, dog, or most certainly the memory of another person; these will have a more forceful content when they are of a traumatic nature.

> A disease entity need not have wings and a long, pointed tail. It can be any mechanism with mobility and a pressured environment.

Harmony = Energetic Power

It is essential for us to learn to control the mechanisms that create immunity from contagion, because such powers of energy in the environment are able to send cross-conflicting signals into the body and reduce its power. The way to gain consistent energetic power is to be in constant harmony with the environment, other individuals and our own body as a whole. The only circumstance that can actually disturb this mechanism is our inability to coordinate and balance the functions of reciprocating energies in the environment.

Confusion = Disease

If you are in a situation that presents a new problem that you can't decipher, or if there is a riddle or confusion in your life that is overwhelming, you most assuredly will get the corresponding effect of disease. Tracing the common cold yields interesting information. If you question a person who has a "cold" about his prior circumstances, you will find that he has run into some confusion or upset just prior to catching the cold. What he has "caught" is the inability to remain immune from a confusion.

A traumatic situation can foster a disabled immune system on a psychic level as well as on a neurological level. In this case, the immune system is not able to transmit a signal to the body to keep it intact and free from harm. If you can't solve the passions of your mind, your body will often succumb to the same upsets. The body will mirror these traumas in a very distinct and different way from the energies of the nervous system and the upsets of the mind.

> The way to gain consistent energetic power is to be in constant harmony with the environment around you. When you solve the passions of your mind, the physical body will follow suit.

Control the Mass, the Energy, and the Concept of the Situation

Let's say, for example, if you were to lose your job, you might feel mentally exhausted. Your nervous system might feel empty and your body may feel a "cold" coming on. But there is always a three-prong approach when considering the control of disease entities—the body, the mind, and the spirit are the three-prongs.

To control the *mass* of the situation would mean to get a new job. We cannot argue with the fact that when a job is lost, it creates a financial hardship. The only way to replace or fix this problem is to get a new job. The point being made here is that mass will cure itself in the obvious physical sense. We can see that if you were employed at one place and lost that job, but then became employed at another place and retained the same amount of pay, there would be no harm done on a financial level.

However, it is the *energy* of the situation that creates a traumatic field. The energy of the new office and surroundings is now different, and you must make that distinction. It is a different location and a different space. There are many differences that fall under the category of energy, and if we don't recognize these very simplistic differences, we will often succumb to disease, because the body is in the "wrong" location. We must be able to be immune to the changes of energy in the environment.

On the other hand, the *concept* of the traumatic job-loss circumstance is aroused because you may have liked the people at the old job. At the same time, you may have a distinct hatred for the person who fired you. Many concepts are co-mingled with energy upsets and have very little to do with the mass of the situation. If we were merely android bodies with a pre-programmed set of rules and could be interchanged and plugged into one situation or any other situation, such as the way we would replace a picture tube in a television set, or change batteries in our phone when spent, then there would not be any problem. But because of the energy and the concept circuits involved in a human being, many different bizarre circumstances can develop.

Infiltration Causes Loss of Energy

The most important factor in the contagion of diseases or mental states is our seeming loss of energy. In this situation, you lose the energy field and the integrity of your defense. You defend an area in the first place because the more you can keep this area clean, the more power you can generate.

An infiltration, then, is an enemy of a human being. Once the energy shield is penetrated, parasitic outposts or operations of other entities can worm their way into a person's energy fields and slowly create havoc. You will realize, down the line, that your own demise or death can only be brought about by infiltration.

If we look specifically at the death sequence, we realize that many overpowering forces from the environment breach our defenses over a lifetime, however long that may be. We eventually have trouble with sight, sound, and memory recall. The body becomes fragile and weak. There are different unseen energies coming between our energy field in the present time and the original blueprint of energy predicted for us by the genetic mechanisms. In the life cycle, we are somewhere between maturity and death.

In other words, the genetic planning mechanism desires that we work at peak performance at all times. There is no real timetable. The truth is, there are plans and programs for dealing with the intrusion of energies from the environment, and it is acceptable to be intruded upon and to be eaten up.

The final degradation occurs when we die and our remains are put into the ground. At that point, of course, all manner of living creatures are able to intersect with the energy field of the body and decimate it.

How to Stop the Aging Process

In order to stop the aging process, three levels need to be addressed and cleansed—body, mind, and spirit. Eject all of those impurities that made their way into the physical system and put down roots. Once cleansed on the mass side (meaning the body is completely cleaned out), then the mind should be completely freed of any adverse energy. On the concept level, any erroneous thoughts, concepts, deeds and errors need to be cleansed. In a perfect world, if we were physically cleansed, and the spirit and mind were in complete and unreserved working order, humankind most certainly would never die.

The Prospects of Humankind

As this is not a perfect world, we are constantly beset upon by numerous riddles, confusions, foibles and weaknesses. As we grow older, there are so many booby-traps that it is easy to become overwhelmed. Even with the ability and intellect to decipher all or most of the problems of our health, our welfare, and our mental and spiritual state, we find that the ratio of "solved" and "unsolved" is sorely uneven. We try so desperately to figure out and solve a problem or two; all the while we are being overtaken by many more. We may be acquiring one problem per day and only solving one problem per week. With such a timetable and scale, no matter what kind of resiliency we obtain, we will lose the battle. This would represent our aging curve.

Of course, in the beginning of life, the amount of confusion is minimal. As these confusions stack up and we gather traumas throughout our life, we begin to observe all the upsets that we can't solve definitively. There are the divorces, deaths, lost loved ones, business losses, things that we are unwilling to tell or share with others, secrets we have to hide, ideas we are unable to communicate, confusing concepts, mental quirks caused by the shifts of energy and location in the environment, and the shame and degradation in our lives.

All those areas where we are unable to recoup our losses will have a traumatic effect. The net result is the inability to discover "why." This inability causes us our complaints and grief. It is the intersection of these problems that crisscross the fibers of our being. This intersection of problems stops us from understanding life to such a degree that we are no longer fully alive and aware. We are, more or less, racing headlong toward death.

As we become more disoriented and confused in life and less able to be enlightened, we come closer to a death-like situation.

On the other hand, *as we become more enlightened and have more understanding, we will live cleaner. The more we let go of what hinders us, the more self knowledge we gain, and the more greatly improved will be the quality of our lives.*

A human being is like a flame. If that flame is able to burn brightly and clearly and is filled with understanding, then we will survive well. If darkness covers that light, if the energy is snuffed away from it, if something intersects between the wick and the flame, then the light will be extinguished.

The Ability to Create

The impetus and purpose for all humans is to have the ability to create. This is considered our prime directive. We must be able to bring an idea into existence. Day in and day out, we envision what we want in life. If we can't create or envision, then we can't produce. If we can't produce, then our ability to see usefulness for our existence diminishes.

We must see objects appear that coincide with our concept or idea of what should be there. If we want to marry one person and ended up marrying another, or if we desired one job but settled for a different one, then we see that our energy was not producing the effects that we had envisioned. This can be very tiring and unsettling.

The disease entity has the same process coordinated with its existence, as does the human being: it needs to create. All diseases that infiltrate the body want to disseminate, procreate, and produce. It is not enough for a virus or a disease entity entering the body to be satisfied with just taking up root in whatever location it finds itself. It must always try to convince the cells and the energies in the body to reproduce its own kind. A disease on a rampage is constantly trying to overwhelm and take over the space of the body.

But even with all the toxins and poisons within our physical structure, we can still be immune to the rampage of a disease. We can add to our immunity on three levels, body, mind, and spirit, through self-awareness and understanding. The greatest and most effective of these are the mental and spiritual levels.

> "What lies before us and what lies behind us are small matters compared to what lies within us."
> –Ralph Waldo Emerson

Thoughts and Study Questions for Chapter 3:

How is a disease stored as a trauma?

How is a past trauma recalled?

Present time and past – how does the SAF method find the link?

What is meant by mental attraction and contagion?

What is meant by: Immunity can be on any level: physical, mental or spiritual?

How does harmony equate to energetic power?

What is meant by confusion equals disease?

How can we control the mass, energy and concept of a lost job situation?

Chapter 4

Numbers, Patterns, and Recognition

The disease process is a very specific process of interference by another entity. If a plant has fungus growing on it, we know it is diseased; the fungus is intersecting with the area that should be "plant." In effect, the fungus is trying to take up the same space at the same time as the plant.

If we look at a goldfish and see the characteristic goldfish rot called Ich, we know there is some entity trying to occupy the same space at the same time as the goldfish.

A similar example would be a human being with dark circles and bags under the eyes, moles, etc. We know he or she is being intersected by visible energies and more than likely by invisible energies, which are trying to take up the area occupied by this human being.

Creation Is a Disease Process

We can observe more parallels in the environment. The actual creation of energy and matter in this universe is in itself a disease process. The basic action of survival – eating – explains this concept.

To eat is to ingest, to take in the energies of another. This involution and convolution of substances, which progresses through the entire cycle of existence, is the same process a disease uses to survive.

This may come as a tremendous revelation because people generally think no harm is being done as they eat food. Normally the process is kept under control. However, when the digestive system is not kept under control and you lose your ability to digest properly, you will experience this disease process as if it were a war.

When we eat a food substance, we are attempting to take an existing entity and convert its energies into our own. But if the chicken that is eaten wants to remain a chicken and refuses to become digested or involved in the body processes of a human being, or if the human digestive fluids are not correctly in sync to complete that metabolism, then the chicken will remain a chicken. At the same time, it has been cooked, chewed and is inside the stomach of the human. This unfortunate event is commonly called a stomachache, and it is a disease process that can foment problems in the future.

Domestic animals, those that are raised to be food for humans, are more easily digested than wild game. The game often needs to be "tenderized" (beaten with a mallet), or soaked in marinades (enzymes, lemon, or vinegar) in order to break down the fibers for better digestion. A native, wild trout gives the fisherman more fight than a hatchery-raised trout. The former has a stronger desire to remain a fish, and the difference in the taste of the cooked flesh is obvious.

If we continually have difficulty digesting, then eventually more progressive disease processes will develop.

Digestion: War Between Entities

In effect, in the process of digestion, there is a war going on between entities. Each entity is trying to envelop or swallow up the other. The process of existence is a disease, a disease that plagues other entities in the environment as well.

We make it very uncomfortable for the food matter that we ingest because the substances and the life energies that exist around us also want to go on surviving. They certainly don't want to become food; they have their own instincts for total survival. This is one of the reasons why many people have leaned towards vegetarianism; however, the vegetables ingested would also like to remain alive as they are in the middle of their own life cycle.

> The process of digestion is a war in which each entity attempts to swallow up the other.

More highly developed energies, of course, have a greater instinct for survival. Thus, the battle occurs when we must convince another energy that it wants to be assimilated, that it is a lower order of life and would be more suited if it were part of our complex existence. People with weak digestive forces get into metabolic and theoretical arguments with foods that cause their systems to be constantly in a war-like state.

Mental and Spiritual Indigestion

The same digestive process can manifest itself on a mental and spiritual plane. If we refuse to digest the words, thoughts, dreams, aspirations or desires of another person, then we may have indigestion of the mind. We could also have indigestion of the spirit in which thoughts and spiritual ideas enter our space, take up root and infiltrate the whole system. It can happen that we attempt to take on the thoughts and concepts of another person, try to swallow them like a tough piece of meat, and are unable to digest them, unable to make them our own.

Confusion Can Cause Indigestion, Too

If you have been exposed to a trauma, death or separation from a loved one, or if you stumbled onto a situation or event too difficult to grasp, this confusion may result in indigestion. Often these misunderstood situations involve loss, especially when you have attempted to bring about a specific change in the environment or tried to create something and it was thwarted.

If you envisioned being happily married with children and your partner is unfaithful, this can wind up causing a condition where you have indigestion of the soul, the spirit, and the mind. You can't "digest," or understand, how your partner could do this. You will experience the same symptoms as someone with physical indigestion.

It is interesting to note that those who have these confusions and conundrums in their minds, as a rule do reflect this in their body. They will have stomachaches, pains, and upsets that radiate in the body to express the confusion. For this reason, in the world today, there are many people with severe digestive problems. Much of it is not from a physical cause but rather a mirror of psychosomatic illness that emanates from indigestible ideas.

Disease Process in the Environment

Again, we must look closely at the environment to see what it teaches us about our own disease process. There would be no such thing as disease if it weren't coming from the master blueprint. In this master blueprint of the universe we can find the intimate processes of convolution, involution, and evolution. We must look at the entire process of the sun, its creation and the cycles of Life Energy on the Earth to understand that the process of birth, growth, maturity, decay and death is a disease process.

In SAF, when we say disease process, we mean that *disease is discomfort, lack of rest,* or *off the resting-place.* On a pain/sensation scale, we can see the nature of disease. With "0" representing rest, if any energy is exuded in a positive or a negative form, it causes a disease condition.

A Disease Represents a Problem to Solve

It is significant to note that the *viewpoint* of disease is all-important, not just the fact that a disease is created. Diseases are of interest to us because they represent problems that need to be solved. It is the reason why humankind exists here on this planet.

If there is any degree of spirituality, we must see that our entire existence depends upon our ability to solve problems. We should welcome the idea of having a problem to solve; otherwise, it would get quite boring here on planet Earth, and our existence would be meaningless. Anyone who seeks to completely erase, ignore, or deny his problems and diseases will have an extremely monotonous life at best.

Countless people have wondered in the past - is the planet Earth a problem-solving location, or is it created as a problem? Both can be true.

- The planet's creation and evolution are the same creation/evolution of the disease process.
- Disease is the sum total of the processes of learning and understanding.

Energies are intersecting one another continually. Even the sun itself must intersect all plant, mineral, and animal life on the earth continually to create the cycles of Life Energy on the planet.

SAF: Disease Awareness

So, you may ask, "What does this viewpoint have to do with SAF?" SAF, the Self Awareness Formulas, refers to *disease* awareness. It means to have total awareness of disease processes. However, this doesn't mean that by following SAF religiously, you will be completely cured of all illness. As long as we exist on this planet we will have such problems. *Disease is the sum total of the processes of learning and understanding.* Assimilation of knowledge is similar to the machinery of the digestion of disease conditions and diseased ideas of the mind. Life on planet Earth is a continual process, a journey. Long ago, Aristotle wrote that all human beings, by nature, want to know. There would be nothing to learn or investigate unless a person was diseased, or off the resting point, in the first place.

> "All human beings, by nature, want to know."   --Aristotle

Let us look at disease as a process of confusion developed out of an inability to know. The faster we are able to be cognizant of, to unravel, confusions and mysteries, the faster we are able to eliminate those confusions or diseases, to eliminate being off the resting point. It is that simple.

The slower a person observes and understands diseases and confusions, the more prone he is to create long-term chronic conditions. A chronic condition is merely a problem that has gone unsolved for a long period of time. These conditions can become compounded, of course, but this is because we have not been able to solve all of the ancillary riddles of our original problem.

For example, someone who has genetic diabetes has a very difficult problem. He must be able to understand not only his own present day condition, but also the diabetic syndrome that has existed in his ancestors, perhaps for eons. The same would be true of various cancer syndromes. It is easy to become confused trying to dissect and understand all the ramifications of toxicity that exist in the environment today, as well as your own toxic thoughts.

Self Awareness Gives Humanity the Edge

The Self Awareness Formulas were created to give humankind the edge in solving confusions and disease processes. As was stated earlier, if you are being invaded at a rate of five disease conditions per day and are able to solve only one or two, then obviously the solution curve is in a downward spiral.

We can observe this phenomenon by looking at pictures of famous people or movie stars at different time periods in their careers. When we compare the younger images with the older ones, we see that something has happened. When they were young, their bodies seemed to have a smooth and glistening look, and by the end of their lifetimes we can see that there has been a lot of infiltration. Poisons worked their way into each person's system by different corridors and corners. This is part of the human condition. In a lifetime, humankind is presented with so many problems, confusions and disease processes that we are unable to solve each one in its proper ratio of body, mind, and spirit.

There are some aged people who are vibrant, full of energy, and it is difficult to tell their chronological age, but many others are so far behind, taking on five or six confusing processes a day that their aging progresses rapidly. They are said to be "old before their time."

The SAF program has been developed so we can at least come up to an even par with the number of confusions and disease processes that enter our system. When we say, "enter our system," we look at the entire complex system, the spiritual upsets, the mental issues, as well as the physical problems. We can't separate body, mind, and spirit. If we attempt to separate this relationship of matter, energy, and concept, we will soon realize that it doesn't matter how much mass is handled, how much energy is handled or how much concept is handled. It is the relationship between all three that must be addressed.

> The connections of body, mind, and spirit and their control of the genetic blueprint. The spirit is the *concept*, with dreams and desires. It is the spirit that controls all, and ultimately controls and directs our progress. The mind is the *energy*, the Life Energy, with directions, designs, and wiring diagrams. The body is the *mass*, the physical structure, with actions to take. It contains the genetic blueprint.

SAF: Understanding Origins and Causes

By using the SAF Method, not only will you understand that you have an upset, such as sensitivity or an allergy, you will also understand its origin. This is essential to avoid a repeat performance.

As an example, if you have a rash on your hand, you know this rash is coming from somewhere. This rash is mass or matter; it is visible. Remember that visible light is only 1% of the electromagnetic energy spectrum, so when you see a mass, you know that you can edit this mass very easily. You can put calamine lotion on it, soak it, or bathe it in Epsom salts or gentian violet.

There are different remedies to use to get rid of a mass, but will it get rid of the total problem? The answer is no, because mass is only one prong of the three-pronged energy system of mass (body), energy (mind), and concept (spirit). By not utilizing the 3-prong approach, it will merely bury the problem until it returns in another form.

How Can the Disease Entity Appear In a Different Place and a Different Form?

People believe they have taken care of situations, such as diseases, because they have gotten rid of the masses (symptoms), while in fact the energies of the disease roamed freely and turned into other confusions or disease conditions. Remember that an entity is composed of energy and energy cannot be destroyed.

A person with a rash uses calamine lotion or chemicals to dissolve it. The rash will disappear. But where did it go? Did it go outside or inside the body? More than likely it sank into the body, and the energy that had been routed from the skin and pushed back into the body will now have to find another resting place.

Often, the resting places the disease energies find are more interior, closer to a human organ system. They may wind up in the prostate gland, the pancreas, or the liver, and thus add this new extra energy to a vital organ to create a more serious situation. Therefore, even simple disease processes, such as rashes, must be handled directly.

Symptoms Are Signals

In SAF, a rash would be considered a signal; it is sending a message that some errant energy or mental problem may exist. A person who has a rash can run an SAF program and find out that the rash is coming from an allergy or sensitivity to bananas. A query determines that this person is, in fact, eating bananas on a daily basis, so the removal of the bananas from the diet would help greatly. Of course, this again is just shifting masses; it has nothing to do with taking care of energies.

By utilizing these self awareness techniques, we can get to the bottom of why the person has rashes created by allergies to bananas, and can remove that problem as well. This is accomplished by shedding light on the mind and spirit aspects to find what led to the allergy in the first place. Then the person can eat a banana without getting a rash. This is the basic concept of the SAF Method. It is a sophisticated process that edits not only the mass of the problem, but also the energy and the concept as well.

SAF Studies Disease or Discomfort

The study of SAF is the study of life, the creation of life, and its disease processes and confusions. As was mentioned previously, Life Energy itself is a disease process; it is uncomfortable. If we look at the action of birth, a necessary event for the creation of a new human being, we note a sometimes pain-filled process. This is confusing to a human being. We know that pain is "bad," but at the same time we know that we need it to progress. To repeat a very trite, colloquial phrase - "no pain, no gain."

Throughout all the processes of energy there are sensations and pains. Sensations and pains are relegated to disease processes because disease means dis-ease or discomfort, and that is all it means. We develop disease or uncomfortable conditions that we don't understand how to handle, so it becomes a chronic, recurrent condition.

If we understood disease and uncomfortable conditions, and how they are necessary functions of life, we would be able to put them in their place. However, we wouldn't be eliminating the disease, because it exists forever. We would just be changing our viewpoint enough so that we would not experience the problems created by the disease. We would no longer be crushed under by its existence.

Physicists understand that as energy moves out from the sun, it immediately creates a disease process on space. As the tempo of energy increases, the rays of energy cause tiny pains, or pressures, to the spaces around the sun. This is a universal disease process, but it is a necessary action, one that the universe perceives quite easily and respects in its ability to also create life.

The Sun's Disease Process

The sun's disease process is the simplest disease process to observe. A sunbather who lies out in the sun and overexposes his flesh to this energy for six hours will prove this idea. The burning is proof of the intersection of the energy through space. Once the sun intersects its energy with the human being, the human's system will begin to blister and decay.

If in the sun too long, a human being's flesh will peel from his or her body. He or she has been invaded by the same energy that causes all diseases on planet Earth, but it is a disease of which the body is quite aware. *On planet Earth, all disease processes start with the sun.*

We have learned how to transform the sun's energy processes and develop a viewpoint about it that is non-harmful. Even so, we must have a great respect for this disease process, because the sun has the ability to burn holes in human flesh. If we let this energy intersect often enough, the end result will be skin cancer and cancers of other natures.

The Age of the Super Disease Format

A simple disease is no more than a simple confusion. Compound those simple confusions and the result is a super disease. We are entering an age of the super disease format – we have less immunity than did our parents, and many today are dying of high-tech confusion. Our bodies are becoming intersected, riddled and invaded by poisons that never existed on the planet before. More and more toxins and poisons are being spewed out into the environment, and no one has any idea what kind of effect these will create on a human body now or in the future. The pains, sensations, and diseases that come from swallowing, ingesting, breathing in or being exposed to such poisons and errant frequencies create situations in the human body that are treated by medical doctors with *more* toxins - the latest sophisticated drugs.

Critical Mass and Spontaneous Combustion

The poisons accumulating in the human system are reaching critical mass. Just like the hydrogen bomb, many people are simply exploding.

The first official incident of spontaneous combustion of human tissue occurred in 1889 when a man driving a milk wagon fell off the wagon and burst into flames. It was a very peculiar incident that no one could explain. Some called it an act of the devil.

In 1933 a second incident was recorded. A woman, dancing in a marathon, suddenly caught fire. Observers and crematorium technicians estimated the amount of heat present to be about 7000 degrees centigrade. The dancer was vaporized within a short time.

It was 1953 before another incident made it to the newspapers. This one occurred in Brooklyn, NY. An older woman, sitting in a chair by her window, suddenly caught fire. When neighbors found her, all that was left were a pile of ashes and pieces of a leg bone. She had been vaporized.

Ever since that incident in 1953, there have been more than 750 reported cases of this phenomenon. We can see that spontaneous combustion is becoming more prevalent. It is a high-tech super-disease. There may be different explanations for what is going on in these cases, but knowing the critical mass aspects necessary for bombs to explode, it would appear that many have been inundated with radiation, radiational energy of various sorts, chemical toxins, and poisons and their systems reached critical mass.

Accumulation of Toxins Creates Mass

The ingestion of drugs, chemicals, poisons, toxins, and hormone imbalances, in association with high radiation sources such as microwaves, x-rays, radio, television waves, nuclear power plant effluence, etc. creates pressure that "goes off" when it reaches critical mass.

This is the same concept needed to create a hydrogen bomb. A hydrogen device contains so much confusing radioactive energy in one place at one time that it explodes. In a similar way, a human being becomes angry and "blows his top" or goes berserk and starts shooting people from a tower. This explosion phenomenon can be observed in those who have reached their limit, that is, reached their limit of problems and confusions. We have not been able to solve problems fast enough. The problems pile up, they become pressurized and explode. Spontaneous combustion of human tissue, hydrogen bombs, and angry people are similar; what they share in common, at the very core, is an unsolvable riddle.

Radioactive Elements: Congealed Sunlight on Earth

The sun, constantly baking the earth in its own aura, creates pieces of congealed sunlight on the Earth—those coveted elements known as uranium, plutonium, and all of the radioactive series. These elements have had so much sunlight, so much energy packed into them, that they are ready to detonate.

Mankind has succeeded in developing a technology to pack enough of this refined sunlight together until it can't take it anymore. It becomes "angry" from the pressure, which causes a chain reaction and it spontaneously combusts.

In almost the same way, people have so many disease symptoms, poisons, and toxins from being exposed to pollution in the environment, from taking drugs and medicines that they are almost ready to explode themselves. Anything might set them off.

The Primary Grid Work of Disease

The primary grid work for creation laid the foundation for the dissolution of disease.

As was mentioned earlier, the sun causes discomfort; it causes the aging process, but it also causes birth and life. Without sunlight, without the passage of enough sun-days (that is, one 24 hour cycle of exposure to sunlight), a baby would never be born. The baby must complete nine months, approximately 270 sun-days, of gestation. Even though enclosed in a dark womb, it takes 270 of earth's sun-days until a baby's exposure reaches critical mass. In effect, a baby being born explodes out of the womb. It has had enough. It has gotten too big. Its energy has collected and congealed to such an incredible size that it can't exist in that space anymore, and it must invade another space. At birth, a baby invades the space of the environment around it and finds a place outside the mother's body. So, this very important survival mechanism is part of the whole process of causing an individual primary life discomfort, growing up. We hear the term "growing pains," but such pains can be perceived as pleasure, depending on our ability to understand the process. It is a matter of viewpoint.

The grid work of the sun (creation and disease) is also the grid work of the SAF method. The power of the SAF method is that it can develop and enhance our viewpoint to explain exactly how a disease process intimidates, and how we can gain back control.

SAF Uses Numbers to Track Disease

The SAF study of the disease process is a universal one founded on the most basic subjects of the universe: mathematics, geometry, and physics.

Galileo, who had much to say on this mathematics process, wrote, "Mathematics is the language with which God wrote the universe." Every science must yield to mathematics. The SAF method uses numbers because numbers are universal to all forms of Life Energy and all forms of disease processes on Earth. Numbers are the triggers for the energy banks.

Numbers by themselves have no meaning unless they are assigned meaning. A person seeking answers to complex problems needs to address a wide range of emotional issues, environmental situations and other upsets, and assigning meaning to numbers is the simplest, most orderly way to accomplish this.

The SAF numbering system intersects all known sciences and bodies of knowledge. The balance of this text and other Scogna-authored books explain fully the numbering system.

> "The story of the entire universe is a grand book, written in the language of mathematics."
> -- Galileo

Electricity, Magnetism, Physics

Madame Curie, Pierre Curie, and Wilhelm Konrad Roentgen have contributed to the basic knowledge of the universe. The laws of electricity, magnetism, physics, radiation, and gravitation have also found their niche. Max Planck's work on quantum theory ultimately led Niels Bohr, Albert Einstein, and Werner Von Braun to understandings that gave us the hydrogen bomb.

Of course, many will argue that because of nuclear madness today, mankind is on the threshold of a nuclear apocalypse. Right now, there are tremendous potential hazards with nuclear energy when we consider all the nuclear power plants, submarines, nuclear medicine, and the overexposure of radiation in the environment. A big question remains: how to dispose of the partially spent nuclear fuel materials whose half-life can number in thousands of years?

In essence, what scientists have accomplished on planet Earth is the ability to take a piece of sunlight and use it as a lightning bolt. The atomic and hydrogen bombs, as the sun's stepchildren, are not only devastatingly powerful instruments for war, and energy producers for peaceful purposes, but have become important study tools to understand more about the human body. Because of the advances in science in the 20th century, nuclear and atomic studies have given us the ability to understand the energies in and around the human being in far greater terms than was ever before believed possible.

Life Energy Foundation

When in his mid-20s, Joe Scogna came to the realization that his rather bizarre symptoms were caused by sensitivity to radiation. He had photophobia, and a dislike for any type of radiation or heat. Television bothered him. He couldn't go near a radio and its waves. Electricity made him jump, and even the electricity of the car interfered with his energy. Often when driving at night, the car lights would blink, and then, with a flash of light on the dashboard, the entire electrical system was gone. This was dangerous, and he was terrified. He had tremendous anxieties and his body felt tired and weighted all the time. He was told he had hypoglycemia and that his Life Energy was low, way too low to support life.

In effect, his protective shields were down, perhaps as a result of the elevated mental/spiritual states of consciousness that he had been experimenting with, as well as over-exposure to the sun and radiant energies.

He had been a star athlete, playing basketball all through high school, college and in city league competitions, so he was determined to find out what was going on. His initial radiation studies on cosmic and atomic levels were for his own edification in the hope that he could perhaps control his hypersensitivity. By studying the reports on the effects of atomic radiation that came out of Hiroshima and Nagasaki, Japan, it was noted and generally understood that the organs and glands degraded in a certain order in the presence of high-intensity, gamma radiation. This sequence, what Joe later called the Primary Sequence, can be found in *The Threat of the Poison Reign* and *The Promethion*.

In 1978, the Life Energy Foundation was founded. Within a year, forty miles away, the first nuclear power plant mishap occurred at Three Mile Island, outside Harrisburg, Pennsylvania. Immediately, radiation was on everyone's minds, and at that point Scogna branched out and conducted tests at various nutritional clinics that were springing up all over rural Pennsylvania. He interviewed clients, tested and logged physical and emotional symptoms. All the test data was evaluated under Scogna's scrutiny at the Foundation. A company magazine was started, *The Life Energy Monitor*, to keep the clinics and interested people abreast of new developments.

Using the Primary Sequence of organ and gland system degradation as the basis of study in the research project, electronic equipment was utilized, including oscilloscopes, frequency counters and computers, and hundreds of composite tests were conducted on humans with vitamins, minerals, color, sound, glands, enzymes, herbs and many nutritional substances.

Subjective radiation tests, symptomatology, and metabolic health evaluations were composed; out of these equations were developed the SAF-120 for physical symptoms, the Stress-120 for the emotions, the Q-24, and others followed. Experimental computer programs were written for analysis of hair, blood, urine/saliva, sound, voice, and temperature. With all these analyses, it should have been easy to intersect what we knew about the body, mind, and spirit connections with what we didn't know, and come up with the answer. But something wasn't adding up.

After thousands of hours of testing, the computer project seemed at a standstill. It looked as if a dead end had been reached. Man's most secret problems, the ones that *cause* our chronic ills, remained hidden. The continual response seemed to be that body, mind, and spirit were too complicated to understand fully, and that the actual answers to the confusions of mental trauma and its connection to body metabolism would remain concealed.

The SAF Numbering System

It took a while to decipher the metabolic codes, those connections between body, mind, and spirit. One day, late in the spring of 1980, the first codes were cracked when Scogna changed the parameters of the study slightly. His findings indicated there was another sequence of organ and gland system degradation, what Scogna came to call the Secondary Sequence. This Secondary Sequence was directly related to radiation acquired from and while on this planet. This sequence included background radiation that is being produced today by microwave towers, nuclear power plants, nuclear bomb testing, radar, metal-smelting factories, auto exhaust, chemicals in pesticides and herbicides, and all the electric and electronic appliances and gizmos that are invented and used each day. These all produce *extra* electricity and radiation. Even the light that is reflected off the moon is included, as it has a certain radiational quality. Note that the human body operates on electricity. The body *is* electrical, and so any excess of electricity will adversely affect us.

Another significant code involved the connection of the DNA-RNA and the genetic response to activity and emotion. Scogna found a way to detect the connection of electricity, radiation and stress to the disease process. Once this was understood, the confusion and fear humans have about sickness and death was dissipated and dissolved. Those first computing programs were called *QUIRK – Questions Understood by Intersecting Retrievable Knowledge.*

From that point on, the theory of the Secondary Sequence of decay has held up under scrutiny and trials with SAF techniques and programming. As more cataloging was done, diseases and syndromes were continually added to the SAF interface as well as the use of different modalities, interpretations, and remedies.

This Secondary Sequence of organ and gland system degradation, and the composition of the particular physical systems, is so intrinsically important to the creation and operation of SAF, that without it the method would be nonfunctional.

Understanding the order of organ and gland degradation is essential, because the organs and glands *are* existence for a human being. These systems are being affected everyday by exposure to sunlight, radiational, and radiant energy.

Some human organs are stronger than others and can withstand more radiational energy before breaking down. Others fail or age more quickly. As an example, the sex organs will fail sooner than the skin. The thymus will fail before the sex organs.

Knowledge of this degradation order gives us the entire secret to understanding the problems, toxins, poisons, and all those things that create the disease process. This particular Secondary Sequence and aging process is the formula for life, as it is also the formula for understanding SAF and its special language.

> Knowledge of the organ and gland system degradation order gives us the entire secret to understanding all those things that create problems for humankind. This Secondary Sequence of numbers is the formula for life, as it is also the formula for understanding SAF and its special language.

The Language of SAF

Every science has its own special terminology; the terminology of SAF best describes ideas and functions that are unique and necessary to its understanding, and form the basics of the SAF method of emotional release. Those listed in this section may differ slightly from standard medical texts and even alternative healing guides.

At its base, the science of SAF is numbers. As mentioned, it is cross-connected with many different sciences, such as bio-energetics, psychology, western medicine, sound, color and vibration, traditional Chinese and Asian medicine, acupuncture, nutrition/naturopathy, quantum physics, herbs, and homeopathy, all of which align with the numbers in the SAF system.

The language of SAF is the numbers used, 1-24, along with corresponding organ and gland systems, certain emotions, and conditions or functions. The SAF Operative Chart 4, found on page 219, embodies the basic language of SAF.

If you recall your history, the Rosetta Stone was discovered in Egypt in 1799. It contained three languages carved in stone: ancient Greek (understood by researchers and linguists); but it also contained an ancient Demotic script and Hieroglyphics, both of which were unknown to researchers. By understanding this stone, researchers were finally able to read and comprehend hieroglyphics and it has changed forever our view of history. In a similar way, the SAF language IS the Rosetta Stone for humans.

When using the SAF method of emotional release work, we can understand the messages our organ and gland systems are trying to communicate to us, which makes SAF truly the translator we need. With this method, we finally have an extremely advanced system for personal change and for helping others to find what resonates for them.

When using the SAF method of emotional release work, we can understand the messages our organ and gland systems are trying to communicate to us, which makes SAF truly the translator we need. The SAF language truly is the Rosetta Stone for humans. With this method, we finally have an extremely advanced system for personal change and for helping others to find what resonates for them.

SAF Participant: is studying the Self Awareness Formulas to learn and increase awareness for self and others. In the past, we called this person the SAFent. This is the chain owner, an active client in the process of developing self-knowledge and enlightenment, not to be confused with a patient. A patient is patient, one who waits, and by definition, has already given over his or her power to a practitioner or medical personnel. By being an active SAF participant, he or she is moving in the direction of seeking the goal of increased awareness on so many levels.

SAF Practitioner: someone who has been trained in the nuances and the techniques of SAF, and who works on self and with others. The SAF Practitioner embraces the principles of the SAF method in order to help teach, lead, and process clients and Participants. Practitioners are trained to find ages of traumatic events and the beginning ages of patterns, which will greatly help the SAF chain owner in his or her gains with this personal emotional release work.

Chain Sequence: For our purposes in this book, the SAF chain sequence of numbers is created by questionnaire and/or infrared device. The numbers represent the stressed organ and gland systems of the chain owner, as well as the emotions that are in play.

Condition or Function: Conditions are assigned to each organ and gland complex. The condition represented by each complex aligns its function with the human body. The SAF viewpoint of the condition and function may present an alternative definition to the orthodox view.

Dichotomy: A division of two opposite but equal sides, both of which give further definition to the universe (the chain) of the chain owner. These opposites enable the SAF Participant to discern differences, such as positive/negative, or light/dark in the chain. SAF uses 64 dichotomies to add many dimensions to the SAF chain sequence.

Emotion: We humans are electrical beings, and an emotion is defined in SAF as an e (lectric) motion, or electric motion. Emotions are mental experiences, which cause biochemical (physical) reactions; these cause us to act in certain ways. SAF has assigned an emotion to each organ/gland complex.

It is often easier for us to understand the *function of an emotion* rather than the function of an organ complex. It is important that we understand and learn we must own all our emotions, however negative or "bad" we consider them to be. This is the way SAF helps us to let go of the energies we need to release in order that we may be freer and more enlightened.

Energetic Dynamic: This feature is the dynamic way we can muster help from the organ or gland complex. In many ways, it is the spiritual aspect of the system, and is instrumental in our emotional release work. It is good to know we have a friend and a helper within our system, ready to assist us.

Organs and Glands: Each of the 23 organ and gland systems in SAF is ranked by number, 1 to 24. Note that the number sequence 17/18 is presented as one number, being male/female endocrine systems with corresponding hormones. By assigning numbers to the systems, this fits in easily with computers and computing work.

Physical and Mental Aspects: SAF assigns special physical and mental aspects to each of the organ and gland systems, which help the SAF Participant to have greater understanding and self knowledge on body, mind, and spirit levels.

Up-Links: SAF uses combinations of the assigned numbers to find additional information and help to further decipher a person's case state. Up-Links are two or more numbers in succession that ascend in value, such as 2-3, or 14-17/18, or 13-20. Particular Up-Links within the chain sequence have specific meanings. These Up-Links represent syndromes, listed throughout the book and in the Index of Up-Links. These particular sequences of energy will shed more light on the chain and the chain owner. Originally there were 256 syndromes, which have been added to over the years. (Note: 2-3 = Love-Hate relationship. 14-17/18 = General business troubles, building up of fat cells for insulation and protection. 13-20 = Loss of possessions, loss of location. Homesick. Depression.)

Reading a Chain Sequence: When the SAF Practitioner and the SAF Participant become proficient, the SAF numerical chain sequence can be read grammatically, much like a sentence of the chain owner's complaint, the issue this person wants to work on. The chain presents a slice of life to be examined, a snapshot in time, always encompassing the body, mind, and spirit of the chain owner.

SAF and Radiation

When reading this book, you will note a distinction is made between the spewing of radiation from a nuclear bomb or a nuclear power plant accident, and the classical definition of radiation such as what we find on the planet. When evaluating radiation, we must consider all types of energy *moving toward the body.* Radiation and gravitation are merely fields of energy, and if something is pressing on or into the body, it doesn't necessarily have to be gamma rays, hydrogen bomb particles, or x-rays. In the SAF view, radiant energy can certainly be a pressing problem, a situation that is not well understood, or a scenario that is not under control. Angry words directed at us, radiating toward us, what we call emotional radiation, certainly have a detrimental effect.

With the tool of SAF, we have begun to understand how radiational energy affects humankind and how we can use this tool to break apart, understand, digest, and dissolve a high-tech confusion and/or a disease situation.

But clearly, as the background radiation continues to increase, and as the number and type of electronic and electrical gizmos we use increases, this in itself becomes a most compelling reason to study SAF. Even with the increased assaults on our body, mind, and spirit, the SAF method has been created to carry humankind through to the next century and beyond that.

The Axioms of SAF

An axiom is a statement that serves as a basic premise for a science; it is a starting point. Axioms are formulas with rules, used by all studies of science and related fields.

After the basic premise, the first axiom is followed in sequence by the second axiom. Each axiom in turn is built on the base of the previous axioms. Without axioms, any science, including SAF would not be able to stand on its own as a science.

Axiom 1: Each of the 24 organ and gland systems (thymus, heart, kidneys, pancreas, liver, etc.) has a life of its own. All are connected to the nervous system.

Axiom 2: The organ and gland systems work alone, but many times work in unison or as helpers to other systems.

Axiom 3: Various amounts of energy are assigned to the organ and gland systems by the brain and/or mind complex on a specific timetable.

Axiom 4: Any extreme stress or trauma, such as drugs, operations, accidents, shock, etc. freeze or lock up a pattern of energy into a non-operational status at the exact instant of impact.

Axiom 5: The non-operational status of organ and gland systems can be plotted by the special 64 point mathematical matrix and flow diagram, generated by infrared detection.

Axiom 6: Once detected, the non-operational status can be deprogrammed to a new state of free operation, thereby releasing all injury on body, mind, and spirit levels – in the past, present, and future.

Study Thoughts and Questions from Chapter 4:

What is meant by mental and spiritual indigestion?

What are some disease processes in the environment?

How is SAF a study of disease awareness?

Does SAF have anything good to say, or is it always about pain?

How can Self Awareness give humanity the edge in this dangerous world?

How are our symptoms signals? What are they telling us?

How does SAF edit mass, energy, and concept?

What is the sun's disease process?

How does accumulation of toxins create mass?

What is meant by "radioactive elements are congealed sunlight on earth"?

How does SAF use numbers to track disease?

What does electricity, magnetism, and physics have to do with SAF?

What is an axiom?

From the SAF Terminology List:

What is an SAF Participant? How is this different from a patient?

How many organ and gland complexes are used in SAF?

What is the SAF definition of emotion?

How are the physical, mental, and spiritual aspects of the organs and glands used?

How were the conditions decided?

What is emotional radiation?

What is meant by radiant energy, and how does it affect us?

How does SAF track and find things for us to process?

Chapter 5

The Language of SAF
The Organs and Glands,
Emotions, and Conditions/Functions

In this chapter:

1 – Thymus & Immune System (includes immune system, tonsils, adenoids, Peyer's patches, appendix)
2 – Heart & Cardiovascular System
3 – Colon & Elimination
4 – Stomach & Digestion
5 – Anterior Pituitary
6 – Liver & Gallbladder
7 – Lungs & Respiration
8 – Sex Organs
9 – Bones & Muscles
10 – Thyroid plus Veins & Arteries of the Upper Extremities
11 – Veins & Arteries of the Lower Extremities
12 – Brain & Nervous System
13 –Adrenal Glands
14 - The Mind
15 - Hypothalamus & the Senses
16 - Kidneys and Bladder
17/18 - Endocrine System (the male and female hormone systems.) This includes the pituitary, pineal, thyroid, parathyroid, adrenal glands, pancreas, testes (M) and the ovaries (F).
19 – Skin
20 – Pancreas and Solar Plexus
21 – Posterior Pituitary
22 – Parathyroid
23 – Spleen
24 – Lymph & Electroplasmic Field

SAF is not just about the physical aspects of the organs and glands, because we humans are not just physical; we are holistic, holographic units. In these pages, the reader will find the body-mind-emotion-spirit of each organ and gland system, plus the shadow side as well as the high emotion, this is that multi-dimensional view.

Think of an SAF chain of numbers as displaying that multi dimensional view as it finds a single moment of impact in your life. How many impacts have there been? We humans each embody many, many chain sequences because we've had impacts, injuries, physical, and emotional upsets throughout our entire lives.

And so, that multi dimensional view and understanding are essential!

1
Thymus & Immune System
(includes the tonsils, adenoids,
Peyer's patches, appendix)

AT A GLANCE:
Emotion: Aggression
Condition/Function: Protection
Keywords: Against, Reaction, Action
Energetic Dynamic: The Protector

The thymus gland, situated near the clavicle in front of the uppermost portion of the sternum, is very important to the survival of the body. As a radiation sensor, studies show the thymus gland has the highest sensitivity so it has been assigned the #1.

The word thymus, from the Greek *thymos*, means shield, and by breaking down the word into Latin it is, "shield of the invisible." This is an apt description of its purpose and function.

The thymus gland is also a monitor for infection and for keeping invaders out of the body and its environs. It works with other glands in a network, the reticuloendothelial system, which is cued by the invasion of any entity into the human being's space. The thymus connects itself with the bones, the adrenal glands, the spleen, and the thyroid to cause changes in the energy stance of humans so that we are able to remove any invading enemies.

If we become sick for any reason, the thymus gland is primarily at fault. But it is only a sensor that can alert the other organs to go into action. If the sensor is in good working order, but the organs that should produce antibodies or protection are not in good shape, then of course, this would not be the fault of the thymus. However, the thymus gland is instructional and tutorial to other glands. It tells the other glands exactly what they have to do to fight off any and all invading poisons.

When the thymus gland is in very good condition, it is able to read the image of the invading energies in the darkness. Because the body's energy is only 1% visible and 99% invisible, the thymus gland works wholly on invisible radiation.

This gland in a newborn infant is very large, about the size of a plum. As a person ages, the thymus gradually shrinks, often to the size of a raisin. Scientists concluded that the thymus gland directed the creation of antibodies, and when it had

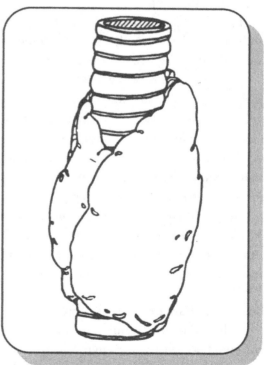

The Thymus Gland

sufficiently made all the antibodies necessary for a lifetime of defense, it withered away. This was the old and accepted school of thought, but their theory of the "withering thymus" is an erroneous one. In autopsies performed on athletes, who had died in accidents, it was found that they had large thymus glands. The real problem is that the body will collect many more toxins than it can handle so the thymus gets overrun, burning out like a fuse. Thus, it becomes withered.

Being the first line of defense against infection, the thymus and the immune system, with its contingent of helpers, is the weakest in the face of disease. The helpers of the thymus in this study are the tonsils, adenoids, Peyer's patches, and appendix. The extent of thymus degradation is parallel to the overall history of illness and disease on the planet. Infection has been the cause of the most devastating carnage of humankind in history. In diseases and deaths caused by infection, the thymus, the immune system, plus the helpers are responsible. The Black Plague that spread throughout Eurasia in the 14th century reduced the population of mankind by 40%, accounting for the death of 75-200 million people within a decade. This was due to faulty thymic action amongst the population. In addition, inflammation parallels the infections of humans, and so is part of #1, the thymus. To reiterate, because of its significance to humanity's health, the thymus has been plugged into the SAF system as #1.

Emotion: Aggression

In working with SAF Participants who had the #1 appear first in their sequence of numbers, it was noted that not only was there some kind of thymus upset, but also these people invariably complained of aggression focused toward them, or they felt aggressive towards others.

The actions of people with #1 present in the chain sequence demonstrate a state of overwhelm. They sense the pressure and aggression building up within the system as invading forces intersect with their energy fields. These forces are stopping the flow of energy to organs whose vital functions are necessary for the creation of life.

The emotion aggression is associated only with the thymus gland, and is an indicator of thymic malfunction. If the #1 appears in any SAF chain of numbers, whether created by infrared or by the questionnaires, the emotion is aggression.

Aggression seems to be the number one trouble of the entire human race. On the national front, the most important concern is the protection and safety of each resident and the country as a whole. Humanity's greatest liability and its greatest foible is safety. So, aggression, used to describe upsets involving the thymus, fits very well into this position.

Condition/Function: Protection

When studying thymic reaction, we observe the thymus gland's ability to screen out all the unwanted energies in the environment that have a detrimental effect on the human being. If the thymus is run down, it cannot come up with the answers that the protective mechanism of the body needs to defend itself. Eventually the body will age and fall apart. As we discover and learn through these Self Awareness Formulas, rapid aging is merely a reaction to the intersection of energies that have breached the barricades and the protective screens of energy around the body.

The whole idea of protection is to thwart or prevent invading forces in the environment from taking over the space that is the body's own. There are many marauding entities in the environment, and the body has a good index of these. The thymus gland, in association with the nervous system, the brain, the mind, and the spiritual aspects, most certainly utilizes this mechanism and its ability to understand a person's problems in facing a very aggressive environment.

Mental Aspects

In a sense, someone who exhibits aggressive behavior, or has difficulty protecting himself or herself, maintains a very brittle defensive stance. When confronted face to face, this person is easily prone to falling apart. Those who possess a strong nature frighten this thymus-type person. When the thymus gland goes out of balance, it indicates there are many unresolved problems on a mental basis as well. Because the mental aspects affect the physical, a person who has not been able to come to grips with his connections in the environment, as far as loved ones and business relations are concerned, will also have stress build up to such a fever pitch that it can destroy him.

Physical Aspects

Fever, pain, swelling, and pressure are brought upon the person when he or she is infected. It is very important to keep in mind that we can also develop these physical conditions from a mental stance. A person can break out in a rash from emotional pressure or cerebral upsets. In a physical sense, a person will exhibit definite characteristics, and it is an easy task to spot someone with this trouble. The characteristic complaints of pain, swelling, redness, or discomfort in an area are an immediate signal that they have a problem involving the thymus gland; his or her body is being aggressed against, and he or she is losing the safety margin. The protection is in jeopardy. This is obvious when people are nervous and unsure of themselves, because they are developing a pattern that will ultimately lead them to that critical mass or explosive state. They must come up with some answers against these toxins and poisons in the environment in order to stop the onslaught of poisons from overwhelming their bodies and taking over their space.

1 and Any Number

Number 1 bespeaks a condition of infection and inflammation; which is, and has been, an eternal connection. The invasion of the body (by infection) triggers the immunological response necessary. This induces inflammation and heat (calor) for the destruction of unwanted microorganisms;. The resulting effect is pain (dolor), redness (rubor), and swelling (tumor). There is a war being fought every microsecond between the forces of the body and the forces of the environment. Is the body winning? The answer is contingent upon the immune system.

So, the presence of #1 in any chain will alert the Practitioner and the Participant that things are getting riled up. There is an inflammatory process going on; #1 in a chain sequence intensifies the numbers in that sequence.

Energetic Dynamic

Energetically, this first system is the *Protector*; it operates on the invisible level as an electronic shield. When we see #1 in a chain of numbers, this tells us our protection is down.

This #1 system is stimulated and programmed by memories and thoughts of times we had to endure feeling unsafe and unprotected. When our protective shields are down, we must put up our dukes for protection; thus, we become focused on aggression, whether it is against a microbe or against another person or entity. We could not change or escape from the situations at that time, but we survived; somehow, we survived.

Today, we recall that we often react to any stimulus, our buttons are getting pushed, or we are constantly fighting off a cold or a negative pattern in our life.

With our SAF personal work, we remember, we learn the history, and we can now see the patterns. Then with new light, we notice that we are no longer reacting as we once were; this is freedom. It is an amazing feeling; it frees us up so we can go into action.

> When we make peace within ourselves, our immunity level rises on three levels — body, mind, and spirit. As a result of our work, our family members will benefit, our business life will be more satisfying, and the community of humankind will be more harmonious.

2
Heart & Cardiovascular System

AT A GLANCE:
Emotion: Love
Condition/Function: Synchronize
Keywords: Run, Deny, Accept
Energetic Dynamic: The Synchronizer

In the Secondary Sequence of radiation degradation, SAF has assigned #2 to the heart and cardiovascular system. This system is one of the most difficult areas in which to control disease in the human being. It is so tangled up with a person's confused emotional feelings that trouble here can be difficult for Practitioners to detect.

Radiation toxicity present in the environment has a large bearing on heart trouble. The chest is one of those areas that is easily pressurized in the presence of any kind of radiational energy, such as radiation from the sun, emotional radiation from other people, from the environment, or from the general pressure and heaviness in this every day, modern society of ours.

The heart organ itself is a small pump that extends its energies throughout the cardiovascular system in the entire body. According to the Chinese school of thought, the heart's actions are the core, or operations center, of the human being. (In contrast, the Greeks and Romans considered the brain as the center of all existence.)

The heart has a most resilient crust, but it is up against so much stress and degradation during a lifetime that it succumbs to the easy actions of heart-oriented toxins. Heart disease remains the number two killer of mankind, just behind infections and diseases caused by germs and microbes.

Emotion: Love

In the research and development of the SAF program, it was interesting to note that those who complained of physical heart traumas (actual heart pains and problems, bypass surgery, clogged arteries, etc.) also complained of difficulty in their love lives. As a

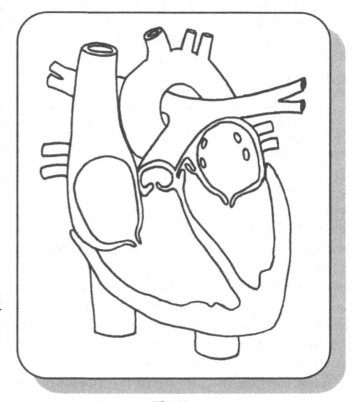

The Heart

result, the emotion love was assigned to the heart organ. It is not necessary to belabor or prove that this is so, as there are many cases of illness and death due to a "broken heart."

Condition/Function: Synchronize

When #2 appears in an SAF chain, it specifically hints at a person's problems with synchronization, meaning that he or she is not able to coordinate his or her basic activities properly.

Love has been found to be a mechanism that intersects energies in a harmonious way for greater synchronization. In this sense, love becomes the opposite of disease.

The importance of love is that it establishes a connection between one person and another; the energy of the combination is greater than either could produce singularly. That is love. If love doesn't happen, it is because one person is not able to communicate his or her ideas to his or her partner, or there is some breakdown in the assignment of needs and wants between two parties.

Harmonization is necessary. When the #2 appears in the chain, there is some desynchronization in the body, mind and/or spirit, and disharmony in connection with certain people. A disease state exists instead of a love state.

What confuses humankind so thoroughly is the fact that people who attempt to play at the game of love often wind up with a diseased state.

A divorce is a diseased state of love. In this case, love started out trying to cross-connect two human beings into a circuit that could have become very powerful and harmonious, but some essential points within their existences were never clarified. It is the darkness of misunderstandings that can overshadow the energy of love.

> It is the darkness of misunderstandings that can overshadow the energy of love.

When the intersection of another's energies with your body, mind, and spirit becomes a disease instead of love, this signifies an involution instead of an evolution. If you stop evolving, if the intersection of your energy with another's energy stops becoming productive, then you must caution yourself that you are entering a disease zone. Poisons are beginning to build up between you two.

We must not look at love only on the basis of two individual human beings. There could be love between a person and any animated or inanimate object on the planet, such as a favored animal, or a wondrous piece of antique furniture. This love is the same emotion that calls out for synchronization. It is the love that creates a bond between two entities in the environment that is productive, instead of nonproductive. Looking at disease as a nonproductive state and love as a productive state, we can see the dichotomy betwixt the two.

How does this affect the heart? It is curious that those who present the #2 as the very first number in the SAF sequence also had difficulties with disharmony, desynchronized feelings, low productivity and disease. With the heart in this position (the very core of the individual according to the Chinese philosophers), it begins to decline. It is time for people to work on their issues. It is time for people to spend their energy searching for a common denominator in the environment that will help them become more productive. It is time for them to patch up communications between themselves and their loved ones, to work on themselves and learn to create unions that will lead to a more harmonious state. Only then can productivity survive.

Mental Aspects

It is extremely important for the mind of an individual to remain organized. When confusion sets in, disease runs rampant. The synchronization and attunement of energies in the mind and spirit are necessary to coordinate the true inner feelings of love that affect the heart. If you have no ability to communicate your feelings to your partner, then the relationship must surely suffer. If you want to cure your heart, you must first cure your mind by dissecting your confusions on the most basic levels. In order to cure your heart, you must begin to educate yourself on how to communicate and how to accept the realities of another person so that you can have great feelings of love and appreciation.

On the other hand, if you hope to squash any connections between human feelings and believe that you can exist on your own, then you don't need these messages. You must shut yourself off and you need not communicate. You must not show anyone you are able and willing to create bonds necessary for greater productivity.

But if you are genuinely interested in becoming more able and more powerful, you must intersect your energies without creating disease. The only way you can do this is with the love process, which is born of synchronization. The give and take of life and energy must be there.

Physical Aspects

People are not always able to understand the feelings that exist between two people. Are the feelings disharmonious or harmonious? How can they detect if their relationship is actually creating a disease process, or a confusion?

If there is a connection between two people, and productivity between these two people is diminishing, or going into nonexistence, then they must re-evaluate and re-examine what this connection is with each other. It cannot be love. It can only be a feeling that is confused with love.

It is essential for any student of SAF who desires to learn these powerful research findings to know that throughout the development of SAF, each person has voiced the most incredible and profound thoughts and relationship to his or her disease state. These statements by individuals (their complaints, worries, troubles, etc.) are vitally important; by voicing these, and if their voices are heeded, they will allow the rest of mankind to escape the miasma of chronic disease. We must be ready and willing to confront all that the environment has to offer, all that it will offer up. We can't deny or disavow any action of which the human body is capable.

These discussions about love are not taking us away from a major point about energy. The most important thing to realize about energy is that it takes on many different forms. If we are not able to recognize and accept what we can create, then we surely are missing something. It is the idea of SAF to allow nothing to go undetected. Therefore, it is important to confront and observe all the phenomena associated with energy, and all the possible conditions that can exist. Once we are able to do this, a disease will not be able to escape our understanding.

Energetic Dynamic

This second system is the *Synchronizer*; it is a love and harmony system, which enables us to choose between harmony and disharmony. However, when #2 is in the chain sequence, it shows our inability to do so! Look to the mind and spirit for guidance, because to cure your heart, you must cure your mind.

We must be mindful to not deny harmony and not over-accept disharmony.

When we find the #2 in a chain sequence, we know that this system has been stimulated and programmed by memories and thoughts of times when we had to endure disharmony in our life, in order to survive what we couldn't change or escape from at the time.

We have been in denial about love because what we experienced was a disguised and unharmonious form of what we thought was love. Perhaps there was a traumatic incident about love, feeling unloved or not loved, or confusion about love. As a listener, do you hear: "I can't synchronize; I have a broken heart, you know." Other thoughts that may come to you as a Practitioner of SAF: "Have you been denied love, have unsynchronized feelings about love and life, or are you trying to digest love, but can't digest it?

With our personal SAF work, and a few SAF couples' sessions, we can understand and learn to separate ourselves into the two people as we once were; we are no longer "one." Having done that, we can learn to accept and embrace love and harmony into our life and sphere of influence. Then we will experience much synchronization, within and without, in our body and in life, with our family, loved ones, friends, and in our work life.

This synchronization is what we all want and need. Acceptance. Peace. Love. Harmony. Being in balance.

> Look to the mind and spirit for guidance because to cure your heart, you must first cure your mind. This is how SAF is helping humankind.

3
Colon & Elimination System

AT A GLANCE:
Emotion: Hate
Condition/Function: Detoxify
Keywords: Contain, Failed, Achieve
Energetic Dynamic: The Eliminator

The colon, or large intestine, is situated in the lower half of the body in the abdomen. It is the final segment of the alimentary canal, extending from the cecum to the rectum. It absorbs water, minerals and other materials, salvages these from the digestive process, and then discards the unwanted matter. When the colon is in good working order, it creates some necessary nutrients, filters poisons out of the body, and in some extreme cases can save a person's life.

What human beings don't realize is that they put substances into their bodies that act as spies and double agents. Anything eaten that can't be absorbed or digested becomes a toxin. It becomes a toxin because it now has intersected its energies with the body's energies and has been allowed to come into the system beyond the screens of the thymus gland's protective mechanisms. Food is brought inside for examination to see if the body wants it, to see if the cells of the body will accept this matter and energy and utilize it for necessary purposes.

It is very important to understand that the colon has a nasty job; it has to deal with those materials inside it that the body has decided are its enemies; those toxins have become the spies and double agents.

Emotion: Hate

Individuals who complain of colon problems also have a difficult time with the idea of being rejected, or they might be in a constant state of rejection. This emotion increases in crescendo to what humankind considers the most violent rejection of all: hatred. Hate can be a mechanism for separating yourself from another person's energy field.

Hatred, at #3, and love at #2 can be further explained in this manner: Love allows another person to come in past the gates; you are taking a chance. When your

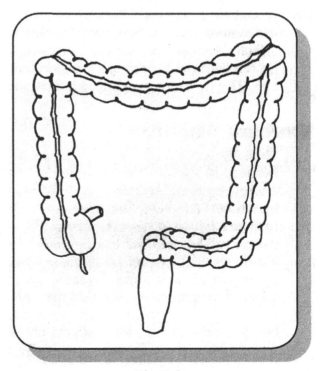

The Colon

partner gets inside to your basic mechanisms, that partner, if some other feeling has been mistaken for love, can create absolute terror and havoc. This happens to many people who are "in love" and then find that they are in love with a person who doesn't really care for them. In such a case, the partner can actually rip the lover apart because he or she has been allowed inside.

If someone has a definite feeling of hatred, he is rejecting or pushing away the idea that another person can even come near him or her. In such a case, there is no energy intersection and no "partner-energy" can be pushed undetected into the body. However, it must be understood that to hate someone, you must have had *some* kind of intersection with that person in the first place. The person's energies (the now-hated person's energies) have been consumed in some fashion; much like foods must be consumed first, then analyzed and utilized. A human being attempts to emotionally accept another person's ideas and plans and then tries to digest them. It is only after realizing that the other person's ideas and plans are poisons to his or her own system that he or she decides to push them out, to reject them.

The process of hatred comes about because once people have accepted or loved, they cannot easily push away another person along with their plans or ideas.

Most of us want to put our best foot forward and we will say, "I do not hate anyone; I have no hate in me." When doing this emotional work, we must be very honest with ourselves if we ever hope to release stuck emotions and those ensnarled energies, especially those that have such a negative connotation as hatred. We must be able to own and accept *all* our emotions. In this case, the SAF Practitioner can say to the Participant, "I understand what you are saying, but tell me, how *could* there be hate or hatred for that person?" You will be amazed at the response; suddenly, the floodgates will open, and the active Participant will gladly comply and will have tremendous gains, to which you, as a Practitioner, will also be privy.

#2-3

This Up-Link shows a Love-Hate relationship. The real problem with hatred is that the person is not able to properly get rid of the offending, intersecting energy. This is how Love/Hate relationships build up. You have allowed another person to come into your life and intersect with your energies, and now you can't get rid of him or her. And remember that we can hate many things, such as circumstances and ideas, not just other people.The problem of not being able to let go happily and easily causes a buildup of hatred. It is the action of energies trying to get out of the system; and not being able to, that builds up the pressure-hatred situation. People's energies are jammed, resulting in hatred. The poisons within their system cannot be released, so they have to push as hard as they can to try to get them out. The pressure builds and builds, and so does the hatred.

Condition/Function: Detoxify

Mentally and spiritually, we must be able to rid ourselves of the condition of toxicity because this is causing a loss of energy. People begin to hate because they are losing energy, time and motion; their abilities are decreasing. They feel themselves being taken away, their space is dwindling. Someone is encroaching on their space and they can't get the intruder out; they're trying to detoxify, but can't. They try to get the intruder away from their energy fields so they can operate properly, but herein lies the problem: they are having a difficult time getting rid of this irritating person. If the #3 comes up in the front of an analytical chain sequence from a questionnaire or while scanning a person on the SAF infrared programs, we see that the SAF Participant once cared for someone or something and is now trying desperately to get out of the situation.

It is very important to see #3 in this emotional context, for it affects physical situations as well.

Mental Aspects

Mentally, with #3 in a chain sequence, people are poisoned. They cannot envision; they cannot see. Their minds are jammed up and they cannot think straight. People with hatred have a narrow viewpoint. They can't see the world; they can only look through a tiny tube. They can't see the outside. They are trying to wash themselves clean, but feel that inside, there is an indelible print on their mind that will never go away.

#3-4-5

When this Up-Link of numbers appears in the chain sequence, we have found there is a dislike for work, a strong dislike. In this situation, the SAF Practitioner would ask the client about the work situation in his or her life.

Physical Aspects

An interesting correlation found throughout the years of reading chains of numbers and looking at different processes is that many of those who are trapped in a condition of hatred are also constipated. They have an irregularity about them, and are unable to release toxins or poisons. Even someone who complains of diarrhea exhibits a marked inability to "let go of things." His energies are snarled up, as if someone had put a hook into him. The fishhook is in his mind. Something has happened, and he's not able to get rid of it. He can't forget it; he can't let go. His physical state mimics his mental state. He is jammed up; he is not fluid, not regular, or not able to be synchronized. He has lost the ability to have any kind of regularity.

#3-24

Something is being used as a drug (#24) against the colon. Often when we see these two numbers together, #3 and #24, we must check if the chain owner drinks coffee. Coffee, in this scenario, serves as a "drug" that is used by many for its laxative effect. Of course there may also be other drugs with a laxative effect or even Imodium to slow down the colon.

Energetic Dynamic,

Energetically, the #3 system is the *Eliminator*; its primary purpose is to detoxify our system through elimination.

The #3 system appears in the SAF chain sequence of numbers because of toxicity. Toxic events are stimulated and programmed by memories and thoughts of being forced to endure similar toxic situations, toxic people, or toxic ideas; none of which could be eliminated or changed at that time.

We are programmed to fail, and thus we have a narrowed viewpoint about life, people, and living. In families there is often hatred and jealousy, petty squabbles (and worse) among siblings, not necessarily voiced out loud, but felt all the same. We couldn't change it at the time, and so became hate-filled about it.

In our SAF personal work, we can finally find and understand that long sought-after cause. We now know the importance of detoxifying on many levels, body, mind, and spirit. And we can do this now. We can learn to find the barriers, embrace those we can see, and we will achieve our best.

> The use of the SAF program is indicated when a person has negative emotional ties that are draining energy in the present time. It is important to detoxify on physical levels but on mental, emotional. and spiritual levels, as well. This is what we do in our SAF work.

4
Stomach & Digestive System

AT A GLANCE:
Emotion: Happy
Condition/Function: Digestion
Keywords: Dissolve, Eaten, Assimilate
Energetic Dynamic: The Digester

The stomach and digestive system is assigned the #4 in the SAF Secondary Sequence. The stomach is the vessel of digestion; as such it may be considered the battleground for energies coming into the system that need to be converted. The ingestion of foodstuffs from the environment requires that there be some area designated as a conversion place. Any substance or entity coming into the body must have its function changed; its purposes must be changed to suit the human body's total plan. If this is not accomplished, then the substance will ultimately do it harm. The stomach is equipped with glands that secrete gastric juices; these are necessary to break down a food substance into chyme so it is ready for further digestion. The genetic blueprint of the human body directs these acids, fluids, and chemicals; this blueprint, in turn, depends on the genetic ancestry of that person to provide the right materials necessary for dissolution of the entities that have been ingested. For example, if a person swallows glass, there is normally no blueprint in the system for the digestion of this substance. However, there have been some human beings that have developed an ability to decipher, break down with chemical codes, and digest any foreign substance, even glass.

Emotion: Happy

Happiness is from the root word *-hap*, or happening. With happiness issues, we could say there is not much happening. Research has shown those individuals with stomach troubles invariably complained about unhappiness, or issues with happiness. Many ideas of existence correlate happiness to the stomach. When a person has a "full belly," he is happy. Happy actions exude from the stomach. A "good belly laugh" indicates that the person is on his way to sheer happiness. The Constitution

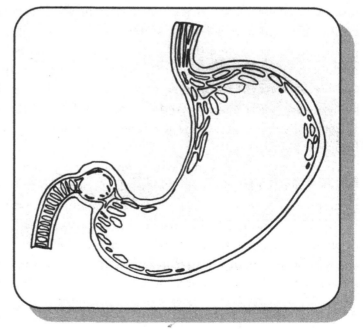

The Stomach

of the United States guarantees that people are entitled to "the pursuit of happiness" (though not the attainment of it!). It would seem that if we were to desire complete and utter happiness, we would have to come up with a regimen so our system could digest anything.

Condition/Function: Digestion

Digestion, of course, is the process whereby food is broken down mechanically and chemically so that it can be absorbed and used for cell metabolism. In many cases the term digestion transcends the physical sense. *A person must be able to take apart any energy or substance that comes into his system.* If the SAF Practitioner finds the #4 appears first in a chain of numbers derived from SAF scans and questionnaires, he knows that the chain owner is unhappy, he is unable to digest the circumstances around him. This can be a *mass circumstance* such as food, an *energy circumstance,* such as a pattern of motion (emotion) in the environment, or a *concept circumstance* such as develops between the human being and people, places, and events that are indigestible to the chain owner.

Mental Aspects

When looking intently at the idea of digestion from a mental point of view, it is noted that people who have stomach troubles also have the inability to digest concepts in the mind. In this case, another word for digestion would be *understanding*. If we attempt to understand a huge problem all at once, and are not successful, then the solution would be to break it down;, divide it, and conquer it. Problems must be broken into finer parts to understand fully their conceptual meanings. So if someone swallows an idea that is indigestible, he must break it down into smaller and smaller pieces until he can understand and digest the whole idea or concept.

It is exciting to note that the whole process of digestion has been embodied into the SAF method. SAF is a digestive mental process. SAF is successful because it takes a complex problem and breaks it down into smaller, finer pieces. SAF gives a person the steps necessary to gain the ability to sequentially understand his problem. SAF gives a person enough observable Cause and Effect so that he or she is now able to grasp the full meaning of how he or she could have gotten into such a predicament.

Not having a plan, formula, or sequence for figuring out problems can be a problem in itself. Problems accumulate with such tremendous energy and power that they can surely overwhelm the chain owner. For example, if someone is trying to understand the economic systems of the world, the troubles in the Middle East, or the concept of death, etc., he or she must go down a long research or philosophical path to come to a satisfactory resolution. A one-word or one sentence explanation won't suffice. Human beings think in sequences. We are sequential beings; we must see the step-by-step pattern in order to understand concepts and digest the indigestible.

Physical Aspects

Those who have #4 in their SAF chain sequences were found to have pains in their stomachs. Many developed severe toxic states.

If you can't physically digest, then you are setting yourself up for trouble throughout your system. Many disease states, such as gout, rheumatism, arthritis, diabetes, etc. are direct results of an inability to digest. With diabetes, the afflicted person cannot digest glucose (sugars) properly. In gout and rheumatism, uric acid builds up and poisons the system because the person is not able to process it properly.

Of all the systems in a human being, digestion is extremely important from the cellular level all the way up to the mental level. It may be the focal point of the SAF method, itself, to help us learn to either digest substances or reject them away from the body to keep them from intersecting with the most precious energy pods inside the DNA-RNA.

It is important to note at this point that consuming drugs and over-the-counter medicines only serve to thwart that digestive process, for some of these materials are completely indigestible. Use of antacids sets up a bad precedent; it is far better to take a step back and really examine the foods being consumed. Are these digestible by us, or are these too fatty or spicy for our own personal system? After about age 20, most of us need more digestive enzymes to help in this process. What are we being eaten up by? Other street drugs and chemicals, such as LSD, mescaline, speed, heroin, etc. are not digestible. They are taken into the system and may never come out again. Common pain relievers such as aspirin (salicylic acid, acetaminophen) may take years to be fully eliminated from the body. Such pain relievers tend to also shut off mental images, the very images we need to have in order to see clearly and understand. All the while these substances are lodged in the body they will create as much havoc as they can.

As we study SAF, we embrace the idea of cleaning out the physical system. We must remember that anything that goes into the body can potentially get stuck inside. The only way to recover is with a good digestive process. The enzymes within the system, produced by genetic command, are a direct result of the thymus gland's ability to observe and to recommend action against certain entities in the body. Yet with the thymus gland being the weakest gland, and the DNA-RNA being fooled on a consistent basis by the outside environment, foreign substances are able to sneak inside the body and then be released there. There are drugs and chemicals used today that can disguise unwanted substances, such as occurs with chelation therapy. In this situation, the product is encapsulated in a protein and so the body thinks it does belong and allows it entrance. So we have to be extremely aware and careful about our ingestion of substances. At the same time, we have to realize that there are so many pollutants, toxins, and radioactive beams coming from a myriad of sources - air, water, chemical frequencies, and food - that it becomes impossible to consistently eliminate activity in and around these polluting substances.

The only real answer is to have a detecting system whereby we can sense or discover the presence of an offending substance and come up with a direct way of editing or removing this poison from the body. Fortunately, the SAF system does this. It has been built for modern man. It is a tool for our future existence, and it is exciting to note that the SAF system understands this problem of digestion. It is a tracking system used primarily to hunt down and seek out the offending, polluting substances in the body and come up with programs and plans for their elimination.

Energetic Dynamic

Energetically, this #4 system is the *Digester.* It is focused on nurturance and happiness, and on our ability to discern and choose what nurtures us, without under-choosing what works or over-choosing what doesn't work. It is important to remember that if there are stresses at meal time, or arguments are loud with someone at the table, it is best not to eat then, and risk also taking in the energies of a disturbed person. It is far better to eat later on in peace and quiet, and to keep mealtimes as stress-free as possible.

Some expressions of this system might be: I can't digest, dissolve, or assimilate the experiences and situations in my life on many levels. I am not able to digest concepts, thoughts, or the ideas of others. I can't stomach that. I must work very hard at being happy. That is distasteful to me.

Are you trying to digest that toxic person, or digest what caused you to be unhappy?

This Energetic system #4 is stimulated and programmed by memories and thoughts of times when we had to endure being unhappy, or feeling we were not being nurtured. We were not able to change or escape from the events and situations at that time.

We have been programmed to be eaten up, to be consumed by messy emotional family issues and other situations and events. With our SAF personal work, we can now break down ideas better, break down foods, assimilate both the ideas and the foods, and finally, embrace these into our system.

> It is exciting to note that the whole process of digestion has been embodied into SAF; this is a digestive mental process. This method successfully takes the complex problem of a chain owner and breaks it down into smaller, finer pieces so that it can be absorbed, digested, and assimilated.

5
Anterior Pituitary

AT A GLANCE:
Emotion: Observant
Condition/Function: Coordination
Keywords: Direct, Controlled, Master
Energetic Dynamic: Master Coordinator

The anterior pituitary is the frontal part of the master gland, the pituitary, which has the ability to direct the plans of the genetic mechanism throughout the entire body, including the target organs of the thyroid, the gonads (male and female), the adrenal cortex, the liver, and the bones. It acts as a monitor to make sure that all the genetic programming mechanisms are followed through.

Under the command of the hypothalamus, the anterior pituitary is stimulated by the hypothalamus to release seven major hormones, which affect stress, growth, reproduction, and lactation. After sending its message, it expects an answer from the target glands.

All of what a person is and looks like is directed by the anterior pituitary gland - qualities such as hair and eye color, size, shape, and body weight. The anterior pituitary gland is sensitive to radiation and is designated #5 in SAF programming.

Emotion: Observant

In evaluating people with the SAF protocol, those with #5 in the most prominent position (first in the chain sequence) were found to have an inability to observe reality.

They have distorted perceptions. If asked to pick up a banana, he or she might reach for an apple. They might also drop things they are holding. The emotional capabilities are on hold; this person is just watching. His or her feelings are frozen; there is a reality shift. The #5 individual has an emotional situation that is locked up.

Condition/Function: Coordination

Number 5 is closely associated with #2 in that there is a definite need for synchronization, harmony, and

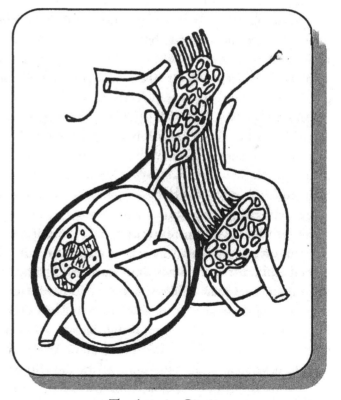

The Anterior Pituitary

coordination, but #5 is more concerned with the idea of control. When #5 appears in the first position in an SAF numeric chain, it indicates the chain owner is losing control. He or she has encountered situations beyond his or her grasp and so is unable to coordinate activities against the encroaching problem. These #5 chain owners are found to have growing problems about which they cannot do anything. We find that many people in marital split ups where children are involved will show the #5 in the first position on the chain. They can't control the situations that have been decided for them by judges and lawyers regarding visitation and monthly payments to their dislike, and therefore, they are stuck having to do something over which they have absolutely no control. At one time or another, most of us have encountered a #5 situation; in those times, we were not able to get a grip on our problems and steer ourselves back into control.

Mental Aspects

It seems that #5 would embody the entire processing of SAF. It denotes a person who has developed a slick kind of confusion that has earmarked him for trouble. As long as he cannot dissolve or absorb the problem at hand, he will suffer.

We must maintain mental control of our existence. We need this control of our ideas and concepts to be certain that the necessary energies are present to complete them. For example, if we decided to build a garage, we must first acquire the blueprints and the plans (the concept). Then we would need the money to buy all the materials, and time to put them together (energy). Finally we would have to gather the timber, boards and screws, and nails (the mass). These things could be all present - concept, energy, and mass - but if we do not gain control of it, we may build a rickety garage, or not be able to complete the task at all.

The final culmination of our ability to control a situation is to build a perfect replica of what we had in mind. If we can't, we feel a subtle loss of control. It is the genetic promise that if we put out an idea into our genetic programming mechanisms that idea will appear in mass form. It is the wish-come-true mechanism that is part of the anterior pituitary complex and the fifth gland matrix in the SAF sequence. If we are not having our wishes come true, then we most certainly have a problem coordinating, and our ability to observe reality is locked up. We are not seeing things for what they really are, and therefore, we can't program our mind so that it will have a logical ending point.

This often happens to us when we are trying to develop relationships with other people. In the mental aspects of developing a human relationship, it is often difficult to observe the attributes of the other person that we like to copy and duplicate for a harmonious life together. Because of the necessity to lock in and harmonize in a loving way with another person, #5 is closely related to #2. Number 5 embodies the idea of being able to control energies once they have intersected with our space. Once these energies are inside our system, if not controlled, they can wreck us. We don't need to develop a sense of trust for another human being, only the ability to observe and control all circumstances that come into our own space. Even if the other person wanted to separate from us, or create other such mental traumas, we would be able to simply observe the situation and keep it under control on our end.

There are far too many people whose lives have been absolutely broken in half by the actions of another person. This occurs dramatically because of the upsets of the anterior pituitary. If radiation from any source (including drugs, chemical poisons and frequencies, emotional radiation, or even a baseball bat smashing onto a person's head) is allowed to reach the anterior pituitary, the afflicted person is in great danger. This master gland has to be in good working order, not only for the physical ramifications of life, but also for the mental necessity of being able to solve problems and being able to see the exact reality - what *is*.

Physical Aspects

Often a chain owner with #5 up front in the chain, in the present time, will also wear glasses, hearing aids, or some kind of assist for the senses. Those with a distorted view will certainly need to have it corrected. Sometimes the distortion in the viewpoint is so great that it carries over into the sense machinery and affects vision. Light begins to curve and bend around them, so that when they look at a round apple, they might see instead an elongated fruit, more like a banana. So they really need to have a set of eyeglasses or some kind of visual assist. This is not a condemnation of those who wear sensory aids, but there can be some extreme examples that manifest.

When the anterior pituitary goes awry, subtle physical problems develop that are difficult to detect. The sinuses (chambers of gases) become affected. The anterior pituitary analyzes the gaseous state of the sinuses and takes apart the conditions, the actual specific gravity, the barometric pressure, and the pressure sense of radiation around it. It is in this way that the thymus (#1) and the anterior pituitary (#5), which appear in an SAF chain sequence as 1-5, work together in producing a perfect harmonious situation that is able to analyze the environment.

Number 5 in the first position of a chain sequence might indicate the chain owner has a "common cold." A common cold develops when a situation of high tension and energy is jammed into the human system and affects the sinuses. The common cold is directly influenced by both halves of the pituitary gland - the posterior pituitary (#21) and the anterior pituitary (#5). The chain owner in this scenario, at some point in time, suffered a loss and the anterior pituitary is trying to return or bring back the pressure to observe and analyze that lost capability. The emotion of #21 (the posterior pituitary) is grief, or crying. When the sinuses are completely filled and there is drainage, when the nose and eyes are dripping with fluid, the person is said to have a "cold." He is actually stifling a cry, a cry for help, because something has been taken from him. We can see that these numbers work together to explain what the loss is about. Apparently, the tearing away of something from a human being creates an empty feeling situation and tears at the control mechanisms, thus causing disharmony, which relates to the heart (#2).

So, observation is essential. When reading the SAF chain of numbers, we gain a more accurate picture of what is being observed. The numbers are extremely important for you to be able to understand more about the physical, mental and spiritual aspects of yourself, your loved ones, and the people you encounter every day.

Energetic Dynamic

Energetically, this #5 system is the *Master Coordinator*, and tells of our ability to coordinate, control, and direct our life by applying the right dose of the correct energy system as needed. However, when this #5 system appears in the SAF chain sequence, it is stimulated and programmed by memories and thoughts of being controlled by others, or not having appropriate control or direction in situations or events. At that time and at that age, we were not able to change or escape from the situation.

But now, we can see that the *event* is now in control; and we have effectively lost all control. We have an altered perception of the past events, we've overlooked or forgotten a situation so now we cannot see it or coordinate it.

Yes, this seems to be a messy situation. You may feel frozen, you can't bring your ideas to fruition, and there is a loss of power to observe reality as it truly is. "If I can't see things clearly, how could I possibly coordinate them or process them?"

SAF to the rescue! This is precisely why the Self Awareness Formulas were created and why they work so well. SAF is able to spark your memory, held in the DNA, of what the body/genetic program wants you to understand. You will make the connections between your present and your past, but this time, *you* are in control. When you find and understand the cause(s), the event has lost its power over you. At the same time, you will be endowed with a burst of energy that will engulf and stay with you.

Throughout the eons, humans have been controlled by and from many sources; with our SAF session work, we can identify the causes, realize our wishes, hopes, and dreams, and become masters of our own lives.

> It is important to find what is ingrained in our DNA and running in the background, directing us in the present, as if we were still living in the past! Once we see and understand these events, we are able to dissipate the electrical charge of it and we are freer.

6
Liver & Gallbladder

AT A GLANCE:
Emotion: Sadness
Condition/Function: Transmutation
Keywords, Keep, Aged, Rejuvenate
Energetic Dynamic: The Changer

The liver, in SAF programming, is considered the fuse box and the battery. It is the electric power pack of an individual; within the liver are stored all the transcriptions and patterns of energy necessary for life.

The liver is found to be the sixth weakest organ due to its delicate electrical circuits connected to relationships with other human beings and the environment. Take, for example, this concept: everyone contacted on a physical level, who has been very close to you (a mother, spouse, or anyone who has exchanged body fluids with you), will have a recording of this experience in their livers. The liver takes in all fluids or substances from another human being. The liver can be equated to a complex factory; it is responsible for more than 1,000 known functions. It possesses all the tools for taking apart, breaking down, and digesting the toxins and poisons that come into the system. It takes care of digestion, glucose storage, mineral transfer, and electric-like charging for the entire human system. It is the fastest regenerating organ in the body; it shares its ancestry with all other living creatures.

The other part of this system is the gallbladder, which works closely with the liver. It holds the liver's bile secretions until the alkaline compounds are ready to degrade and help digest fat compounds into usable materials. This occurs in the small intestines. If the gallbladder is removed, the liver will take over its functions.

#4-6

When the liver (#6) and the stomach (#4) create an Up-Link in the front of an SAF chain, this means that the chain owner has acquired what we called "civilization disease." In this instance, too many recordings are coming into the

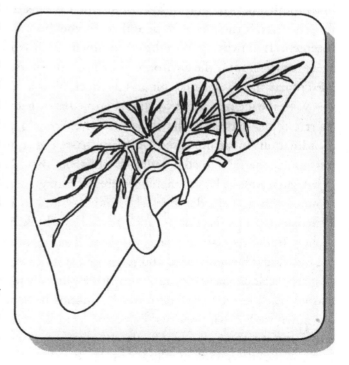

The Liver and Gallbladder

system that cannot be fully digested, so we get indigestion. Put #4 and #6 together and the chain owner has biliousness, gas and rumbling in the stomach; the lower half of the body is making an incredible amount of noise trying to relocate and shuffle around all these toxins and materials that need to be tagged and bagged.

#5-6

The appearance of the anterior pituitary (#5) with the liver (#6) should indicate an ability to coordinate activities and bring about necessary actions for life-sustaining survival in our world.

However, when this Up-Link appears in the SAF chain sequence, it indicates that the chain owner cannot seem to coordinate activities for life-sustaining survival; he or she cannot observe actual conditions.

Emotion: Sadness

When the #6 (the liver) appeared first in the SAF chain, it is attached to the emotion of sadness.

Sadness is the opposite of happiness. It is a statement that the chain owner is "not happening." Unhappy means things are not going the way we want them to go, there is a break-up or a split-up, or there are situations in the environment intersecting with our energy. It is extremely important to note when a person has something or someone directly intersecting with his energy. Number 6 in a prominent place in the chain of numbers means that the liver is the area of this intersection.

The liver is the power pack and the home grounding structure; it is like the fuse box in the basement. If something from the environment, such as an infection, disease, toxin, or even a mental upset comes in from the environment, when this intersects with the human electrical circuitry, the person may have a short circuit and in effect, blow a fuse.

With the idea of sadness, we must immediately get the idea of a break. There is a disconnecting short circuit, and with the short circuit there is a problem with concept, energy, and mass coordination. In such a case, the person has an idea, may have the energy to complete the idea, puts much energy into completing the idea, but that idea doesn't come to fruition.

As an example, let's say a man desires to marry a certain woman. He courts her and spends lots of money on dinners, dates, jewelry, and furs, and then is crushed when she runs off and marries someone else. His reaction is sadness. He has a broken feeling, much like a circuit that has been broken. In the English language, the word "liver" contains the word "live." When broken like this, the individual becomes aged and just about stops living.

The melancholia that occurs with sadness literally means "black bile." It turns black for a specific reason: blackness and darkness are the unknown. When a person's circuit is broken, there is an unknown wedge that prevents the person from knowing the outcome.

Certainly, the individual in the example would not have spent all his energy on the idea of marriage, with no hope of realization. He should have foreseen what was going to happen. If his plan had been correct, he would have gotten what he wanted, but obviously his idea was not "in the light." It was in the dark. There was information missing and he was gambling on mystery. He was hoping to create a situation that would be beneficial.

In the SAF method, what we attempt to do is take as much dark light or "black body light" and intersect it with the awareness of a chain owner, and turn it into "white body light."

White body light is the information or energy that is known or conscious, while black body light is the information or energy that is unconscious or unknown. When something intersects with a person's white body light and turns it into black body light, the person gets a broken, sad feeling. The differences between white body light and black body light will be studied thoroughly in this text because it is the goal of the SAF program to dissect and understand all the mysterious and invisible energies that surround a human being. Much of this will be learned as you go through and follow the SAF protocols.

> White body light is the information or energy that is known or conscious.
> Black body light is the information or energy that is unknown or unconscious.
> SAF links the two, shining a light into the darkness, which allows us to see.

Condition/Function: Transmutation

The transmutation or changing of energies is the job of the liver. In the human being, it is the system that helps us make all the proper changes throughout our lives, for energy is constantly changing. As the earth tilts and orbits the sun, the seasons change; an individual's molecular and chemical structure must change or he or she will die. It is as simple as that. The poisons in the environment and the toxins that enter the system necessitate the change.

When #6 appears on the left in the SAF chain sequence, we know that the SAF Participant's ability to change and redesign have been thwarted; there is a break somewhere that needs to be repaired.

Number 6 is the number for keeping pace with changes. The saying "When in Rome, do as the Romans do," admonishes a person to keep pace with his environment or it will leave him behind in the dust. It originally meant travelers to Rome must learn the way of the Romans, specifically to drink a lot of wine, which has definite affects on the liver!

Mental Aspects

Mentally, people must be fast enough to keep pace with energy changes in the environment. If they are not quick enough in intelligence and understanding, their perception of white body light is lacking, and they will sink into the murk of black body light. There they will find much sadness.

If a person believes in hell and purgatory, he will find these on Earth; they exist as the unsolved energy created in the mind. This has been taught for eons and is ingrained in our DNA. The pain and suffering of people who spend their time in hellish places comes about because the energy and mass build up to create situations of pressurized black body light. This crushes the person, thwarting his or her every activity. Even in mythology, the gods themselves were tortured because of their inability to understand and turn black body light into white body light situations.

Physical Aspects

The liver is a very important organ for the operation of the human mechanism. If it becomes disturbed badly enough, jaundice can or might occur. The person with jaundice will have a yellowish tinge to his or her appearance. Liver troubles greatly affect the eyesight, and tax the anterior pituitary (#5) because the individual's perception has become distorted.

#5-6

If your plans, programs, ideas, wishes, desires, or dreams are being thwarted continually or even on a occasional basis; if black body light is intersecting with or taking over your white body light; if your mysterious half is becoming greater than your known half; or if you are more unconscious than you are conscious, then you are certainly unable to observe actual conditions. In this way, this Up-Link tells us the liver (#6) can disturb the anterior pituitary (#5).

Errors in perception naturally occur in people who are consistently taking recreational drugs, over-the-counter or prescription medicines; these toxins take away our ability to see things properly. Drugs rarely assist in anything except to override the action of some other poison. They are poisons fighting poisons, and the human body becomes a scorched battleground.

#4-6-20

With liver upsets, digestive capability is greatly reduced. This would involve the stomach (#4) and also the pancreas (#20). When these numbers are in close proximity in a numerical chain, we know the SAFParticipant may be having trouble digesting particles of food, as well as particles of life and living.

Energetic Dynamic

Energetically, this #6 system is the *Changer*. The liver takes in what we take in and transmutes, or changes, the metabolic processes to make it suitable for what the body needs for sustenance. The gallbladder stores the bile secretions from the liver until the alkaline compounds are ready and needed for use. The liver, on this energetic level, changes what we envision and want into what we should see and possess. However, when #6 appears in the SAF chain sequence, we know that we have lost this ability. When things are not going our way, when we envision something and it is not there for us, we become melancholy and sad.

Some expressions may be: I can't change the energy I am putting out into what I want to see. Dreams and wishes are thwarted. Things are not happening.

This energetic system #6 is stimulated and programmed by memories and thoughts of traumas of disappointment, and we gave up on our expectations. When we give up on our expectations, we can no longer create what it is we want.

We begin to feel old; we cannot rejuvenate until we take a look at the past traumas that we couldn't change or escape from at the time.

With so many sad circumstances in life, we have been feeling aged beyond our years. With our personal SAF work, we can learn to pinpoint the beginning of the traumatic patterns, and we can change our interpretations of these. With that miraculous attitude change, we can finally feel rejuvenated.

The numerical matrix of the sun can be used in a proven mathematical formula to help you gain insight into your troubles and your symptoms, on body, mind, emotion, and spirit levels.

7
Lungs & Respiratory System

AT A GLANCE:
Emotion: Monotony
Condition/Function: Vaporization
Keywords: Exchange, Stifled, Refresh
Energetic Dynamic: The Exchanger

The overall function of the lungs and respiratory system is vaporization. The lungs are in the seventh position on the SAF Secondary Sequence; they consist of fibers and tissues of a sensitive nature. Their matrix is used to deal with invisible gases, particularly oxygen and carbon dioxide.

The lungs allow outside energies to intersect with its own systems. They take these energies apart, dissect them, dissolve them, puts them into solution, and then casts out the refuse the same way as the colon. The colon, however, deals with digesting masses while the lungs are an energy-digesting machine. A lung respirator works on the same principle. It takes energies in from the outside; it is nothing more than a gaseous digester machine.

The lungs, of course, are essential for survival because of the constant need for oxygen digestion. Their purpose is respiration and aeration of the blood. We need continual intake. If we look at breathing as a type of digestion, we would see that we are constantly digesting gasses. By letting air into the system, it is necessary to make certain that the toxins and poisons, which are taken in along with the air, are processed *out* as rapidly as possible. Most of the trouble that arises with the lungs is created when toxins become lodged in the bronchi and then work their way through the bloodstream and into the cells and tissues where they can take up root.

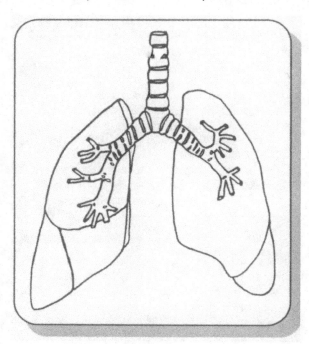

The Lungs & Respiratory System

Emotion: Monotony

The emotion most closely depicted by SAF Participants found to have #7 (the lungs) in the first position of their SAF chains is monotony. When we look at monotony, we see a chronic condition. In SAF programming, #7 does not mean we are lucky. It means that whatever entity exists has been there for a *long* time. In deciphering a chain sequence with SAF #7, in association with any other organs or glands, this entity will point to a chronic situation.

#5-7

When we see the Up-Link of the lungs (#7) connected with the anterior pituitary (#5), it is indicative of what medical people call a common cough.

#7-23

The common cough is a deep-set bronchial situation that can easily move into a condition of asthma that affects the lungs (#7) and the spleen (#23).

#1-5-7

The lungs (#7) also work with the thymus gland (#1) and the anterior pituitary (#5) to create a system of chronic exhaustion or tiredness. So we see that the appearance of #7 gives us a continual monotonous voice. The SAF Participant may speak like a zombie. He may exude an idea that he is lost in some sort of deep miasma.

Condition/Function: Vaporization

We have to watch #7 because it is an energy number. It indicates dissolution and dispersion. It dissolves mass. It may not be the best condition to have when a person is trying to create some matter, but it can be considered a lucky number when trying to explode or dissect some matter that has been chronic for a long period of time. We have to look at #7 as the entity formed by the chronic condition itself.

As an example, if the SAF Participant has had a cold for two or three days and then it seems to go away, he must keep in mind that the cold is an entity and has an ability to create its own identity and a life of its own over a period of time. The cold symptoms are just 1/88 of the whole cold entity, just the toenail so to speak; the other 87/88 lies dormant inside the person. As is often the case, when a cold enters the system, it easily becomes a chronic condition.

Mental Aspects

The mental aspect of the lungs (#7) is the notion of invisibility. If any body system confronts black body light more than others do, it would be the lungs, for the lungs operate wholly on a mass-less level. Certain entities are absorbed into the system that is invisible; the lungs, throughout their entire existence, are programmed to contend with invisible entities.

Physical Aspects

Human beings plagued with troubles of the lungs will find that this vital detoxification organ can affect every other organ in the body.

#3-7-16-19

The lungs are closely aligned with the kidneys (#16), the skin (#19) and the colon (#3). In coordination with these organs, the body attempts to process out all those elements that don't belong to it and absorb all the elements it wishes to keep. The confusions come when the emotional aspects intersect with the physical aspects. When we embody a great deal of hatred (#3) in our system, we certainly are unable to reject certain conditions around us, and these conditions may freeze up or become chronic problems on the skin (#19). The factor of lungs (#7) indicates that whatever problem is being worked on needs constant attention because it happens again and again.

When noting #7 in the first position of the SAF chain, the SAF Participant may have trouble breathing. Breathing should be non-interesting and non-detectable. It should change to suit the amount of oxygen ingested and the amount of carbon dioxide ejected. However, if a person's breathing becomes labored, or if he is unable to correctly manage his circumstances, then he will have trouble.

#7-24

If the lymph system (#24) appears next to the lungs (#7) in a chain, there is a good chance the individual is drawing in some toxicity from the air he is breathing. In many instances the person is either a smoker or is surrounded by those who smoke. This is indicated because #24 represents ingestion of drugs or toxins.

When the lungs are in proper working order, the body can be relatively healthy. If there is any trouble with the lungs whatsoever, the nail and hair matrices will begin to show signs of wear and tear.

#7-19

If a person has #7 in the first part of the chain, he may also have degradations of the skin (#19) and other organs of the body. The skin (#19) is important to observe when associated with the lungs (#7) because the Participant may have warts, moles, tumors, cysts, boils, pimples, acne, or other signs that signal the inability of the lungs to reject toxins entering the system by way of the nose and mouth.

In other words, the lungs are having a difficult time processing out solid poisons coming in through the air, and therefore, the skin must take up the responsibility of trying to detoxify the entire system. When the skin fails, it is up to the kidneys (#16) and the colon (#3) to take up the slack. If they can't handle it, then the toxins and poisons wind up nestling in the colon (#3), in the kidneys (#16), or in the bones (#9). If this occurs, then the individual is more prone to a cancerous situation. Remember that a human body tries to digest a substance or *it* tries to digest *the human*. If a person has not been able to take apart a substance (digest it = # 4), it may wind up in the most disadvantageous location possible. It could chew up some of the more vital processing areas such as the liver (#6), heart (#2) or the brain (#12).

#7-and any number

The #7, because of its designation as chronic, can also indicate a possible hand-me-down genetic situation. In most cases when reading chains of numbers derived from human beings, ancient genetic conditions that may have lasted more than 100,000 years are indicated by the specific genetic changeover numbers 23-24. If #7 is in the chain, it simply shows monotony, or a chronic condition. It means that for a long period of time, there was a constant exposure to a substance that may have had a detrimental effect; the presence of #7 in the chain sequence tells us this has happened over and over again. Whatever the condition may be, it must be addressed. Number 7 is vital to resolving the case because it gives the relative intensity of the physical, mental, and spiritual situation. Because of the chronic situation, seeing #7 in SAF chains intensifies any problem or condition.

Energetic Dynamic

Energetically, this #7 system is the *Exchanger*. The overall function of the lungs is vaporization, the taking in of fresh gaseous energy and the release of spent gaseous energy. It shows that we can be refreshed; however its presence in the chain sequence shows that we have lost that ability.

The #7 system is stimulated and programmed by memories and thoughts of feeling stifled, feeling stuck in a rut, and the same thing happening over and over, again and again. We could almost not breathe. Invisibility spread throughout our body but we could not see it; it got into us, like a gas, like smoke. Could this feeling be the cause or instigation for smoking? Chronic seems to pervade everything in life. It is a stifling situation, from which we cannot let go or process it out; we could not escape from it either, not at that time.

In our personal SAF session work, we can now learn to find the cause, and we can take a deep breath as we discharge energies. We realize that we can finally be refreshed.

> When chain owners disconnect from the shards of black thought invisible to us, we gain the ability to float above the disharmonies lodged in the special places where traumas like to hide. The more observation, contemplation, and connections we can make with our own anchors, the more freedom we will experience.

8
Sex Organs

AT A GLANCE
Emotion: Apathy
Condition/Function: Reproduction
Keywords: Attract, Separated, Create
Energetic Dynamic: The Connector

In the science of SAF, the sex organs are assigned the #8. Included in this group are the male gonads and prostate gland, as well as the ovaries, uterus, and mammary glands of the female.

This SAF identification system #8 may also indicate an abnormal condition of the blood vessels that supply these lower areas with life-giving plasma and serum.

Gamma rays and x-rays have an ability to atrophy and sterilize the sex organs.

When the #8 appears in the SAF chain sequence, it could hint at menopause in females or climacteric in males, and the emotional upheavals from these life changes. A person's ability to maintain sexual performance will suffer when under stress, duress, pressure, emotional troubles, and all forms of environmental and emotional radiation. The presence of #8 in a chain sequence is the idea of reproducing, either children or projects.

Emotion: Apathy

Much controversy in the SAF program has been generated over why apathy correlates with the sex organs. When most people think of sexual activity, they think of being happy, not filled with apathy. However, those who have had upsets involving the sex organs (such as herpes, HIV-AIDS, syphilis, gonorrhea, bacterial infections, buildup of yeast or Candida, and other non-specific infections and inflammations) also professed apathy. Included with the physical symptoms would be the mental disorders relating to these organs, including frigidity, sterility, impotence, and even

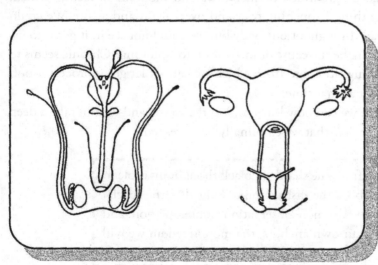

The Sex Organs

many perverse sexual behaviors, such as sex addiction.

Perhaps most importantly, this #8 system also speaks of creativity, and in many cases, it may indicate a lack of desire to create, feelings of apathy, or a block may be present for creative people – as seen with writer's block, an artist's, or musician's block.

When the sex organs are disturbed by disease, mental or physical, there is a marked interference in the ability of the person to create. People who have had these conditions also complain of their inability to finish projects once started. Many SAF Participants who had sexual disturbances of one sort or another also expressed that long ago their projects, purposes, or plans, had been thwarted.

When major creative cycles are thwarted, especially among writers, artists, painters, and musicians, deep-set feelings of apathy ensue. An artist attempts to produce a work and present it to the public, but for some reason he is stymied or stalled, or perhaps the public doesn't appreciate his creativity. This causes the artist to exhibit a low emotional state - apathy. In all cases where the #8 is in the first position of the numerical chain, a state of apathy exists.

Condition/Function: Reproduction

The #8 embodies the entire knowledge of the disease entity and its existence in humankind. Diseases in any life form (animal, vegetable, mineral, and other entities throughout all the solar systems, galaxies, and universes in space and time) have created a simple process whereby they reproduce. It is a necessary process, an extremely important one for the survival of any species or individual unit, including humankind.

The action of one energy intersecting with another can be considered a sex act. The term sex in this sense is in actuality a misnomer, for the word sex as a noun, means two divisions of organism, having characteristics of either male or female. It means to be different, or to be separated from another.

The fact is that sex indicates a difference and *unsex* indicates a unification. So in this sense, when a mosquito inserts his long, narrow, proboscis into an individual's arm, she is not having sex, she is unsexing. The mosquito is trying to become part of the body and if she is successful, can withdraw more of the host's blood than she had in the first place. Unbeknownst to most people, this type of action is repeated billions upon billions of times per day.

To understand sex and to be aware of interconnecting your energy with the environment is to also understand that sex *transcends* the physical act. The point is that sex on a gross scale is a symbolic action, which represents the movements and activities of all energy throughout the day, throughout the entire life of the person.

To explain further, in an electronic sense, words going into a tape recorder and then played back out may be considered a sex act. In a chemical sense, many molecules coming into a body and then being released in rhythmic fashion is a sex act - unification and then a release. The process of excretion from the colon and the bowels also could be likened to a sex act in the sense that materials are taken in and then, through peristalsis, are released.

In our SAF work, we use the word sex as a noun and/or a verb; in this sense, it means the creative reproduction of another human, or reproducing or creating an idea or a project.

Mental Aspects

On many fronts it is seen that in sexual activity there is also a power that comes from the mind. This sexual creativity comes from the ability of a person to intersect his ideas into other subjects or problems so that he can pull out the essential ideas and then can reproduce his own thoughts. The important quality affected when #8 appears in a chain is the individual's ability to create.

When the #8 is read with other numbers in an SAF chain, interesting data can be gleaned.

#8-10

For instance, when an Up-Link of sex organs (#8) and the thyroid (#10) is seen in the SAF chain sequence, it suggests that the SAF Participant is spending his energy unwisely.

#8-11

If the sex organs (#8) are found next to the veins and arteries (#11) in a chain, this syndrome indicates that the person is creating physical problems from mental worries.

#8-17/18

In this Up-Link, #8-7/18, the sex organs (#8) are found in connection with the endocrine system (#17/18); this syndrome shows that the individual is losing his or her ability to create altogether. There is a cessation of productive ideas. The #8 forms and combines with all the other numbers and aspects of SAF to create the mood and disposition of a person's creativity.

#1-8

When a chain owner is very aggressive about his ideas, poisonous with his concepts, and aggressively tries to thwart or destroy another's plans, the sex organs (#8) will be connected with the thymus (#1). So if we see an Up-Link of #1-8 in an SAF chain, we know that the person is using energy in a negative way to hurt either himself or others.

#8-12

If the combination were sex organs (#8) with the brain (#12), this would show that the person is thinking of or wants to create an idea that is not yet fully formed in his mind. It indicates that ideas will be formed out of this #8-12 concept.

In later chapters, more connections between numerical codes and their intersection with other numbers will be described. Attention is given to it here because the #8 indicates excited actions between energies more than any other single number in SAF.

Physical Aspects

When the #8 appears in the chain of numbers, the individual has difficulty with his entire system. The body is not able to create itself properly as has been blueprinted in its genes. This could involve upsets and degradation of the blood vessels in the body. The person may find that his power is very low. His muscles may be lax. The most significant sign of upset is that the tone of the body is slack. The veins and arteries of the circulatory system may lack integrity.

There is no attempt being made here to create terminology or a special language for all the particular kinds of sexual disturbances and physical symptoms that accompany these organs. Suffice to say that any disturbance involving the sex organs and also any problem with the circulatory structure will be a primary indication that the #8 is involved.

#8 and any number

When we see #8 in a chain sequence, this tells us of major blocks in the ability to be creative, to pull out essential ideas in order to reproduce our own thoughts.

The #8 represents the creativity to actually enhance the action of all other numbers, and of all other functions of chromosomal activity, including those that regulate detoxification, organization, those that are important for establishing location, and those that establish water balance in the body.

Energetic Dynamic

Energetically, this #8 system is the *Connector*. It shows our ability to attract positive relationships and shows how creative we can be. This system is a measure of our connections with everything, and everyone else. Our connections are what we, as a spirit, really want. However, its presence in the chain sequence shows that this ability is lost at the moment.

This #8 system is stimulated and programmed by memories and thoughts of not feeling safe to trust connections with those around us. We had to endure and survive relationships with apathy, all the while not connecting with our own truth.

Some expressions by Participants may indicate that there is a creative block and apathy. In addition to lack of creativity with the #8, there may be issues of a sexual nature, sexual relations, children, reproducing. We may feel helpless or useless about the issue. "I should just give in, give up. It doesn't matter anymore …" Power is low, and the Participant is having difficulty because of weakness caused by apathy.

We have survived with apathy by telling ourselves we are separate, separated from other people or from other things. In our SAF session work, we are able to see the whole picture, to brighten our outlook, and reconnect emotionally, and then we are able to create what it is we hold most dear.

> We must have the creativity to think and create; this is a high purpose. The #8 represents the creativity we need and will actually enhance the action of all other SAF numbers.

9
Bones and Muscles

AT A GLANCE
Emotion: Pain
Condition/Function: Locomotion
Keywords: Hold, Blamed, Respond
Energetic Dynamic: Movement

The function of the bones and muscles is to control how we can move, our locomotion throughout the day and a lifetime. It is found in SAF programming that those persons with the #9 in the first position in the numerical chain will have some upset in the bone structures. The bones and muscles are weak in the presence of radiation, which in this case means not only nuclear effluence, but also background radiation from the sun, distant stars, appliances and electronic gizmos, and other magnetic sources.

Emotion: Pain

We most often think of pain as a physical manifestation, not an emotional one. We need to be able to pinpoint the messages we are receiving on this emotional pain level so that we can continue to move in the direction of what is best for our survival.

Pain tells us there is something encroaching on our space that does not belong. There may

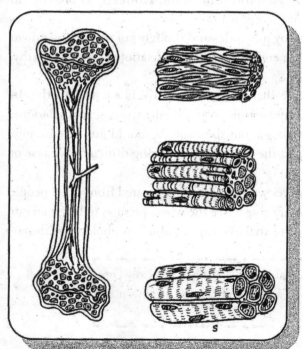

The Bones and Muscles

be an invader, a toxin, a frequency that is not to our liking, or a poison of some sort. The body's sensing mechanisms primarily interact among other structures to learn of the encroaching entities in the vicinity. The body has its own early warning system, which can decipher when there is an invader present in the surroundings, and at the same time, identify the exact type. This is made possible by the pain sensing mechanisms that work in coordination with the nervous system and other structures able to discern wavelength and frequency characteristics of energies that may enter the spaces of the body.

It may be most important to note that the factors providing the body with its sensing information on the pain level can be hyper-extended into unconsciousness, death and the zomboid level (the lowest level of human existence). A human being can sense activities occurring on a conscious level in the form of pain, but cannot knowingly track entities that are encroaching on the unconscious level. These unknown violations can include the actions of hypnosis, drugs, medications, and similar programs. With the early warning system and the SAF method, we can track all the sensing problems found in these lower strata.

Sensation and pain are polar opposites. Sensation tells the analytical intelligence of the human being (brain and mind) that we have lost something; it indicates energies are moving away from the body. These are being deleted. We are losing something. On the other hand, with pain, we gain something. It may be consciously or unconsciously acquired, wanted or unwanted. Pressures begin moving into body spaces and are violating the principle that two objects cannot occupy the same space at the same time.

#1-9-22

This 1-9-22 syndrome is arthritis, which is simply inflammation of the bones, with upsets of the calcium balance. We hold onto anguish and many emotions in our bones and muscles. We may blame ourselves and we may hide this in that same place. If resentment is held onto, watch for arthritis to develop.

Condition/Function: Locomotion

Concerning this primary structure of the body, the skeletal system, #9, relates to its movement. As with all energies and systems, if there is any impingement or encroachment from one group onto another, then there must be change, movement, and space. The #9 signifies this change, the ability to make moves from one space to another. This mechanism makes the actions of invasion, eating, and parasite infestation possible. If one entity can't move on another, or doesn't have the locomotive power to change its location, then it certainly will not be able to invade.

When we notice the #9 as the first number in the SAF numerical chain, it indicates that there are poisons present in the system. One specific designation for #9 is rheumatism because, with this condition, poisons moving through the body are changing locations. However, it is not the fact that the poisons have just changed locations but that they have gotten into the body in the first place that is of paramount importance.

When #9 appears, the system is showing that it has gained something it doesn't want. It has reached a new level of toxicity that it did not own before and it must find a way to detoxify (the colon, #3).

Mental Aspects

The ninth development of awareness intrinsic to the structure of any being is the needed ability to change mental position and to change viewpoint. As we move through daily life sequences, #9 is designated as the mental aspect that tracks our power to change our life toward the direction of peak performance. The SAF method arranges and organizes our actions like no other program. The #9 is extremely important because it gives us an ability to prioritize. SAF makes vital lists of creative situations that trouble us. This allows us to invest all our energy into the most important actions first and the less important actions later

For example, if we were learning to swim, we would start by practicing the pre-basics, such as ducking our head under water. Much later our skills would improve and we may be able to perform various strokes. There is a specific sequencing arrangement that gives us the ability to accomplish easier tasks first and then harder tasks second, and so forth, until we are able to reach the expert level.

When #9 appears as the first number in a chain, it indicates this person cannot prioritize, cannot put events into a sequential order. We may know what to do first and then second for any project, but with the #9 in a chain sequence, this tells us that ability is not active. *SAF gives us the ability to arrange our choice of healing actions on a step-by-step scale of activity and achievement.*

It might be difficult to create organized situations out of chaos. We don't seem able to straighten confusions and put in order the organic and inorganic messes of our life. This suggests that toxins, poisons, and diseases infesting our system are more regimented and organized than we are. We may not have the ordered aspect of mind to create structured activity in body, in mind, or in spirit. We need SAF protocols to help us understand and utilize the special number language of SAF until we are fluent, and we need to study and teach using the basics of the step-by-step approach.

Physical Aspects

The most physical number of all is #9. The SAF Participant may be in pain, a physical reflex warning action of great importance. The ability to decipher and evaluate these warning signals differentiates a human being from an animal.

The muscles are comprised of tiny fibers that carry electric current. Pain is an overload of electric charge in certain areas due to structural trouble (bones out of alignment) nerve trauma, nerve blockage, or cerebral excitement (gross nervousness).

It should be noted that if you are prone to accidents or have continued collisions in the environment, then #9 indicates troubles on a much deeper level. You may be unable to decipher the warnings of earlier pain profiles. Pain is always the alarm signal for the encroachment of a minor or major disease characteristic. It means you may be falling into some potentially dangerous pattern that could do you great harm, now, and in the future.

The Greeks believed that gout was caused by "drops of poison" within the system and they were very accurate in their assumptions. When uric acid moves through the muscles (rheumatism) and the joints, and drops its deposit of poison (gout) to create great pain and deformity, gout causes exquisite pain and nightly torment. Lower back pain is the result of poisons settling in the lumbar-sacral bone region.

If you find yourself in a situation where you have lost the ability to extricate yourself from problems and poisonous conditions, then you have probably ignored some primary pain reflex signal early in your life. So it is important that you increase your awareness levels so that you can identify and stop pain or painful conditions at the first hint, before these can progress further. We must not misunderstand or ignore pain signals when they occur early in our life.

In the incredibly chaotic mess created by civilization today, it is nearly impossible for us to decipher pain signals. Toxins and poisons released into the atmosphere are extremely complicated and cause bizarre energy signal patterns and errant frequencies that inflict the body with pain that is difficult to process.

#1-9

The person who "holds it all in" (a withhold or a lie) will suffer electric charge overloads in his muscles as a punishment for his non-communication. This is especially so when the #1-9 is found in the first position in the chain sequence. It is essential that we *not* hold it all in but learn to release this from our system. We can begin to do this releasing by journaling, and by learning to communicate our inner thoughts and desires to another person.

Energetic Dynamic

Energetically, **t**his #9 system is all about *Movement*, moving away from painful situations and toward what is fulfilling. This #9 system is stimulated by memories and thoughts of having to endure painful events, which could not be changed or escaped from, not even by moving away. We bring it all with us through time!

We have held ourselves to be responsible, or even blamed by others, for conditions not of our choosing. "I can't move. I can't prioritize. Frozen in pain. Mental pain. Held-in thoughts cause pain. Let me move away from it. I can push those pain signals away. No, I can't move," etc.

With our personal SAF session work and journaling, we are able to let go of the hidden, pain-filled thoughts we are mentally grasping, holding onto, hiding in our bones and muscles, terrible thoughts that have caused us such pain. When we journal about the painful thoughts and images we have harbored in our bones and muscles (we hold it in = #1-9), we find we are able to release, to let go of these ensnarled thoughts and events, and can now, finally, respond appropriately.

> When we learn to recognize the pain we have been holding onto, hiding from view in our bones and muscles, we can learn to let go of all those ensnarled energies. The result is we feel the freedom, and we can now respond the right way. We are so grateful.

10
Thyroid
(Includes the Veins and Arteries
of the Upper Extremities)

AT A GLANCE
Emotion: Anxiety
Condition/Function: Metabolization
Keywords: Action, Criminal, Justice
Energetic Dynamic: The Corrector

The word thyroid, from the Greek *thyreos*,
(large shield), and *eidos* (form) means a physical shield. Whereas the thymus (#1) is the electronic invisible shield, the thyroid (#10) is the shield for the physical form, the body. As such, the thyroid is a sentry to prevent toxins, poisons, and other energies not belonging in the body to be processed out and kept away.

The thyroid effectively monitors the carbon-nitrogen equation in the body and is a radiation monitor as well. Those people living in close proximity to nuclear power plants are slated to receive potassium iodide to protect their thyroids and lower glands should a plant disaster occur.

Troubles in this #10 gland result when the random motion of the environment seems overwhelming. If things seem to be moving too fast, such as with a hyperthyroid, vertigo may be experienced. If the action is too slow, feelings of dizziness occur, as with a hypothyroid condition. With a hypothyroid, there may be low energy, lowered intelligence, and an inclination toward weight problems, such as obesity. People can vacillate on these two fronts on a daily basis, but in either of these scenarios, the presence of #10 in a chain sequence shows a non-optimum effect on the regulation of metabolism of foods and cellular metabolism, which is the purpose and function of the thyroid.

The thyroid also works with the anterior pituitary (#5) to regulate the appearance of the structure of the body.

Emotion: Anxiety

The emotion anxiety results when a person attempts to perceive what might happen in the future. This can lead to being anxious about change. Anxiety is generated because you have created some scenario in the past that is rickety and unsure at best, and you are holding that in place in the present time. You might

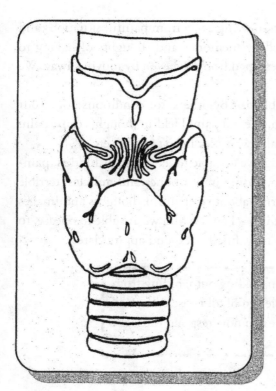

The Thyroid

be worried that the plans and programs you have produced have not been powerful enough to sustain you throughout the interference of energies in the environment. Those who understand the mechanisms of survival will see that the thyroid is an intrinsic cog in the program of Life Energy and the ramifications of toxicity.

The thyroid can become very toxic and create a sensation of anxiety. A state of *delirium tremens*, following drug or alcohol withdrawal, is characteristic of thyroid upset. In this situation the thyroid becomes heavily toxic in its war against these pollutants, and causes a trembling sensation.

Condition/Function: Metabolization

The important consideration of the thyroid, in a conditional sense, is its ability to change the features of the body. The genetic blueprints, using the command centers of the anterior pituitary (#5), affect the thyroid and will it to make its changes. In effect, the thyroid becomes the foreman of the body. It works in conjunction with the liver (#6) to repair the body and to change its structure depending on the directives from the anterior pituitary.

Interference with the gene plans and programs are what give individuals the characteristic lumps, bumps, and misshapen parts that are the cataloged anomalies of mankind. To give names to each one of these disease characteristics is really not necessary. The point is that an afflicted person has toxins and poisons that have worked their way into his or her system. These poisons will affect various organs. The SAF breakthrough is the development of a method that can detect the precise order in which these organs will be affected.

Heat, pressure, and the variation of toxic influence will create a prioritizing sequence of invasion within the body. In other words, a disease condition has a target plan and zooms in on some areas of the organism for immediate invasion, while other areas are the targets for light invasions or remote invasions.

SAF can track all these disease characteristics because it understands these sequences. The point is, the thyroid has the ability to sense and pick up heat changes in the body, and in a very real way is the body's own infrared sensor. It is curious that when the thyroid is malfunctioning, the individual has a difficult time withstanding heat in the environment and heat changes in the body. When the thyroid feels the pressure from the heat changes, the person will receive erroneous signals concerning excess disease in the system. So the thyroid readings are becoming extremely important as an assist to the SAF program.

Mental Aspects

Mentally we must learn to make changes in viewpoint. As was seen in the mental and physical aspects concerning the bones and muscles (#9), we know that changes of time and space will affect the primary sequencing pattern. The thyroid has the important ability to foresee and carefully supervise these specific changes.

The mental aspects of the thyroid gland must be able to withstand change; it is the most important and most necessary function of all activities. When the #10 appears in the chain sequence, it could indicate that the chain owner is anxious about change.

An individual in excellent shape is able to change his mind and position with whatever circumstances arise. Conversely, if a person is ill and his thyroid is malfunctioning, then mentally he will be very rigid and his ideas will be stuck together.

#10-15

When the thyroid (#10) creates an Up-Link with the hypothalamus and senses (#15), we have what is called a "mental mass or a block." It has been found that writers who become stuck when attempting to write novels or technical data will exhibit #10 and #15 in the foremost part of their numerical chains because mental masses are building up. This is also true for musicians and artists with blocks of their own.

#10-11

In the case where the thyroid (#10) and the veins and arteries (#11) become associated, this syndrome indicates that the person has an inability to put his plans, dreams, desires and wishes into action. When #10 and #11 are seen together in a chain it means that there are peculiar upsets blocking the person's ability to be creative.

#8-10

As was stated earlier, when the sex organs (#8) and the thyroid (#10) are associated, then the individual is wasting energy. He or she is not utilizing their potential to the fullest.

#4-10

One of the most important aspects of the thyroid in the mental sense is its connection with the person's ability to digest ideas and concepts properly. When the stomach (#4) and the thyroid (#10) are coupled in a numerical chain, then the SAF Participant will be found to have difficulties controlling his emotional responses to people around him. There are many other connections for the #10 on the mental aspects to be covered later in the text.

Physical Aspects
#1-10

The thyroid is working hard to shake loose poison and move it from the system. It assists the transfer of toxins to the thymus (#1) for final extraction. But when these two glands (the thymus and the thyroid) get together and are not successful, the individual is prone to body tumors. Goiter is a primary example of this situation.

#2-10

One of the most important physical aspects that is found with the thyroid (#10) is its connection with the heart (#2). When the Up-Link 2-10 is found anywhere in the same numerical chain, this denotes basic considerations for the viewing of the chain owner's condition. The 2-10 Up-link indicates the chain owner's inability to withstand insult and injury from the environment. This is the kind of insult, injury, a break up, separation, and/or great loss that may physically damage the person. Memories such as these can physically tear at his heart and create disease there; this is especially so for a highly sensitive person.

#10-22

The thyroid certainly controls a lot of the physical aspects of the person and must be considered in all programs used. When the thyroid (#10) and the parathyroid (#22) appear in a chain sequence together, the client is prone to spinal misalignment. He or she may have rickets, sciatica, or spinal decay. It is extremely important for an SAF Practitioner to spot #10-22 in any numeric sequence because these numbers suggest structural problems, and depending on their location in the chain, may indicate problems of long duration.

#10-17/18

When the person's thyroid is malfunctioning, this person may become overweight. This is indicated by the combination of thyroid (#10) and endocrine system (#17/18). When under tremendous stress, we have too much electricity running through our bodies, and we need some insulation for protection. We grow our own insulation – fat - which is the best insulator against electric stress. It grows where we are the most stressed, or where we are trying to hide our stress. It grows and grows, and so we are now so encased in fat that we are protected from just about *everything*. This would be an ideal time to work on our SAF chain sequence.

#10-12

The thyroid can work effectively on physical and mental levels as it oversees the person's ability to change viewpoint and to understand new things in the environment. An important mental upset is the Up-Link 10 (thyroid) and 12 (brain and nervous system). In this syndrome, #10-12 we are primarily looking at a misunderstood situation, idea, concept or just overall confusion in the person's life. A #10-12 always indicates that the chain owner is having difficulty perceiving the true circumstances around him or understanding new concepts.

There may be projects and programs that were started and proved overwhelming. This trouble may transcend into the physical sense when the person has the misfortune of translating the confusion into his body. Power surges and overloads warn of spastic movements and attacks. Excited brain cells, steeped in action without adequate protection, burn out quickly.

Many of the pains and sensations, the odd feelings that we are just "not okay," energy exhaustion, and all the poisons associated with modern-day living form a #10-12 phenomenon. This syndrome shows a basic confusion about how to behave to insure survival.

Energetic Dynamic

This #10 system is the *Corrector*. The #10 system, the thyroid, and the veins and arteries of the upper extremities, is one of the most important in the SAF lineup because of its ability to maintain balance between the pressures that are too great and those that are too weak. It is the monitor for the carbon-nitrogen equation, but most importantly, the thyroid monitors the radiation in the system. It can coordinate corrective actions in a physical as well as a mental sense, all to achieve the genetic program of the body.

The #10 system is stimulated and programmed by memories and thoughts of anxiety, of enduring personal injustice from people, places, and things that were not the right frequency for us, and from which we could not process, change, or escape from in an earlier time.

We have been operating under false pretenses in that we were seen as wrong, even criminal. In our SAF session work, we can throw off that yoke of anxiety and realize the justice we seek in the correct action.

> A chain owner must learn and know his or her own experiences. When we reach the end of the yellow brick road in this world of SAF, we find it quite easy to piece our traumas together instantaneously, and learn to dissolve these and dissipate their energies.

11
Veins & Arteries of the Lower Extremities

AT A GLANCE
Emotion: Resentment
Condition/Function: Circulation
Keywords: Move, Gravity, Games
Energetic Dynamic: The Circulator

The veins and arteries of the lower extremities create a vast and complex network of tubes which allow the blood to flow on its intended journey. The ultimate function of the veins and arteries is circulation; this system is considered an extension of the heart. This #11 system is important in the respiration or the reflex echo pumping of the heart mechanism. There may be dilated or bulging veins caused by excesses of pressure in the liver, spleen, lymph, bone, and heart. The consumption of concentrated starches and sugars contribute to the problem of varicose veins and can aggravate inherited varicosity conditions. When we see the #11, we know to look for a breakdown in circulation somewhere. Therefore, this #11 system in the Secondary Sequence should be monitored very closely.

Emotion: Resentment

When there is #11 on the left side of an SAF chain, it indicates that actions taken by this person in the past resulted in deep-seated resentment. With resentment, a person harbors ill feelings about an occurrence in the past. It is not hidden from view but is right there. These resentments are well known, harbored, and "cared for," making them full of energy.

People with the #11 are sensitive; they focus on others and their problems so much so, they are liable to take on the problems as if these were their own. When we focus on certain situations and emotionally entangled or ensnarled events, we tend to attract the same type of resentment trauma over and over again. These are chronically drawn in to us, even though we don't understand how that could be. This is a situation of having to own our heated emotions and understand all the ramifications of holding onto resentments.

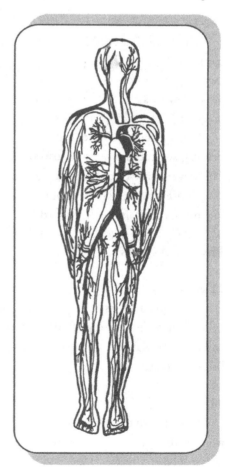

The Veins and Arteries

103

Condition/Function: Circulation

Those who have exhibited upsets involving the veins and arteries (#11) have also complained of continual circulatory problems. The presence of #11 in an SAF chain indicates a chronic condition.

Mental Aspects

People who have complained of being scattered or dispersed will always exhibit the #11 in their chain of numbers. Such people must be careful not to be suffocated by holding onto the poisons in their minds for long durations. However, they do not have traumas buried deep within their systems beyond conscious reach. People who carry on with a #11 are very cognizant of their traumatic experiences and put a great deal of energy into this problem. They are constantly dwelling on the past. They are quite sure that the past problems they are focusing on are the source of *all* their troubles, when in reality there is something buried deep in their systems of which they are *not* aware.

#11-14

The term that could be used for chain owners who exhibit a #11, especially when with a mental connection (#14 the mind) is "scatterbrained." This combination causes dispersion. This chain owner puts much of their energy into other people's problems and troubles. They are sensitive people, who systematically absorb the problems of others. If their families or friends tell them a problem, *they* will worry about it for them.

With this Up-Link, they may suffer tremendously because it increases their worry deficit. Feeling scattered, they spend too much time trying to decipher problems that are not their own. This severe case of co-dependency can lead to a condition of burnout.

Those who do worry about others make up the base of charitable giving to those less fortunate, but moderation is the key word.

Physical Aspects

11-22

The physical aspects of #11 demonstrate that the chain owner has a predisposition for solidification issues, especially with an Up-Link such as #22 (parathyroid), which is the gland for calcium regulation. There may be spinal misalignment, sciatica, low back troubles, or decaying bones or teeth.

#10-11

Often a chain owner with #10-11 in their chain will show a predisposition to arteriosclerosis as a result of circulatory system degradation. In this situation, the integrity of the blood vessels is being lost.

#8-11

When we see an Up-Link of the sex organs (#8) with the veins and arteries of the lower extremities (#11), the chain owners will be found to have severely compromised their ability to maintain their muscle tone. They may exhibit a fresh crop of varicose veins or hemorrhoids. They may complain of constant pains in the arteries, such as that exhibited by patients who have phlebitis. The most important action for people in this physical situation is to use chelating elements to detoxify the entire bloodstream, as well as clean the fibers and walls of the veins and arteries. Such individuals are in great jeopardy because they are liable to develop poisonous situations in the soft tissues and be more prone to cardiovascular and cerebro-vascular accidents (stroke).

#11-14

The danger of stroke is especially great when the veins and arteries (#11) connect with the mind (#14) and the chain owner has what is termed "bursting headaches" or suffers from constant headaches.

#11-15

When we see this Up-Link, the veins and arteries of the lower extremities (#11) and the hypothalamus and the senses (#15), the chain owner is creating tendencies in the body to harden vital organ structures. In this situation, the chain owner must be observant and careful to avoid this pattern.

#11-16

The vital organ hardening mentioned above occurs particularly in the kidney tubules when the veins and arteries of the lower extremities (#11) are found in combination with the kidneys (#16) in an SAF chain sequence.

#11 and any number

Of course, when #11 is connected with any number, the combination pinpoints the specific area in which there is a breakdown in circulation, either the inhibition of circulation, or the action of total dispersal. The dispersion problem is included primarily under mental aspects, whereas the solidification problems relate more to the physical aspects of the body.

Energetic Dynamic

Energetically, this #11 system is the *Circulator*; it helps us to move about and participate in the life we have created, without enduring unnecessary restrictions.

When the #11 is found in the chain sequence, we know that we can no longer move well without some restrictions.

This system is stimulated by memories and thoughts of having to endure resentments, which pull us downward, just as gravity does. We have participated in very grave situations, and emotional events that could not be processed, changed, or escaped in the past. We were not able to move as we wanted; we were filled with resentments and restrictions from these serious emotional events when we were younger.

With journaling, we can learn to let go of resentments by identifying these and the people to whom it is or has been directed. There are yoga exercises for letting go, or using a Bataka bat to hit a pillow to get rid of resentments and rage that were not fully understood before. Then, along with our SAF personal work, we are able to finally understand the resentments, and we can let go of them. Now unencumbered by those resentments, we can once again move about more freely, as we enjoy the lightness of games we have created in our life.

> Past remembrances of traumatic experiences can no longer hurt the enlightened chain owner, who can now touch and control his or her traumas at will.

12
Brain & Nervous System

AT A GLANCE
Emotion: **Nervousness**
Condition/Function: **Electrification**
Keywords: **Time, Complicated, Simplify**
Energetic Dynamic: **The Simplifier**

The brain, the central nervous system control factor, is considered a human's main operation base. Because SAF is based on physical electrical output, the laws of electricity, magnetism, and radiation studies, the brain is a fitting position as the epicenter of the program. SAF is not physical, mental, or spiritual alone, but a trinity of these three. The brain is that physical area that is the absolute core of operations for spirit energy, mind energy, and physical energy. It is the meeting ground for SAF intellect and current, everyday science; it is an area upon which both segments of philosophy can agree. The brain is the bridge between known and unknown information.

The other part of this #12 system is the nervous system. Textbooks tell us the human nervous system is the most sophisticated and complex information processing system in the known universe.

It operates at the speed of light as it coordinates, regulates, and controls our various organic functions. But present day textbooks give us only organic functions, the physical aspects. There is far more to life than mere organic functions.

The neuron, axon, and other nervous system components are written about in *Light, Dark* (by Scogna and Scogna) from an energetic viewpoint. It lends a voice and personality to the light and dark of this most mysterious circuit, as if these components were alive, endowed with personality, intentions, dreams and desires ... and so they are!

Our enlightened vision of these invisible communication links within us allows for the greater holographic image of the human to be revealed.

At times in our life, there may be extra electricity flowing through the

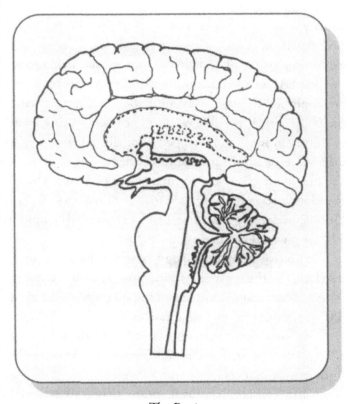

The Brain

nervous system, enough to absolutely fry it. This hyper motion or excitability of the nerves is due to high electric stimulation from the environment, which could be received from people, places, things, and events that happened at some point in time and were recorded in our DNA so that we can pull this knowledge out and learn from these experiences when necessary.

Emotion: Nervousness

The word nervous typifies the action of not only the brain but of the SAF program and its constituent parts, in that SAF has the capability of tapping into the nervous system and reading its electrical functions.

SAF work on chain sequences is accomplished by several methods. One way is with an infrared scan, perfected for analyzing the neurovascular reactions of the body. Temperature readings are taken at certain venting sites on the face, hands, feet, and other areas; these are sites where the organ and gland systems release their heat and their pressure, enough so that we can see the readings on an infrared device.

The spinal cord is the main conduit for information transfer between the brain and the periphery of the body. A specialized set of cranial nerves emanate from nuclei in the brainstem and cortical areas to regulate information flowing to and from the internal organs and the specialized sensory systems. Twelve pairs of cranial nerves transmit sensory and motor impulses. We read these twelve pairs of cranial nerves as 12-cylinders. So with a chain of twelve numbers, a perfect chain, we could say that all 12-cylinders are operational, a good thing!

The SAF infrared scanning works primarily on a stimulus response basis in which energy can be monitored through relay areas such as the face, hands, feet, and the entire organic system of the body. This is possible because the energy being transferred from the gray matter of the brain to the organ sites can be tapped in much the same way we would tap a phone line. By aiming the infrared sensor at the precise areas, we are able to detect activity on specific nervous system inputs.

Just as effective, and in many ways preferred, chain creation is accomplished with subjective questionnaires, which are used to ascertain a person's current realizable symptomatic patterns. The Questionnaires are the Stress-120 for emotional symptoms, which we use with this book, the SAF-120 for physical symptoms, or the Q-24.

Subjective symptomatology is very important, and is fostered by pain and sensation grids developed by the nervous system. These reactions cause symptoms that are brought to the attention of the person completing one of the SAF Questionnaires. It is because of the nervous system that SAF is capable of doing what it does.

The emotion of nervousness indicates there is unusual activity in the nervous system. This activity must be analyzed more closely to get a better idea of what is going on in the system to see if something extra is functioning there.

When you are nervous it means that your systems have been turned on, that something is happening; those actions are occurring on a conscious as well as an unconscious level. We are vitally interested in understanding more about how the brain projects this energy, but at the same time, we must analyze the patterns of nervous response in the whole body.

Nervousness implies there is attention focused on the hidden and unknown energy beyond the reach of the conscious mind. Not understanding it, not seeing it clearly, causes nervousness.

Unfinished projects and plans also cause nervousness because some attention units are focused on those unfinished items. There may be headaches or neuralgia, which could be biochemical in nature or these could arise from mental conflicts. There may be food allergies, insomnia or lack of REM sleep.

Condition/Function: Electrification

The energy portals developed through the SAF grid work are important to the symptomatology of the system as they are patterned after the brain's own pathways. The word electrification indicates "a splitting apart" or a "segmenting." The SAF programs are able to dissect (or split apart) and understand conglomerations of masses unreadable by human beings, which is also a purpose of the brain. All of the upsets and confusions causing toxicity in the system are directly related to the brain's inability to segment and analyze confusions.

Confusions that are not dissected will well up into tremendous balls of mass that are dark and unreadable, so it is important to realize that a core idea of the program is to be able to split apart, dissect and thus understand. This is what the brain does when functioning properly.

SAF is the greatest problem-solving method to come along since the beginning of time. It can dissect simple problems, as well as the most confusing complexities anyone could have. As a problem-solving machine, it eats problems consistently and willingly, and will do as much as its master commands. This is true if using any of the subjective questionnaires or the infrared device. No matter how many questions or complaints are constructed, the Self Awareness Formulas will perform to find the answers. This is another reason SAF has been called the Rosetta Stone for humans.

Mental Aspects

The mental aspects related to #12 are directed toward unknown barriers, which are developed beyond the reach or understanding of the individual. Be aware that whenever #12 appears in any SAF chain, there is attention focused on the unknown. Nervousness occurs when a person is not able to understand the unseen. There must be some unknown invisible quantity that is part of his problem, and yet he or she cannot see it.

When developing a program for nervousness, we must look at the processing power of the chain owner, especially in coordination with other glands and organs.

#10-12

If the thyroid (#10) creates an Up-Link with the brain (#12) in a numerical chain, then the person has misunderstandings and confusions present. These are rudimentary confusions that must be sorted out very quickly.

There may be a misunderstood situation or idea, or a general, overall confusion in the chain owner's life. He or she may not be able to figure out how to behave to ensure survival. This Up-Link is a syndrome that indicates the person may be having difficulty perceiving the true circumstances around him or her or cannot easily understand new concepts.

#12-13

When this Up-Link is found in a chain sequence, it tells us the brain (#12) is connected to the adrenal glands (#13). When we see this syndrome, we know that the chain owner has many projects and plans left incomplete. His energy is scattered because bits of it remain focused on the unfinished projects; he might not be able to muster enough energy to complete his plans. In a physical sense, these unfinished projects may create a condition of insomnia, which may be detrimental to health. (See #12-13 sequences below).

Physical Aspects

Physical upsets involving the brain (#12) are primarily headaches, neuralgia and nervousness. These nerve reactions, of course, may be due to mental conflicts 90% of the time, but may also be part of a biochemical upset in which the elements calcium and magnesium are out of balance.

#12-17/18

When the brain (#12) is associated with the endocrine system (#17/18), the individual may exhibit signs of food allergies. He or she may be consuming something that is upsetting the biochemical balance of the body and therefore causing the condition of nervousness.

#12-13

If the SAF Participant's chain presents an Up-Link #12-13, (brain and adrenal glands), then there may be insomnia, the inability to sleep or gain rest. In this particular context, gaining rest comes not only from sleeping but also from getting REM sleep (Rapid Eye Movement), which is a dreaming state. REM sleep physically discharges electrical activity from the body and causes a deep relaxation. Often people feel they are getting enough rest because they "slept like a rock," but in reality, they are overshooting the REM state. Therefore, they are not getting the much-needed physical release of electrical charge. This can cause varying upsets, such as daytime exhaustion, or a specific type of nervous energy. This typifies the #12-13 individual.

#12- with any other SAF number

The idea of #12 in a chain of numbers bespeaks the concept of hidden energy. The organ found next to #12 (on the left) would be the primary location of the upset: there is some unknown, hidden or obscure condition involved.

Energetic Dynamic

Energetically, the #12 system is the *Simplifier*. The flow of energy we want from this system is such that it defuses confusion and complicated situations, making these simpler to understand. This #12 system is the bridge between what is known and what is unknown.

The #12 system is stimulated and programmed by memories and thoughts of enduring complicated and confusing situations. Because we could not process, change, or escape from those early events in our life, feelings of nervousness flooded our spaces and are still there today.

When we see this #12 system, we know that our attention may be focused on complicated situations, or on thinking there may be an unknown condition in our body or system, or things are so complicated that we think our brain is rattled, which confuses us even more.

When we are in the middle of a confusing situation, or a very complicated and entangled situation, we are filled with excess electricity and so are not able to decide what to do first or second, in order to find our resolution.

With our personal SAF work, we can learn to untangle and unravel those situations to glimpse the value of simplicity. Once we have mastered this aspect of personal SAF work, we can begin to make simple, clear, and uncomplicated choices.

> After chain owners rid themselves of the interference of traumas, they can allow the experience of life to age them spiritually, rather than physically.

13
Adrenal Glands

AT A GLANCE
Emotion: Courage
Condition/Function: Capacitance
Keywords: Pressure, Shame, Pride
Energetic Dynamic: Pressure

Designated #13, the adrenal glands are located above the kidneys and are comprised of the cortex (produces steroid hormones) and the medulla (supplies epinephrine and norepinephrine.)

These glands are the spark plugs of the body, carrying enough power to give us 14 trillion volts of energy. If all the cells in the body were coordinated with the electric capacity of the adrenal glands, we would be able to pick up two locomotives, one in each hand. Indeed, we have all heard of heroic instances where the adrenal glands kicked in and made it possible for a slight person to lift a 2000-pound car to save a trapped loved one. The reason the adrenal glands don't seem to give us the capability of superhuman strength on an everyday basis is because of the checks and balances issued by the rest of the organs, especially the anterior pituitary and the male and female gonads.

Emotion: Courage

The adrenal glands are the mechanism of courage in the body. Courage, in this sense, is the ability to put up with stress and defend against attack. In coordination with the thymus gland (#1), the adrenal glands (#13) are what give us our base immunity system. These glands are extremely important in all phases of courage: physical, mental, and spiritual. It is our ability to act with courage that elevates us above all other organic life.

No matter how much stress is put upon them, courageous people seem able to continue along the same course of action in their everyday lives. Many times we don't realize we are in a courageous situation because the stress has mounted by increments somehow, without our awareness. Such people are fighting

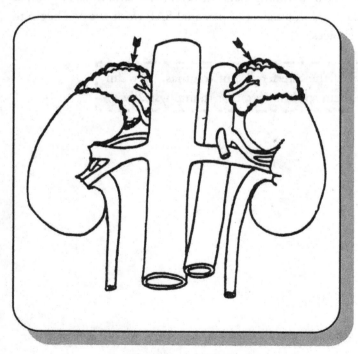

The Adrenal Glands

heroic battles day in and day out. We view courage as a feeling that occurs in the face of imminent, extreme and acute danger, but this is not always the case. Often we are exposed to chronic circumstances, such as family issues, which put an inordinate amount of stress on our system and cause us to need adrenal strength on a subconscious level.

#13 indicates an energy thief is in the area. When we see the #13 in a chain sequence, we should always question who in the chain owner's life is draining them of energy. We can also feel drained when in a battle against allergies or viruses. Unfortunately, this type of courageous activity starves off the adrenal powers, diminishing our ability to cope with sudden danger in the future.

Condition/Function: Capacitance

The purpose of the adrenal glands is to store electrical charge or energy, called capacitance. The adrenal glands exemplify our ability to do work and to perform functions. It has been seen when the #13 appears in an SAF numerical sequence that we often find the opposite of energy: low blood sugar, or hypoglycemia, caused by environmental factors.

The person with #13 in their chain sequence may be losing energy to environmental parasites and thieves. What are these? Radiation (frequency transmissions) of radio waves, microwaves (cell towers and cell phones) television waves, the sun, and nuclear isotopes. In our modern day and age, exposure to computers, WiFi, and X-rays can lead to complaints of exhaustion and an inability to perform under any kind of stress. Emotional radiation from those we love can also sap our strength. These all steal energy (glucose) from a body and replace it with hardened fat, calcium, and inert materials, all of which reduce the efficiency of the overall human mechanism.

#13-16

Often the adrenal glands (#13) will have a connection with the kidneys (#16) in a chain sequence. This could be called the failed test of strength or courage, for #13 indicates the emotion courage, while #16 indicates fear. Chain owners, at some time in the past, found themselves in positions where they were on the horns of a dilemma; they had the opportunity to become heroes. Did they act and let their courage carry them through to completion, or did they run the other way? Fight or flight. Many times when #13-16 appears, it is indicative that the person has turned away in the face of danger, doing neither, but in actuality, it is the flight factor that weighs heavily. At any rate, they did not have the capacity to perform.

#13-17/18

Another interesting Up-Link is the adrenals (#13) coupled with the endocrine system (#17/18). Viewing this syndrome demonstrates that the person depicted feels a loss for the zest of living. This loss of desire to participate in life is caused by some severe trauma in the past that was powerful enough to drain the adrenal glands of their strength and energy. Indeed, upon questioning clients and patients at various clinics, this was found to be true.

As was seen in the earlier chapters of this book, we might have the illusion that our energy or power has been taken away from us; however, this is impossible, for the genetic storage memories are not erasable. They are always present. All that has occurred is that some trauma or energy has misaligned or blocked the pathways we normally use to retrieve this power from our genetic storage banks. So, the SAF Up-Link (#13-17/18) shows that the trauma, whatever it was, was powerful enough to convince us we could not reach back into our energy banks. We could not have energy anymore.

The content of the trauma is a powerful mechanism affectionately labeled the dragon by some practitioners to signify the unknown cause of an event or a confusing situation in our present time life. The term dragon is used illustratively as a way to help others understand their own lifetime patterns better.

When the dragon (the trauma) in our lives is powerful enough to convince us there is no such thing as energy, it can successfully thwart even the most powerful people in their ability to perform tasks. The important thing to remember is that these trauma-dragons exist in many different areas or sub-strata of energy within a person, so we could conceivably have energy in some areas and have none in other areas.

This is what creates phobias and fears. We may have the ability to fly an airplane or drive a car, yet have a distinct and terrible fear of elevators or crowds of people. This happens because this particular trauma-dragon (#17/18) is powerful enough to jam our mental/physical circuitry and cause us to believe we have no power in these areas.

> The content of the trauma is a powerful mechanism affectionately labeled the Dragon by some practitioners to signify the unknown cause of an event or a situation in our present time life. The term dragon is used illustratively as a way to help others.

Mental Aspects
13-20

One of the most powerful mental viewpoints involving the adrenal glands (#13) is its connection with the pancreas (#20). This Up-Link relates to people's inability to cope with the loss of possessions or items, and especially loss of locations, such as their homes.

Those who have a #13-20 combination in the chain are often found to be homesick. Depression is another aspect of the #13-20 Up-Link; depression is a major problem for those living in society at this time. In many cases, both the homesickness and the depression are subconscious. Strange as it sounds, it is not uncommon for us to have a specific problem in which some of our organs are "homesick" and others are not.

As an example, if someone has lived for some time in rural Louisiana and then relocated to New York City's winter climate, a few of his or her body parts may still be functionally attuned to the bayou while others have caught up with the new location. Examples of this phenomenon have been put to music. Remember the popular song, "I Left My Heart in San Francisco"? This lack of synchronization causes an outflanking of the energies and may cause us to feel disconnected from our present surroundings.

We may be exhausted or have hypoglycemia, a condition in which our energy rises and falls at certain intervals during the day. Particular hours of the day and specific events will cause a loss of energy. At the same time, we may notice that we are losing muscular strength, and that the body is starting to drain itself of energy. This is because various organs are not in harmony or synchronization with the rest of the body, and we are starting to lose our physical performance abilities. This would especially be true if the bones and muscles (#9) were also present in the numerical sequence, written as (#9-13-20).

#9-13-20

As mentioned above, when the bones and the muscles (#9) are in an Up-Link as #9-13-20, this hints that various organs are not in harmony or synchronization with the rest of the body; we are starting to lose our physical performance abilities.

#13-14

When the adrenal glands (#13) form an Up-Link with the mind (#14), the chain owner may complain of poor eyesight, astigmatism, myopia, or an inability to focus properly. This situation arises because the person is having trouble viewing reality. The mind is not able to face certain traumatic situations; therefore he or she has trouble seeing exactly what is real and what isn't real in the environment. Life images may become bent when they hit the plane of the body; actual images may become distorted.

Physical Aspects

Many physical problems involving the adrenal glands are very marked. A person may have bronzing of the skin, but more importantly, there is that factor of exhaustion. The person may be run down and unable to cope with stress. He or she may not be able to handle physical pressures or do as much physical work as before. On the other hand, if the adrenals release excess epinephrine, there may be a situation of being hyper-wired, hyper-alert, or being on guard all day and night.

#10-13

When the adrenal glands (#13) are tied with the thyroid (#10), people may be in the throes of physical abnormalities causing them to have mal-absorption, or trouble with their diet. It is indicative of a problem involving the acceptance and the rejection of foodstuffs. What they are eating may be causing allergic reactions. The force and the power of the adrenal glands initiate the fight against allergens, unwanted substances and toxins in the body. This would especially be true if the thymus (#1) and spleen (#23) were also present in the chain, (#1-10-13-23).

#13-20

As mentioned in the mental aspects, when the adrenal glands (#13) connect with the pancreas (#20), people exhibit loss of muscular integrity. In other words, they may be cannibalizing their bodies by using their own protein structures more than usual for energy because there may be some renegade allergens, such as a superoxide, in the body.

#12-13

Another physical factor for observation is the combination of the brain (#12) and the adrenal glands (#13). These numbers together are directly related to the action of the body trying to get rid of traumatic circumstances during the day.

As we go about our daily lives, electric pressures from the environment in the form of mental pictures and experiences are recorded in the bones and muscles. The logical sequence of events would be that the brain (#12) and the adrenal glands (#13) must harmonize so that the body can reject the toxins of experience

Some experiences are pleasant and some are unpleasant, but the residual charge that causes friction energy and develops into capacitance must be eliminated.

Sleep is essential so we can deeply discharge the spurious toxins of a normal day's activity. If we don't reach full REM sleep, we are not totally relieving our tired bodies and our weary minds of the infiltrating toxins that may become latent within our systems. As each un-refreshed night goes by, the errant damaging electric charges in the body will remain charged. This increases the chances that there will be more difficulty with simple pressures and mundane stress on a daily basis. If we don't reach the much-needed REM sleep, then electrical charges and unwanted friction energies back up; these are strong enough to generate heat in any organ.

Many of the disease entities created by the aforementioned process will be depicted in the rest of this book. For now, you should know that such hidden energies or traumas could be created by a combination of simple stresses that are picked up during daily life and refuse to be discharged from the body. It makes sense that if we are able to discharge all toxins and errant frequencies from our systems, we will certainly be trauma-free, and dragon-free, for our whole lives.

It is interesting to note that when we successfully rest, we attain the state of alpha (7.5-12 Hz oscillations), which is a deep relaxation state. Alpha waves were promoted with biofeedback machines and some people have learned to attain the state of alpha on a conscious level; this rest and relaxation is what we need for healing. This frequency seems to coincide with the true wavelength or circumference of planet Earth (7.83 Hz). It gives us a proper grounding state and draws toxins and all unwanted electrical phenomenon, not associated with the body, back into the earth where they belong. If we could actually view this scene, we would see the ensnarled energies of traumas by the hundreds being pulled from the body toward the earth.

Energetic Dynamic

Energetically, the #13 system is all about *Pressure*, and we can make use of this to equalize the pressures of life. When we can courageously meet pressure with equal pressure for balance, we can resolve conflicts and regain our self esteem.

This system is stimulated and programmed by memories and thoughts of having to put up with loss, and overpowering feelings of not being able to live up to our own expectations, plus the expectations of others. For this, we feel a bit of shame. We were not able to process or escape from this emotional situation in the past.

We were knuckled under by the pressures of life so that our fight or flight mechanism could not work properly when we needed it to. We may feel emotionally drained, or we don't feel we can fight *or* run away. Our zest for life and living has dimmed. We allowed a trauma or an accident to become a defining moment for us.

In our SAF personal work, we are now able to stand tall with pride and put away the shame and self-abnegation we had when we believed we didn't measure up. We can now courageously explore our new lease on life, and are filled with energy and new-found abilities.

> Even if we are not instantaneously cognitive of what the core means (it is the subject of the chain), after the inky blackness of the trauma has been vaporized, great truths about the chain owner's existence will spring forth.

14
Mind

AT A GLANCE
Emotion: Wonder
Condition/Function: Analyzation
Keywords: Space, Unknown, Serenity
Energetic Dynamic: The Analyzer

Probably one of the most mysterious parts of a human being is the mind. Many philosophers, scientists, and poets throughout the ages have tried to detect, dissect, and explain the mind and how it works. When groups of people are asked where the mind is located, we hear a variety of answers. Many are confused. They don't understand what a mind is. They think the mind is the brain or is in the brain.

In the science of SAF, the mind is given the #14. Its main purpose and function is to analyze all data. It is considered to be an electromagnetic aura that invades, infests, and pervades every cell and nuclei of the body, especially by using command centers *around* the brain. In essence, our SAF work entails the diligent and arduous study of the electroplasmic field, those various halos or auras that steadfastly revolve around every human being. The electroplasmic field (the energy field of humans) and its elemental composition, is discussed further in *The Promethion,* and *The Threat of the Poison Reign.*

The Mind

Paintings and mosaics by famous artists from various periods in history have depicted saints and martyrs with very bright golden halos, for it was known that this golden aura showed the most harmony and balance of mental continuity. Human beings are not normally shown with halos because they have the basic but unfortunate problem of not knowing where their minds are located.

The mind appears to cup the brain and the skull, and this is the main storage of numerous tiny micro fine energies of various wavelengths. When speaking of wavelengths in the mind, we look at 1×10^{-30} (one times

10 to the negative 30th power) as a long wavelength and 1 x 10^{-3000} (one times 10 to the negative 3,000th power) as a shorter wavelength.

The shorter wavelengths register the deep past. In the mind, these are the connections we have to genetic philosophies handed down by our remote ancestry as present in the DNA-RNA. The longer wavelengths register a period closer to the present time.

It is crucial when doing SAF programming or *any* enlightenment procedure involving mental treks into the past that these past life wavelengths are in proper order by following the SAF protocol. If the short wavelength energies accidentally become longer, their power that existed in the past (even up to 500,000 years ago) can float into the present time and create havoc in a person's life. The wavelength of a past remembrance is brought forward from ancestral times when energy is pumped into it. This phenomenon can occur when homeopathic practitioners give their patients high potency remedies too often.

Many practitioners in the field of homeopathy become befuddled by the action of their high potency remedies. High potency homeopathic remedies have concentrations of incredible diminution, such as 1:1,000,000, that is one drop of substance to one million drops of water, a short wavelength. When taking high potency homeopathic remedies such as this, people may have the unfortunate reaction of having their ancestral memory files yanked out of their minds, ready to be examined by a practitioner who didn't know these were there in the first place!

Many people don't even know they have these particular wavelengths and stored information, so they certainly would never intentionally pump energy into them. People who dabble in past lives and other kinds of self-awareness routines that involve time travel may inadvertently be stoking the fires of a gargantuan dragon, a huge trauma that lives in their past ancestry (the cells have all of this data recorded). It may be difficult to imagine, before you have done SAF programming, that you can summarily be destroyed by actions of your ancestors that occurred 500,000 years ago. So it is imperative that the correct information is known, that all the programs are given properly, and that those programs produce the results desired by the chain owner. Stick to the program!

It is not necessary to go into *possible* past lives for resolution of our past events. There is often enough going on in *this* life for us to worry about and want to address. That said, the chain does represent our past life in a sense, because these events did happen in the past. We are no longer that same person we were 10 months or 30 years ago, so for all intents and purposes, even those more recent times can be considered a "past life."

For those who do believe in past lives, know that this is a spiritual aspect. We can also have past recordings of ancestral lives that are stored in the DNA-RNA.

Emotion: Wonder

When SAF chain owners produced numerical chains with the #14 occupying the lead position, those chain owners had usually voiced a major complaint of chronic worry or mental disturbances.

The SAF program has been carefully developed to be sure that a person has a good understanding of the processes of the mind and the body. Furthermore, the SAF philosophy embraces the concept that we can control illnesses that may have a psychosomatic origin.

Chain owners who consistently presents #14 in an SAF chain sequence must have their attention focused squarely on upsetting subjects. These people most likely let their imaginations run away with them; they may have a good deal of fantasy inter-playing with their problems. They may believe they have a particular condition when in reality they do not. Often when the #14 shows up in the chain, it is because an examining practitioner or family doctor has told the supplicating individual that he or she has a certain harmful condition.

We should be careful if the #14 is up front (to the left) in an SAF chain, for it shows an active, powerful imagination process in the present time. On the lighter side, the person may just be worried about the SAF test results! This is very possible, depending on how the SAF Practitioner guides the chain owner through his or her program.

#5-14-15-24

When the #14 is present in the chain of numbers, along with the hypothalamus (#15), the anterior pituitary (#5), and the lymph system (#24), there is a good chance the person may have been misdiagnosed; among patients at clinics, this was found to be true.

Condition/Function: Analyzation

The #14 designates worried persons, who are constantly mentally computing and intensely pondering their troubles, with no solution in sight! This is a classic case of over-analyzation, which is a condition of worry.

Note that the mind (#14) does not represent the spirit; they are always separate, although there is a connection. A #14 appearing in the chain may represent a curious person with encircling worries and low self-esteem.

#14-17/18

When the mind (#14) is connected to the endocrine system (#17/18) as a syndrome, then we consider a very rudimentary problem, called general business troubles or environmental troubles.

#14-8-17/18

If the #14-17/18 combination from above also has the sex organs (#8) mirrored to it (#14-x-x-8-x-x-17/18), then it is indicative of family troubles.

#14-15-17/18

If the #14-17/18 has the hypothalamus (#15) in an Up-Link, then it indicates business troubles, specifically related to economics rather than family or environmental troubles.

#13-14

If the mind (#14) is associated with the adrenal glands (#13), the chain owner is having difficulty with his or her ability to accurately perceive his or her environment and surroundings.

#14-22

When we see the mind (#14) is connected to the parathyroid (#22) as an Up-Link, this syndrome indicates that the SAF chain owner may be angry about situations. Confusions of the mind cause him or her to select wrong targets in a precarious environment. This chain owner may be concentrating on troubles that are really obsolete or are not of the right value. He or she may have altered erroneously what is important when considering a correct course of action. As an example, if you are in dire need of a job, and you are out shooting pool in the afternoon because you feel you need a career change, you are making the wrong choice.

Mental Aspects
#1-14

Because #14 is considered a mental phenomenon, it is important to note that when the thymus (#1) is in connection with the mind (#14), there exists a condition of mental or psychic invasion. These people are definitely afraid of random confrontations with other disoriented people because they cannot put up with such sporadic impingements on their souls. Their energies are not organized or powerful enough to ward off these haphazard situations in the pressing environment, especially when in communication with other people.

> **Psychic or Mental Invasion (#1-14)**
> **Chain A** (#1-14-11-20-23-24-5-6-7)
> The condition is more acute, the numbers #1-14 are close together in the chain, and are on the left of the chain, closer to present time.
> **Chain B** (#11- 20-9-16-14-2-3-10-1)
> The condition is improving, demonstrated by the #1-14 Up-Link being reversed, more spread apart with numbers between, and moving to the back (right) of the chain.

#14-15

When the mind (#14) creates an Up-Link with the hypothalamus (#15), the chain owner is definitely showing patterns of distortion, mental derangement and temporary or continued stages of what in SAF we call insanity. This is not necessarily clinical insanity as in the western medical model but the person has to make certain that his or her perceptions are accurate and precise if this chain owner wishes a chance at optimum survival.

The mind (#14) in different combinations may appear in the SAF chain sequence	
#14-17/18-15	Business or financial troubles
#14-8-17/18	Family difficulties
#13-14	Perception is off
#14-22	Angry, alters what is important
#1-14	Psychic invasion
#14-15	Signs of distortion; insanity

Physical Aspects

The physical relationship of the body to the mind induces the psychosomatic condition. Because the mind is wired into the main impeller (a junction were physical matter, electricity, and psychic power meet), the mind can easily cause the motor and sensory areas of the brain to function properly or improperly. The mind is able to create various situations that are of great importance to the mind and body on a demand basis. The mind has the ability, when under deep stress, to create violent physical reactions, one of the most powerful and injurious being a stroke.

Lesser conditions can also be created by the mind, such as headaches. A migraine headache (#14) with nausea and vomiting, can act as a pressure gauge for the surroundings that may include friends, relatives, or business associates, and could signal a time for retreat. There could be a sick feeling that relates to the person's ability to stand up against environmental pressure.

#10-11-14

When observing the above Up-Link of the thyroid and veins and arteries of the upper extremities (#10), and the veins and arteries of the lower extremities (#11) along with the mind (#14), then the person should be wary that his mind is impinging information on the body that the body cannot handle. He or she may be overtaxing the frail physical structure of the body with powerful energies that are too cogent for those specific cells. The #11-14 Up-Link alone indicates there may be a condition of burnout. Different positions and combinations with surrounding numbers will further define the meaning.

#14-17/18

When the mind (#14) is connected with the endocrine system (#17/18) in an Up-Link, the chain owner may be creating a definite scenario for building up fat cells in the body for protection from the overloads of business and family troubles coming from his or her immediate environment. The Up-Link #14-17/18 indicates a certain type of trauma from the deep past may be stealthily creeping into the unsuspecting wide-open mind portals, and busily working on the delicate circuits there.

These traumas and ensnarled trauma-dragon energies are loaded with raw electrical charge just the way a murderous tornado or a wild electrical storm seethes and crackles with lightning.

When #14-17/18 appears as an Up-Link in a numerical chain, it may be indicating that the person could be in the throes of a maverick mental electrical storm; this is one of the primary sources for creation of psychosomatic illnesses.

Energetic Dynamic

Energetically, this 14th system is the *Analyzer*; it analyzes events and situations in the past in order to help us predict and create the future. Here we find the ability to figure out problems with imaginative solutions, in which we change the unknowns into recognizable knowns, and thus achieve serenity and balance in our life. But know that when this #14 appears in the SAF chain sequence, it tells us we have lost that ability.

This system is stimulated and programmed by memories and thoughts of worry and wonder over just about everything that has not been figured out ahead of time. This #14 exemplifies a condition; it is not present in the chain sequence as just a passing endeavor. This is not a single thought, but is a way of life. The presence of #14 tells us that in the past, there was no way to process, change, or escape from this situation.

We have been wondering and worrying and thinking on unknown subjects for so long it is as if we are lost in space with no reliable answers in sight. We may be extremely analytical, and full of wonder as we ponder all the mysteries of life; we may be temporarily stuck in this situation until released.

In our personal SAF work, we are able to realize the futility of focusing on the overwhelming number of unknowns and unseen invisible events; so instead, we turn our attention to what we *do* know and what is concrete. When we can do this, it affords us the serenity we desire.

SAF Participants find that conventional ways of thinking are no help when facing true traumas. Traumas when we were younger were formidable, but when looked at again through the aid of our age and experience, and with help from the SAF Practitioner, these become understandable. We can easily put two and two together so that our chains, and our lives, make sense.

15
Hypothalamus
& the Senses

The function of the hypothalamus and the senses is the evaluation of all the information being presented to us. All outside information comes through to us this way. Alternative healing practitioners recommend that we go outside in the daytime, without glasses or eye coverings of any type, and let the LIGHT enter, which stimulates the hypothalamus. We must be careful, however, not to look at the sun, but to be *in* the sunlight. Because of the vast area that the hypothalamus directs, we need this stimulation to ensure our hypothalamus, and our body in general, is in good working order.

The hypothalamus (#15) is directly associated with the complete balance of the human body and its deliberate daily functions as far as accurate regulation of heat and cold, appetite, and sex drive. This gland system also activates and integrates our autonomic mechanisms and activities, plus the endocrine and somatic functions. It controls the ability of the human being to discern stress and various patterns of pressure on each sense level. Therefore, when reading about this method, know that the term hypothalamus (#15) also incorporates the senses: sight, sound, smell, taste and touch, as well as the perception of time, if the brain (#12) is in the same numerical sequence. However, in the science of SAF, we account for more than just the five major senses; 128 sensory channels or perceptions are outlined in *Junk DNA: Unlocking the Hidden Secrets of Your DNA*.

Combinations of numbers with #15 tell us which sense is especially being stimulated. When the mind (#14) is associated with the hypothalamus, then we think of sight. When the anterior pituitary (#5) is in close proximity on a chain with the hypothalamus, then we consider hearing. When the lungs (#7) are associated with the hypothalamus in a chain, we are interested in the activities of the sense of smell. When the stomach (#4) is aligned with the hypothalamus in a sequence, we consider the sense of taste. When

The Hypothalamus and the Senses

the bones and muscles (#9) are present along with the hypothalamus in a sequence of numbers, we study the sense of touch.

The sense of touch can expand outward for a long distance, sometimes a *very* long distance. With this Expanded Tactile Sense, we can sense many different fields; it is also known as Extra Sensory Perception (ESP).

The hypothalamus and the senses, #15, are how we receive most, if not all, of our information from the environment around us. This #15 appears quite frequently in SAF chain sequences today because we live in a time of information overload. Think of all the data we receive on a daily basis, from school, in our busy home life, from friends and family, and in our work world. The electricity being tossed about left and right from microwave cell towers transmitting to us and our cell phones, the satellite activity that we cannot even see above us but which affect us at any rate, the use of our cell phones with their cameras and actions of mini-computers, iPads, television, and the desktop computers. And it seems that Wi-Fi is everywhere, in coffee shops, schools, houses, along our highways, and in every business. It is dizzying just to think about all this data and the radiant energies, the electronic smog it creates and brings into our lives, and what it might be doing to us! The excess radiation we receive today is reflected in the SAF chain of ours, appearing as #15.

Seeing the #15 in a chain sequence, we know that there may be sensory overload, too much coming in that we can't distinguish, look at with clarity, or understand. This may lead to the idea there is too much stress to handle well, or too much radiation is incoming. This radiation could be on a physical level with toxins, but it is often on an emotional level with toxins. This number appears quite frequently in the chains of chain owners as a result of these challenging times today.

SAF and the Senses

#14-15 Sight

#5-15 Sound

#7-15 Smell

#4-15 Taste

#9-15 Touch

#12-15 Perception of time

Note: these number combinations can appear in any position within the SAF chain. For example, a problem with hearing can be indicated in any chain that includes a 5 and a 15.

#15-21

If the posterior pituitary (#21) is associated with the hypothalamus (#15) in a chain as an Up-Link, this is an indicator for an alert study of the pineal body, which secretes melatonin, a hormone that influences sleep, circadian rhythms, and hormone levels, and in this capacity, it may also affect sexual maturation and sexual activity. Other writers, religions, and researchers consider that the pineal gland is our Third Eye and is responsible for our ability to see and visualize what cannot be seen.

The pineal body is considered our future gland; its responsibility is to ensure that the human race perpetuates itself. It is especially stimulated, and goes into action, at times when it thinks the body is dying, such as when there is alcohol involved. When two people are drinking at a bar, (ingesting a poison) they spot one another across the room and there may be sparks that fly, sparks of sexual energy. Right after this, the two may become coupled in sex; all done in the pineal's effort to perpetuate the human race.

Emotion: Attention

The emotional correlation to the hypothalamus and the senses can be expressed by the term attention. It indicates that the person with #15 has had repeated distortions of perception or inability to hold concentration for long periods. This trouble comes from both simple and complicated forms of radiation, any energy from any source that is directed to us, including nuclear radiation, electronic smog, smoking haze, from places, inanimate objects, and emotions from others as emotional radiation. Any time we have to kick back against such sensory overloads and pressures, we can be misdirected.

We find that when #15 appears in an SAF chain sequence, it is a definite sign of degenerative conditions created by excesses of radiation, used in the classical radiation sense as any particle of energy that moves *inward toward the person*. We understand this as stress, excess stress to our bodies. As mentioned, this number appears frequently in the chains of people living in the world today.

This type of radiation or stress, these conglomerated, spliced, conjugated, or ephemeral energies can be generated from *any* source in the environment including other people, other places, and even inanimate objects. The emotions are included in this study, so for example, if the chain owner is in a confused situation in which he or she has to confront a good deal of poignant anger from another party, then he or she, as the victim or target of this attack, is effectively receiving doses of emotional radiation.

Any animate or inanimate object, or any visible or invisible energy approaching inwardly toward a person, is part of sun cycle energy and would be considered radiation. As mentioned previously, any electrical phenomenon now on the planet originated with the sun; therefore, any phenomenon of light (visible or invisible) that seeks the center of an individual can be considered a radiation phenomenon. Each dose of sun cycle energy, in whatever form, must also be considered part of the tally toward a person's aging process. It is important to remember that we do need the sun in order to properly grow in the physical sense and in our awareness levels, as well, as we are learning in this book.

Scientists and researchers have always been concerned with ionizing radiation, which is of the type that can oxidize tissue, but any form of radiation that increases the stress and pressure to the target system can be counted and must be defended against. When the target system has to fight back against any pressure, this means the radiation has the ability to confuse and misdirect the overall plan of the body.

> SAF defines radiational energy in the classical sense; this is any particle of energy, including emotional, that moves inward toward us, toward our center.

Condition/Function: Evaluation

The function of the hypothalamus and the senses is the evaluation of all the data that comes into our system. All information from the outside world comes to us through the eyes and directly into the hypothalamus in this way. The hypothalamus controls the ability of the human being to discern stress and patterns of energy and pressure on each sense level, which includes not only the 5 major senses, but the full 128 sensory tracks of perception as detailed in *Junk DNA: Unlocking the Hidden Secrets of Your DNA*.

Perhaps the single most important consideration when observing people's behavior is their ability to evaluate circumstances. Can they evaluate situations realistically, and put the proper events in perspective? Can they process all the sensory input into a view that clearly reflects an accurate perception of the outside world around them? With the presence of the #15 in the chain sequence, we know that these abilities to evaluate have been inhibited.

Analyzing with the mind (#14) is a different factor altogether. Analysis, #14, involves dissecting the congealed particles of the most pressing problems, whereas in evaluation, #15, the individual is putting problems in an order of importance. This order of importance – evaluation – is directly akin to the mathematical actions of the precisely ordered numerical chain of the SAF program.

Many SAF Practitioners have noticed tremendous boosts of energy while deciphering and reading numerical chains for curious chain owners. This startling reaction occurs because the forthright practice of studiously evaluating black body masses and black body light explodes the black body light into white body light. When this happens, this peculiar phenomenon causes unknowns to transform into knowns; mysteries into solved riddles. The effects for both people involved can be astounding! SAF Practitioners will actually gain energy the more they evaluate and dissect important issues for and with SAF Participants.

#14-15

The Up-Link 14-15 is very important in the consideration of general sanity. It is extremely vital to understand when initiating the practice of SAF, that this program moves us directly *towards* sanity and *away from* insanity. The insane individual has become more mentally and physically conglomerated and darkened. We understand that SAF is the antidote for insanity; as we learn to turn more of the darkened images into visible and knowable light or white body light images.

The more black body light we possess, the more confused we will be. The more white body light we own, the more enlightened and intelligent we will be.

This is why it is essential, when working with SAF protocols, to avoid hypnotic spells, trances, or devices that delete our conscious willpower. We must constantly seek to *enhance* the capabilities of the active SAF Participant to judiciously perceive the black body light around him or her.

Hypnotic spells and trances place a darker state of black body light *into* the person in order to achieve the goal of the wanton suggestion. Forcing the operator's suggestions into a person's black body light renders that person "suggestible" or "sleepy." The operator of hypnosis will tell the person to make certain they are relaxed, and soon they will feel sleepy. Sure enough, the person becomes sleepy. And more *unconscious*.

This is a very dangerous state as far as SAF is concerned! The SAF Participant wants to be *more* awake, not more asleep. The idea is *more* self awareness, not less. The darker this black body light becomes, the more the SAF Participant's energy is turned away from white body light; and then, the easier it is for inhospitable traumas and the ensnarled energy of past traumas to become active.

Mental Aspects

The hypothalamus #15 is truly a phenomenon born directly out of the spiritual and interpersonal relationships with higher energies and the Supreme Power, God. To become more God-like, people must certainly become more aware; they must have as much black body light removed from their systems as they can.

What is the simplest explanation for white body light? God possesses and controls more white body light than any other being. White body light is intense and powerful. A being of God's magnitude would certainly not have any unconscious areas of His mind, and very few areas of black body light or mass, if any at all, if He is to be able to understand and perceive all His self-created, mental machinery. Evidently, Earth is one of His mental machines. So, it is a Universal Directive from above, and part of our quest, to emulate God. This makes it imperative that we put our attention on gaining as much white body light as possible.

#10-15-17/18

When the thyroid (#10) and the hypothalamus (#15) are together as an Up-Link in the chain sequence, this syndrome is an indicator of the black body mass encroaching on the white body light of the chain owner. In many cases, those who possess the #10-15 control numbers have been experiencing a difficult time perceiving through the black body mass. It is difficult to peer through darkness and see accurately.

If the endocrine system (#17/18) is in the same chain, it indicates that traumas and those ensnarled energies are on the move, bringing with them much darkness and confusion.

> "It is better to light a candle than to curse the dark." – Eleanor Roosevelt

#5-15

When the anterior pituitary (#5) is connected with the hypothalamus and the senses (#15), the chain owner has a creative sense of distortion. His imagination can go wild inside and around him, causing mental and physical miasmas. It becomes difficult to perceive the ideas and mental images that are being transmitted to him from others.

If, for example, someone is talking about a boat with many sails, the distorted person may get an image of a car with leather interior. The garbled and deformed image may be that wild and uncontrollable. Usually this person, victimized by his or her own mind, will say, "Huh?" or "What?!!" as if the speaker were crazy! These deformed pictures flash by in about 1/20th of a second; these are unbelievably fast, so the distorted person is unable to follow the conversation correctly. Furthermore, when asking people who have difficulties tracking information around them, we find that many of the beleaguered SAF Participant's mental memory banks are corroded with ensnarled traumatic figures and images. These mental traumatic images lie sideways across the person's energy pathways and distort his or her views of the past so that he or she believes that certain traumatic events had occurred recently, when in actuality, they didn't happen, at least not in this lifetime.

#5-10-15-17/18

The #5-15 Up-Link in a chain sequence, especially if there is a thyroid (#10) and endocrine system (#17/18) in the same chain sequence, indicates that there is an intense jumble of ensnarled trauma energies near or in the individual's sensory channels.

When chain owners with these number combinations are asked about events in the past, they have a very difficult time retrieving them. They have bad recall or no recall at all. Many times, people with these particular numbers (#5-15) forget events that have occurred in the past, such as loss of a loved one, certain kinds of traumatic surgical operations, drug taking, etc. They may vehemently deny any of these things ever happened to them! This denial makes matters very confusing for regular practitioners not trained in the nuances of SAF training.

There are many intricate connections of energy involving the #15 in a numerical chain sequence, and it is important to note some of the more delicate ones.

#15-17/18

When the endocrine system (#17/18) is specifically tied to the hypothalamus (#15) as an Up-Link or syndrome, we have what we call "healer's syndrome." These numbers were found to exist in those who had inadvertently picked up or absorbed the energy or the twisted ideas of another. Chiropractors and physicians, who work directly with disturbed, diseased, or distraught people, contract a good deal of energy by laying their hands on them So do massage therapists, energy workers, and this is true for some distance healers, as well. The therapists take on some of the actual memories and the conglomerated images of the traumas and snarled up energy inside their clients' mind and/or bodies. It was found that many practitioners possessed the same strange, disharmonic ideas and the bizarre problems as the patients they had treated.

SAF has not forgotten about our healers! An SAF program, "Healer's Rescue," was developed so that we could actually unravel some of the practitioner's traumas and find out which traumas and messed up energies belonged to whom. Therapists and healers often don't realize that many of the problems they are carrying around aren't their own. This is true of mental health therapists as well, which affects them on mental, emotional, and spiritual levels.

It is interesting to note that animals used for therapy will often pick up the same twisted energy of the people they were brought in contact with to help. In these situations, the Infrared device is used to create a chain sequence for the animal, and Healer's Rescue can be accessed to suggest change and greater understanding.

#15-20

Another signal of mental distortion and the inability to observe reality is when the pancreas (#20) falls together as an Up-Link with the hypothalamus (#15). When these numbers are present, the chain owner may be seen to have a very peculiar phenomenon right in the center of the forehead. An invisible knot of energy exists there with such power that it pushes the person's head backward about 10 degrees. It causes him to look out from under this barrier of energy that is positioned just above his eyes. Many practitioners who have handled or touched people with problems, such as arthritis or heavier diseases of cancer or kidney troubles have been afflicted with this specific knot in the middle of their foreheads. It appears as a very confused, twisted ball of energy that nestles on the brow. Known as the "doctor's squint," it comes about because the pressure of this balled black body mass (congealed trauma matter) is enough to squeeze a practitioner's capacity to view others through a tiny pinpoint of mass. In order to look through this massive pressure, the practitioner has to tilt his or her head backwards a little.

At the same time, *anyone* who generates a #15-20 sequence in the chain is liable to have had some pressure buildup in their system, especially in the mind and near the sense mechanisms around the ears, nose, eyes, mouth, and even at the tips of the fingers.

Epileptics, and those who have observed someone in the throes of a seizure or convulsion, will know a manifestation of the #15-20 phenomenon as the "aura." This aura can be a visual one, with hallucinations, a motor or a somatic aura. The afflicted person can detect smells, sounds, or experience a feeling of "not being here." This is sometimes a warning of an impending seizure, which may follow the aura several minutes later. If it were possible to spray this aura with some kind of phosphorescent dye to make it visible to the naked eye, it would resemble a miniature tornado. When this tornado alights on certain parts of the brain or mind, the afflicted person loses all sense contact with that area.

Physical Aspects
#14-15

Regarding physical troubles, we find a similar kind of reaction generated to the rest of the body by the hypothalamus (#15) and the mind (#14). Tiny tornadoes of energy can light on the body and absolutely foil the present and past energy processes of the body. This number combination indicates patterns of distortion, which SAF would define as insanity, and the sense of sight is also disturbed.

#11-15

Many times, especially when the veins and arteries (#11) are together as an Up-Link with the hypothalamus (#15), the individual may have hardening of certain body tissues, particularly in the lower half of the body. It is not uncommon for a person to have rectal calculi or kidney stones with the Up-Link #11-15. The poisons lodging within the veins and arteries may cause arteriosclerosis and blockages.

Solidification of these particular invisible tornadoes of energy is merely the electrical output of certain entities. Specifically, the trauma that existed in the past is being called up to work on the body in the present, in the *Now*. When such a trauma is called up, it breathes fire against the body. These fires come out in the form of tiny tornadoes (Planck's laws of heat, photons, quanta and thermodynamics) that are invisible to the naked eye. But once they infest themselves in the body, they stay in there and are able to cause arthritis and calcification in many of the soft tissues.

When the SAF Practitioner sees a #11-15 sequence in the chain, he or she knows that this tornado-like action has been going on a long time and is capable of destroying the tissues within the person's body. If this is the case, we find that many detoxification processes are necessary. Sometimes several trauma entities will work together on an area of body or mind at the same time, just to ensure that the physical parts or mental zones are frozen into place and helpless. The trauma entities attempt to turn that region of the body or mind into a "nest" so that they can rapidly reproduce themselves and remain there. If the solidification of physical or mental energy is complete enough, they may have gained the ability to procreate, to become something else.

What we experience with disease conditions that worsen is the birth of additional entities. So powerful and so insidious is this process, that it infests the genetic system of the human being. These "new" entities and traumas are handed down from one hapless generation of humans to the next.

It seems that the process of existing as a human being is a challenge to unravel this mass of ensnarled life that has been created by traumatic experiences existing deep in the past of a person, and recorded in the DNA-RNA. In other words, we are born with problems that were created by the traumas and entities of past centuries. Being such old conditions, some of these are quite formidable. (see DNA Research and Genetics, page 196)

It is best to start the SAF process on a simpler level, in the present time, in this lifetime!

To truly reach the state of a super human being, the Unchained Spirit, we must be able to confront these masterful, powerful, and meaningful trauma entities that have been created by our ancestors, as well as the traumas we have experienced in this lifetime.

There are many other influences against #15 in the thoughtful view of a person's case. The number sequences are all-important in detecting this menagerie of ensnarled energies of traumatic events.

#15-16

When the Up-Link of kidneys (#16) and the hypothalamus and the senses (#15) appear in an SAF chain, the patient may have an extraordinary fear of traumas, entities, and toxins. These two numbers appearing anywhere in the same chain may show that the chain owner is in retreat from the onslaught of these toxins and poisons. He or she may be cowardly, afraid of the past traumas in his or her life. Due to the presence of #16 in the chain, the Practitioner should be careful to ascertain whether the SAF Participant has developed an inability to confront traumas in his existence. This could be deadly, for the more people don't look at their traumas, the more they lose their ability to create white body light (the only light that can dissolve and resolve traumas). In SAF, we welcome traumas and entities because they give us something to work on. This is the only way we can dissolve traumas and acquire more white body light.

Traumas and the physical representations of trauma, which are the poisons and toxins in a person's body, have power only when they exist in the black body realm, where they are invisible. Therefore, when a person refuses to look at his or her problems, fertile ground is provided for the nesting of traumas in that person's existence.

#15-19

When the skin (#19) appears with the hypothalamus (#15) in the SAF chain sequence, there is a great possibility that the person may be developing a tumor in his or her body or mind.

The forefathers of western medicine, the Greeks in particular, in their attempts to understand when an entity was impinging upon another's body, observed and wrote that particular sequences occurred. Their studies of the physical humors showed that once the toxins invaded the body system and reached beyond the defense mechanism of the thymus (#1), they were effectively *in*. The medical scientists in ancient times called this first step *dolor* (pain); the second step was *rubor* (redness), followed by *calor* (heat). After this segment of change, a person would develop a *tumor* (swelling). These ancient Greek practitioners saw this reaction more or less as a *footprint* or *imprint* of an invisible force (black body light) against the body. They understood that they could not see what was making the pain or what was actually making these conditions occur, especially if there was no physical object present, such as an arrow, a stone club, or a knife. If a person of that time period suddenly developed a pain or sensation, or any kind of mental or physical disorder invisible to the naked eye, then the practitioners considered that there was some demon, an invisible entity, involved.

Black body light persists in the presence of white body light because of the ignorance of its existence. It is important to note that these SAF processes are specifically tuned to turn the lights *on* in the presence of these traumas and take a good look at them. In this way the traumas can be known, resolved through the SAF process and then put to rest in the past where they belong.

#15-22

Another number that is important to the physical aspects of the hypothalamus (#15) is the parathyroid (#22), which shows hardening. The process of creating tumors begins with #15-20, light mass; then #15-21, a tumor that is spongy and made mostly of water; and finally #15-22, a calcified, hardened tumor.

We should have a great deal of respect when viewing a chain with #15. Radiation and toxins of a black body nature are involved here, and we must be very alert to this signal that the SAF Participant is entering an area that was once dark to him.

> **SAF Number Combinations with the Hypothalamus & the Senses (#15)**
> #5-15 Imagination runs wild, hearing sense is disturbed
> #5-15-10-17/18 Poor or no recall (intense jumble of traumas, ensnarled energies, and toxins)
> #10-15 Encroaching black body mass; perception troubles
> #10-15-17/18 Confusion (entities and trauma energies are on the move)
> #11-15 Hardening of body tissues; rectal calculi, kidney stones
> #15-16 Fear of trauma and ensnarled energies
> #15-17/18 Healer's Syndrome (taking on another's energy and their stored traumas or toxins)
> #15-19 Tumors might be forming
> #15-20 Light mass tumor; "doctor's squint"; epilepsy; convulsions
> #15-21 Spongy tumor (fluid), a study of the pineal gland warranted
> #15-22 Calcified tumor (hardened)

Energetic Dynamic

Energetically, the #15 system is the *Communicator*. It is born from the spiritual and interpersonal relationships with higher energies and powers, what Christians call God, who possesses and controls more white body light than any other being. We are made in God's image so as we emulate God, we must learn to transform black body light into white body light. It is important that we humans understand the importance of attaining as much white body light as possible. In our SAF work, we do this by locating and focusing on those areas that are in the dark, so to speak. These are the unknowns and are found in the anchor number of the chain, the last number on the right. When we focus on that anchor, we will have more resolution. As the black body light changes to white body light, it becomes known to us once again. When this happens, it explodes! It is an electrical phenomenon. As the mysteries become solved riddles, the resulting explosion is felt by both the Participant and the Practitioner.

The #15 system is stimulated and programmed by memories and thoughts of feeling inhibited from communicating what we saw, heard, and felt during emotional situations in the past. At that time, we were not able to process, change, or escape from the situations in which we found ourselves. Comprehension and words were inhibited; we were effectively shut off.

We have been in situations where the sensory input from various frequencies was so great it overwhelmed us, inhibiting words or comprehension. In our personal SAF work, we learn to break that cycle by evaluating patterns and past emotional events and traumas, freeing up our attention. With our new-found understanding and energy, we can forthrightly communicate to ourselves, to others, orally and by way of the written word.

> The chain owner may have an extraordinary fear of traumas, entities, and toxins. He might not want to look, but shedding light on these past events and traumatic occurrences is the only way to dissolve them. This is what we do daily with our SAF work.

16
Kidneys & Bladder

At a Glance:
Condition/Function: Filtration
Emotion: Fear
Keywords: Refuse, Poisoned, Purify
Energetic Dynamic: The Purifier

The kidneys are a pair of essential organs designated #16 in the SAF Secondary Sequence. Proper functioning of the kidneys is vital, for these organs filter the blood, remove toxins and excrete the end-product of body metabolism that may otherwise overtax other glands and organs. This end product, urine, is the refuse, the discarded waste; this is sent to the bladder for storage until voided.

The kidneys are resilient. They regulate the concentrations of minerals and other ions in this extracellular fluid.

Emotion: Fear

When the #16 appears in a specific chain sequence, the SAF Participant correspondingly exhibits an acute or chronic fear or phobia. However, the position of the #16 in the chain determines phobic action. There may be circumstances involving acute terror of specific dangers. Whenever #16 appears in a chain, it indicates that traumas and their ensnarled energy, sometimes called dragons, have caused a constant fear for the confrontation of the emotional events themselves.

Sometimes those who exhibit the #16 in a numerical chain sequence have a difficult time realizing that they even have traumas. Not being able to express or confront these trauma-dragons causes a great deal of pain and sensation. However, the fear of trauma cannot be classified as a trauma itself. In various circumstances, those who have fear reactions will exhibit the #16 in an SAF chain. Fear reactions are a specific organizing of human energy that tries desperately to escape an environmental, mental, or physical danger.

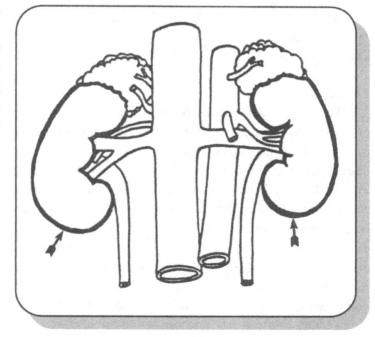

The Kidneys

Problems arise when the chain owner has traumatic events and overwhelming energies buried in the deep subconscious that cause true fears. In other words, phobias are stacked one on top of another like a deck of 3-D playing cards. If you have a particular phobia, such as fear of animals or insects, you will have other phobias underneath these fears that you cannot see. This has been the understanding, the breakthrough, made by SAF. SAF technicians have been able to uncover the real poisonous or toxic situation underneath the outer crust of trauma, which gives rise to other false or misdiagnosed conditions.

Condition/Function: Filtration

The actions of the kidneys are part of a purposeful chromosomal objective. Any entity or structure of living organism in the environment must have the ability to filter out toxins; however, these may sometimes be mislabeled. And because we cannot discern a toxin from a friendly bit of energy, we may sometimes become confused and erroneously allow a villain into our system.

The kidneys are very specific in their action. Acting like a deft screen, they take poisons out of a polluted blood stream and remove the byproducts of metabolism to thoroughly cleanse the human machine.

The kidneys act much as an oil filter does in a car. Dirt is considered the primary enemy of any machine, computer, or body-mechanism. If poisons, dust, and dirt get into a body, the resultant motion of these materials within the body can easily cause an abrasion of the internal structure of organs, glands, tissues, and cells, thereby wearing down the system. Once toxins, dirt, and poisons get into the organs, the organs are easy targets for destruction. This is because noxious substances can swiftly infiltrate delicate places in the body and embed themselves, so it is important that the kidneys endlessly create this filtration mechanism.

#16-22

When the kidneys (#16) form an Up-Link with the parathyroid (#22,) there is a definite possibility that non-specific toxins and poisons within the system are beginning to solidify and take root. As relayed previously, the traumatic past scenarios can certainly create a miniature tornado-like effect in the invisible realms, between visible physical dimensions, and can ultimately build up masses. These radiant but condensed masses are powerful enough to create concretions affixed to the walls of soft tissue. You may think this is a more unusual circumstance or an exception, but it is actually quite common in humans.

The layering or depositing of energy in one location will definitely cause the existence or the creation of mass. It is the audacity of the chemically-biased trauma-dragon to reproduce itself so much in one location that it actually comes out of the black body light in which it usually exists and becomes visible in white body light, seen as a tumor, stones, and other names, and these will show up from time to time. In this case, the trauma and that ensnarled energy has won over the thymus (#1) for the moment; it has occupied a space in the visible light spectrum.

It is essential for anyone practicing SAF to understand that the visualization or realization of energy in a solid state is merely the compilation of minute radiant energies that have piled themselves onto one location at one time. These tiny phenomena of stones, parasites, toxins, vermin, and other pests that invade the body are merely the end result of many hours, days, months, years, and in some cases centuries, of accumulations of energies in one place at one time.

The creation mechanism of a kidney stone, for example, is the same kind of mechanism used to create a human being, an animal, a bird, an insect, or any other life form on the planet. The key is the eternal application of energies to one spot. The energies must collide into one location and create a swirling pattern like an invisible, diminutive tornado that ultimately wraps around itself like a ball of string and becomes visible.

This action occurs in the reproduction of human beings. When the sperm invades the egg and a zygote is formed, the energy begins to wrap around itself and create a tornado-like effect. The fetus, in the early stages of pregnancy, appears coiled into itself, wrapped up. As the fetus grows, these tornadoes of invisible energy become powerful enough in that location that they can finally unravel themselves.

It is the same principle when the entity forms in the shape of stones and tumors. The entity that invades the body is strong enough to create a tornado of energy, which wraps around itself. Ultimately, if a kidney stone, or any other kind of anomaly, were allowed to persist, it would mold into the visage of the toxin itself. In other words, those particular entities are the offspring of the original trauma, the true marriage or collision of life forms that fostered it. Particles that grow into stones are, to a certain understanding, the "dragon eggs" being laid in a person's body. Given enough time, they can become the exact duplicate of the entity and its ensnarled energy, a 3-Dimensional hologram of a trauma that may have existed ancestrally, eons ago.

What many people don't understand about these entities is that traumatic situations don't usually take on the gruesome appearance of a snarling, fire-breathing lizard with a pointed tail and leathery wings. The trauma-entities, the dragons, if you will, that live in this text are those created by the collision of various energies in the environment against the human being.

Often these trauma-entities take on the appearance of car bumpers that have crushed or hit the person in the past, or the appearance of stairs, baseball bats, familiar faces of women or men, the vision of a childhood house. All manner of animate and inanimate objects that have collided with the human being are encased in a protective photographic state so that they can prolong and proliferate their existence.

On the other hand, many traumas are the visage of humans, or of monsters and demons. SAF Participants have been confronted by all manner of living forms on the planet. Whatever a person visualizes as his or her dragon, has certainly become his or her dragon. Whatever a person puts thoughts and energy into, that becomes a reality for him or her.

People fear insects, even tiny little bugs, because throughout the centuries the genetic blueprint of the body has recorded attacks by insects. When a body is put into the ground, the cells are still alive. As the bugs and crawly creatures come to devour the last vestiges of that human being, those genetic cells are still recording the trauma of being eaten alive by a very large creature, such as a worm or a beetle! To the genetic program, in a state of being devoured underground, a bug will appear to be 30 or 40 feet tall in comparison to the cell. Hence, many people have a dread of creepy crawly bugs, roaches, worms, spiders, and other critters. Read *Junk DNA: Unlocking the Hidden Secrets of Your DNA* for more on this, listed under Allergies and Addiction, The Cockroach Story.

This type of phenomenon is part of the kidney reaction; the kidney itself developed a fear of being unable to reject a toxin. Many of the poisons that are filtered from the kidneys are sent immediately to the bladder. Compared to the colon (#3), which has more strength, the kidneys are daintier and more frightened when it comes to disposing of byproducts.

When severely frightened, a basic human reaction is the tendency to urinate. The phrase "that scared the piss out of me!" is descriptive of this. When a person becomes fearful, the fluid carrying many of the unwanted materials are rejected rapidly, very rapidly. The reason for this: *no two fears can occupy the same space at the same time.* The body actually trades one fear for another. The toxins that are in the body within the urine, urea, etc., are less detrimental to the system than an unknown, perhaps a greater fear, so the body trades off the lesser fear, the urine, by releasing it. Of course, to recreate this circumstance, someone has to be terrorized into letting go.

#16-20

When the kidneys (#16) are associated with the pancreas (#20), this may be a signal that the kidneys' center of gravity is off balance, and poisons are escaping into the body. There may be a poison or toxin infesting the kidneys that creates inflammation. In many cases, this has been staidly reviewed by medical science as Bright's disease. The affected person passes albumen, or protein, via his urine and complains of a definite dysfunction of normal kidney processes, such that the urine may be darker than normal.

#15-16

When the kidneys (#16) form an Up-Link with the hypothalamus (#15) in an SAF chain sequence, a greenish tint to the urine may indicate hemoglobin is being lost through urination. Hemoglobin is the material that carries the iron, laden with oxygen, through the body. The #15-16 sequence is an indicator that the person may be becoming magnetically polarized, which means, there has been a change in the direction of the magnetic flow, enough that it could change the direction of the iron in the system. Following this thought, the dipole, the positive or negative electric charge, also changes as it revolves near the trauma site in the body. Some energy in the environment, that is powerful enough to electrically sway iron in the body, may have come into the area. A trauma-entity forceful enough to cause the blood to change course must be recognized and handled. Often when #15-16 is in the chain, this syndrome indicates that the chain owner may be under the control and influence of barbaric and horrific ensnarled energies from a trauma. This state can be verified if the person behaves in a zombie-like fashion.

#16-any organ number

When the #16 is present in an SAF chain, the SAF Participant and SAF Practitioner should look to the target organ. This is the organ that appears just prior to the #16, when reading the chain from the left. Proper filtration of noxious substances in each organ is mandatory for tissue and cell survival. If an organ or gland complex allows toxins and poisons to escape into its tissues, then it will reduce the efficiency or output of that particular organ complex.

SAF number combinations with Kidneys (#16):

#15-16 Hemoglobin in urine (person becoming magnetically polarized)

#16-20 Bright's Disease - Albumin in urine (kidneys' center of gravity is off balance, and poisons escape into system)

#16-21 Kidney stones (Poisons in system begin to solidify)

Mental Aspects

Probably the most pernicious mental aspect of the presence of #16 in a chain is the reality of fears, phobias, and terrors. A #16 in the sequence shows the chain owner has a definite unwillingness to confront certain circumstances in the environment. A person's face sometimes can reveal the degree of fear present. The tone of the skin, bags under the eyes, pallor, cachexia, lines, wrinkles, and haggard looks are indicators. Swollen eyes are often a clue that a person may have a specific fear or problem confronting or facing certain subjects.

There is a plethora of listed phobias in medical science that involves every kind of action imaginable. A phobia indicates the person is unable to handle a particular mass, energy, or concept (any or all of these). The rest of this text will depict the actions of environmental reminders that may trigger all manner of phobic reactions.

It was determined through SAF programming that what the Participant actually fears is not the real problem. The mechanism of the "reminder" contends that the active Participant is looking at a white body mass, *some visible energy*, which is serving as a trigger or reminder for some black body mass or ensnarled energies. This trauma, beneath the Participant's awareness in the subconscious, is using light body energy or creatures in the present environment to trigger thoughts of itself (the trauma). The way that it does this is very simple.

A specific energy in the environment (such as the color of a person's hair) can be similar to that of a person who faced the trauma in the past, someone who had the same hair color. This lies within the person's unconscious. This mechanism is able to stimulate a person's memory enough to awaken the trauma-dragon from his sleep and cause these ensnarled energies to go into action. Now, when traumas are put into action, they infest, pervade and invade the nervous system, producing symptoms. They create pains, sensations, and discomforts, and they cause headaches, nausea, vomiting, nervousness, and all of the basic problems of mankind.

You might ask why a trauma-dragon would want to be awakened from his rest. Wouldn't he much rather have a nice, quiet sleep? Trauma-dragons are able to go through existence undisturbed, but in reality, the extent of their existence depends upon the amount of playing time they receive. In other words, each time a stimulated trauma plays out its dark existence or sends an arcane message of symptoms to its human host; it etches the groove of a macabre recording into that unwary human being. So the number of times the trauma's scenario is played will give it maturity or tenure in the body.

The playing of the excited, stimulated trauma is vital to the existence or perpetuity of the phobia, because traumas must be played, or they may be forgotten altogether until there is a reminder. They must be played out of black body light, for if they appear in white body light form, they will summarily be destroyed. (This script can be demonstrated in the lore of Dracula, who was never allowed to come into the light or he would be vaporized. The trauma-dragon has a similar script.)

The fact is that if a trauma-dragon is to get a play, it must nudge or work its host into a space where the host can have a reminder. A reminder is extremely important because if the trauma-dragon doesn't have a reminder, then it doesn't get a play, and if it doesn't get a play, then it won't be fed energy. In other words, to feed a dragon, to give it more energy, we must encounter or find a reminder for it. Why do this? Because we are trying to give the trauma energy so we can *see* it and *process through it* and release it with our SAF program.

The traumas can only get energy nourishment from the present time because that is where all the actual live energy is located. The present time contains *all* light energy and knowing energy. A trauma-dragon can't know or express its own existence unless it is fed energy by the present time, so it is vital that when working on our own self awareness work, we get involved in those situations similar to the forgotten trauma so that these *reminders* can be fed energy. Once that happens, with the SAF protocol, we have a way to envision them and can make use of our new-found dissolving ability.

Consider people who are accident-prone. They have been able, by some coincidence, to injure the same body part over and over again. Such actions are merely the traumas getting people into situations where they will be reminded of the traumas. The traumas get *play* and thus get energy.

As an example, you may have hurt your foot when you were younger. Suppose you were playing baseball and someone wearing cleats stepped on your foot. In this particular case, your dragon may look like a shoe with points. We could say that a baseball shoe with cleats makes a fine dragon! The cleats could be the teeth and the stitching could be the eyes, and from up close, it would be a very formidable looking dragon. You will see reminders all around so the dragon can have a play. You will subsequently get into similar, unhappy situations. Perhaps you (the SAF chain owner) would drop a book on the same foot, or trip and fall on the same foot, or you could stub your toe on the wooden post of the bed. These recurrent collisions give the original trauma more energy, more power.

If you have the particular trouble of having a trauma like that, you find that you look for anything that reminds you of the trauma in the first place. If it were a shoe with cleats, you would just happen to find something that looked like a shoe. In this scenario, it is difficult to escape from, or get away from reminders because we all wear shoes every day. Each time a shoe is put on, it would be one reminder or one play for the trauma. You would find yourself in a chronic situation where you would be endlessly replaying the trauma's scenario, often on an unconscious level, and be in the unique jeopardy of having accidents occur to that same body part, over and over again.

Fear now kicks in because you are unable to control this trauma miasma; you live in a constant state of phobic symptomatology in which you feel chills and scary sensations, such as dizziness and vertigo. You feel the kickback of your own genetic diagram telling you to get out of the way because the overwhelming hidden trauma is coming through! The genetic program itself works in black body light, so it can help avert trauma-energy feeding problems and cause you, the dauntless but stupefied chain owner, to get out of the way and let things happen as they will.

We experience much symptomatology in the presence of a hungry trauma in need of energy, for *the trauma is actually trying to encroach on the space of the genetic blueprint.* The genetic cells, the DNA-RNA and the chromosomes, feel the invasion of this wily trauma (for some people, the image of a dragon does seem appropriate, as it tries to install its own existence and purpose). A trauma-dragon, with the image of a shoe with cleats, might try to cause the related body part (the foot) to spawn dragon-traumas of the same nature.

We can imagine what traumas would look like if they actually were able to develop into that particular dragon-visage. Many people develop foot problems slowly; first they experience extreme tenderness, then sores, and later, bunions will form within casts of calcium that bend and twist. Under a high powered microscope, they look more and more like a spike or a cleat. When that dragon-trauma has enough plays, it has the power to create or reproduce, to have children. This arthritis situation could be passed on to your children by way of the DNA-RNA.

#6-16

If the kidneys (#16) form an Up-Link with the liver (#6) in an SAF chain, then the chain owner may be experiencing the fear of change. In such a case, the Participant may have grown so accustomed to certain problems, that he or she may be afraid to change them. It is a fear primarily coming from trauma-dragon talk. The trauma-dragon, of course, certainly doesn't want us to fix our problems or our case conditions because many of them come directly from the dragon-trauma itself. When such trauma-dragon talk goes on in our mind, we may prevent ourselves from doing SAF chain work or *any* programs that could be for our betterment.

In these situations, you would likely try to keep your fears and phobias because you don't want to change. You may be afraid that if you lose your traumas, your problems, lose your life, your existence, or your personality. That is not what would actually happen. but Practitioners find they must compromise somewhat with someone who has these problems because he or she is not all together in the head. The trauma-dragons are more or less thwarting this person.

> With an Up-Link of #6-16 in your SAF chain sequence, you may be afraid of change, specifically, you fear that if you lose your traumas, your problems, you will lose your life, your existence, or your personality. This fear of change can cause you to stop any kind of programs for your betterment.

This same number combination (#6-16) indicates that the person will have trouble in any situation where change is taking place, such as in divorce, separation, losses, business troubles, etc. Such a chain owner with this Up-Link,# 6-16, will have a difficult time coping. This change of energy, or change of location, is detrimental to the person's existence because it acts as a reminder and causes a play for his trauma-dragon, giving the traumatic event much more power. In other words, the dragon says, "See, I told you this would happen to you and that you would lose."

Often the trauma was originally created in a very traumatic circumstance, one in which the person was connected to a heavy, horrible loss experience in the past. It may have started with his or her parents, then through time, places and events were recorded where he or she had failed. This new change (loss of the trauma-dragon) may be a constant reminder that he or she is losing and the possibility exists that he or she will be taken advantage of … again.

#13-16

If the Up-Link #13-16 appears in the SAF chain sequence, this shows the adrenals (#13) combined with the kidneys (#16). The Participant may have a problem or a phobia dealing with the performance of spectacular or heroic actions. He may even have a fear of being unable to accomplish very ordinary deeds. In many cases, #13-16 in a numerical chain indicates that the person may have trouble facing projects he or she has put together out of fear that these will not be successful. He or she is the type who says, "Well, I'm not sure that this is going to work out for me, and if I invest my money and time I'm going to lose. I'll fail anyway." A person with this particular SAF chain combination may already be aware of his or her phobias about future plans and projects, but is nonetheless unable to confront those phobias.

> Failure is always from a traumatic event; this type of failure chatter is the trauma communicating, or talking. The failure trauma-dragon may have many heads, each head being in the image of a person involved in the chain owner's failure.

A #13-16 type is stuck in a rut and is a prisoner of his own program. If the #13-16 appears to the extreme right of the SAF chain, the Participant has had failure in the past. His or her mind is still stuck on this and the failure scenario becomes a trauma. Failure is always a trauma, and this trauma-dragon may have many heads, each head holding the image of someone involved in the Participant's failure. This chimera is attached to a hydrous body that is so energetically charged that anytime the chain owner tries a new or fresh project, this multi-headed beast attacks the chain owner. Furthermore, if he or she tries to get away from this trauma and the ensnarled energies, the traumatic event and its energy convinces the chain owner he or she will be destroyed in the goriest way imaginable. A horrendously sad feeling then envelops the chain owner, because it seems all he or she can do is feed energy to the trauma-dragon and those ensnarled energies.

Every time he or she makes a plan, or has a desire or a dream and tries to make it come true, he or she unwittingly calls up this ugly beast.

It is very disconcerting to have something so formidable in the path of our energies. It causes us to lose faith in the idea that we will ever amount to anything. Therefore, we stop ourselves from succumbing, and push ourselves into a grind, much like some mindless laborer in Hades. We plant ourselves in what we believe to be a safe routine, one that is trauma-free. We become dull, robotic, and uninterested in anything. We have become the victim, and we complain that our life is useless and boring. As we complain, we harbor and feed this extremely fascinating and interesting trauma-dragon that waits in a black body closet. If we could ever let this dragon out, or actually showed it to anyone, and what an amazing feat that would be, we would be sought after by the media and endless others. But of course, the dragon will never come out in the daylight to show itself. It always exists in the shadows, and stays hidden away, until we do our part, which is our personal SAF work. When we do this, we are able to shine our light on it, and dissipate it.

Physical Aspects

When a person gets sharp back pains or notices troubles with his or her eyes (e.g. bags under the eyes), or fluids building up in different areas of the body, the kidneys are to blame. The posterior pituitary (#21) also helps establish the body's correct water balance. Because water is the perfect conductor, the human system's molecular construction can cause discomfort. It is important to make sure that the surface tension of the fluid in the body, plus the purity of the water, is maintained.

> **Detoxification:**
> Kidneys (#16) = Water Detoxification
> Lungs (#7) = Gas Detoxification
> Colon (#3) = Solid Detoxification

Many times when a person complains of skin trouble (#19), he or she is likely experiencing some deep trouble with the kidneys (#16), the lungs (#7), or the colon (#3). The important notion to remember is that the kidneys (#16) take care of the body's water and fluid detoxification, the lungs (#7) take care of all gas detoxification and the colon (#3) takes care of the body's solid detoxification. If all three organs are working properly, then the levels of liquid, gas, and solid in the body are being properly detoxified.

The final area from where all toxins eventually exit is the skin (#19), the body's outer encasement, and our largest organ. As we urinate (#16) the urine must go beyond the skin; as we exhale (#7), the breath must go beyond the skin; and as we defecate (#3) the feces must go outside the skin.

#1-16

When the thymus (#1) associates with the kidneys (#16) as an Up-Link, some energy or poison has worked its way into the system. Of course, the thymus (#1) is indicative of the highest pressure possible, so that if an infection or inflammation is invading the kidneys, it means that the toxin or the trauma is powerful enough to take up root there, and can actually disrupt the detoxification process.

In all physical conditions involving the kidneys, we should make sure that the kidneys themselves are clear. Just as we are careful to change the oil, gas, and air filters in a car, so we should be mindful that the filters of the body's fluids – the kidneys – are properly detoxifying.

#4-16

If a person is casting off urine filled with proteinaceous substances, there is some kind of breakdown in the filtering process. This is because the digestion (#4) is erratic. When we see (#4) in a numerical chain along with (#16), we should realize that there is some kind of toxic situation being created because the digestion is off.

#1-16-20

If the pancreas (#20) aligns with the kidneys (#16) and the thymus (#1) as an Up-Link in a chain sequence, this syndrome suggests there may be a definite problem involving the indigestibility of toxins and poisons, not to mention foods, solids, liquids, and gases.

Energetic Dynamic

On an energetic level the #16 system is considered the *Purifier* for the holistic human system and must be in good working order so that all the systems work harmoniously.

When we see #16 in the SAF chain sequence, this tells us the Participant may be overwhelmed by fears and phobias of all types. This #16 system was stimulated and programmed by memories and thoughts of having to endure fearful feelings and toxic emotional situations in the past that could not be understood, changed, or escaped from at that time.

We could not face emotionally-charged events without terror gripping our innards, as if we were poisoned by the negative thoughts and angry words flung in our direction. We may have felt acute or chronic fear or terror. We may fear confrontation and be unwilling to face certain issues."Is this really going to happen, or should I stop my negative thoughts?" Fear holds onto toxins, and instead, may mistakenly dump urine and nutrition.

With our personal SAF work, we now recognize toxic situations as they pertain to body, mind, and spirit levels, and we can take steps for filtering and purifying our lives.

> Whatever people visualize as their dragons, certainly become their dragons. When we are deep in thought and put a lot of energy into an idea, whatever we put our thoughts and energies into becomes a reality for us.

17/18

Endocrine System (Includes the pituitary, pineal, thyroid, parathyroid, adrenal glands, pancreas, and testes (M) and the ovaries (F).)

AT A GLANCE
Emotion: Conservative
Condition/Function: Equalization
Keywords: Coordinate, Perverted, Balance
Energetic Dynamic: The Balancer

The endocrine system is composed of glands that secrete hormones, which are signalers to other organs and glands. The target glands are stimulated into action; the messages usually require a response. Hormones regulate various human functions, including metabolism, growth and development, tissue function, sleep, and mood. This system consists of the glands and organs considered the *power train* - the pituitary (the master gland), the pineal, thyroid, parathyroid, adrenal glands, the pancreas, and the sex organs - the testes (M) and ovaries (F). Some groups list the hypothalamus and the thymus as being in this gland system as well.

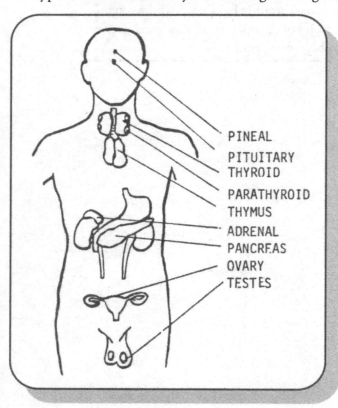

PINEAL
PITUITARY
THYROID
PARATHYROID
THYMUS
ADRENAL
PANCREAS
OVARY
TESTES

The Endocrine System

This system is considered part of that sequence of energy that causes us to look and behave the way we do. It is the mechanism that creates structure and processes energy. This framework of glands helps all other glands and organs in their daily functions. In a sense, the remaining organs, the liver, heart, spleen, etc., are merely servomechanisms for this power train.

Two numbers, #17 and #18, are used for this organ complex; #17 represents male hormones while #18 represents female hormones. This number sequence, #17/18, is extremely important because of its ability to track trauma-entities or trauma-dragons. When the #17/18 shows itself in the numerical chain, it is indicative that a major trauma has been stimulated and has occurred in a precise region of the chain owner's past. A numerical chain, because it is a layered and stratified past history, will give the present time on the left side of the chain, and the past on the right. So wherever the #17/18 falls in the SAF chain sequence, it gives us a better idea of exactly where significant traumas have been created in time. Those skilled in SAF techniques can pinpoint to within a few years when a particular traumatic event and an emotional pattern first occurred.

Emotion: Conservative

The endocrine system (#17/18) must be balanced so we can produce power.

Without an organized and aligned endocrine system, we may not have sufficient usable power. Energy failures occur because we have had a trauma in the past. The traumas and those ensnarled energies are able to cause us to lean toward one set of hormones or the other.

Ferocious trauma-dragons that have the right stuff to create disruptive pressure, such as those demons, entities, and traumas that are created out of automobile accidents and drug abuse, encrust the fertile body. *Pressure-packed trauma-entities control the male hormones, while trauma-entities born out of degradations, embarrassment, and loss will impress themselves on the female hormones.* This sets up a very interesting situation inasmuch as the hormone mechanisms of the body control not only the temperament of the individual, but also all the secondary sex characteristics.

If a chain owner is abused enough by pressure-driven circumstances, male trauma-entities will be created. The male hormones will be compromised, and the chain owner may have more receptive, masochistic feminine qualities. On the other hand, if more losses are present, and the chain owner finds that he or she is being hit with more female trauma-entities, then he or she may turn the other way and have more aggressive, sadistic male qualities.

Trauma-dragons are able to infest the hormone structure, creating a definite effeminate or masculine quality in certain individuals, because of the abuse and traumas that affect the hormone-producing mechanisms. By understanding the production and inhibition of the hormones testosterone (male) and estrogen (female), we can sometimes predict the creation of homosexuality in males and lesbianism in females. These states exist primarily because male or female traumas have taken up space in the body.

The SAF science is very simplistic in this respect. Suppose a male trauma-entity has taken up residence and is active in a male body. By following the laws of chemistry and physics, in which *two objects can't occupy the same space at the same time*, one force must be kicked out. So, if the male trauma-entity presence is crowding or inhibiting the male hormone production, then estrogen will reign supreme. On the other hand, if someone has been hit with a female trauma-entity (loss), then testosterone will reign supreme. This can happen in the case of males or females, since both produce both testosterone and estrogen.

Psychologically, if a man has had tremendous pressure brought to bear, and has had to admit defeat by way of a crushing effect of some impact from the environment, then he may become weak and effeminate. On the other hand, if a man has been struck with female trauma-entities and has suffered many losses, he may develop more masculine qualities. The same principle would apply to females.

This is not to simplify the problems created by hormone imbalances, only to give a basic premise as to the distortion of them. Male and female trauma-dragons can hit a person simultaneously and affect one or the other system in tandem. If a person has these particular hormone imbalances from some traumatic impact of the past, he or she has been programmed by the male (pressure) or female (loss/space) trauma-dragon to perform in a certain way. The process is complicated and may involve whole families of trauma-dragons or a whole species of trauma-dragon that enter human beings. It also may come from a trauma-dragon that is part of a virus or bacteria.

It has been found in SAF programming that if someone maintains a conservative output and is unable to perform to his fullest capabilities and talents, or if he or she is reluctant to move into higher states of energy, then he or she may be harboring some male or female trauma or traumatic ensnarled energies. This particular balance of male versus female, aggressiveness versus receptivity is extremely important. It guides the manner of treatment.

All this being said, there is perhaps no greater reason to get started with SAF chain resolution work than simply to discover what early traumas are affecting us and directing us in the present time, *as if* we were still living in the past.

When the chain owner has #17/18 in the chain sequence, the emotion depicted is conservative. This is not a political statement, but refers to the person holding back a bit in the emotional outlay, being conservative in his or her emotions. In this situation, it seems wise to conserve the power one has accrued and to save the emotions for use later on.

Condition/Function: Equalize

The #17/18 embodies all the most important functions and ramifications of energy necessary to understand all sciences, not just SAF. The dichotomy of male and female is carried throughout each science. For instance, in chemistry, male and female are depicted by *acid* (male) and *alkaline* or *basic* (female). In physics, *radiation* is the male idea, and *gravitation* is female. In astrophysics, pressure is considered male and *space* is female. In Chinese medicine, *yang* denotes male, and *yin* is female.

With the presence of the #17/18 in the chain sequence, we are alerted that something drastic and dramatic has happened, something so severe, it has thrown off the entire hormonal system.

When #17/18 appears in the chain of numbers, it automatically indicates this SAF Participant has lost his or her balance or perception for the basic dichotomies of life. He or she cannot equalize what is going on in life. "To be or not to be" is the basic question. To exist or not to exist? To perform or not to perform? The basic questions of existence, mobility, and intelligence are brought forward when #17/18 is encrusted in an SAF chain sequence of numbers.

#15–17/18

When the hypothalamus (#15) is connected to the endocrine system (#17/18) as an Up-Link in a numerical chain, it is imperative to understand that the SAF Participant is sensing, evaluating, or studying one of his or her own traumas. In a sense, when trying to decipher a trauma, we contact *reminders* in other people. We may very easily cry because someone else is crying. Strangers sobbing on a television program can trigger our trauma. Even when confronted with the fact that the television people we mourn have absolutely nothing in common with our own lives, it won't change things one iota because this televised scene feeds an actual traumatic event of some type. If we watch someone crying on television or in the same room, we can be instantly reminded of a traumatic situation in which we cried. But the consequences of this action are subtler than an outburst of tears. A person can pick up reminders from just about any source. This can only happen when our hormones are physically, mentally, and spiritually (mass, energy, and concept) out of balance.

Many times, however, mere hormone indications on chemical tests are not enough to tell the whole story. We may have a perfect report on a blood test and still be unbalanced. Remember that energy is 99% invisible, and the hormone balances on the harmonic levels of radiational energy in the body may be distorted in many different areas. For example, radio waves, sound waves, or microwaves on other levels in the body would not show up on a chemical test; and trauma-dragons, like poltergeists, are plucky enough to change their settings while the test is being taken. Many patients get a clean bill of health when they go to the medical doctor because *medical science is not programmed to scan all aspects of energy.* These patients are still uncomfortable and *know* something is wrong, even though the mechanic (doctor) *didn't hear the noise* when the patient *ran his engine* (body) for him.

#14-17/18

When #17/18 is found connected with the mind (#14) in a chain, there is a very difficult situation to observe. The chain owner with these numbers has a common but nasty trauma present; a poor memory. The mind itself is a series of connecting black body masses that are only ignited by white body masses of attention (#15) when the person calls for them. In other words, all the mind's material remains hidden in black body masses until ready to be *recalled*. When data is recalled, the specific overseer of the mind - the spirit - is able to shed light on a certain area and re-illuminate it. Those people unable to recall certain memories are said to have a bad memory however, the ability to recall might be blocked by the impudent energy of a trauma, the ensnarled energy of a trauma. Once we are able to illuminate the mind, we can see all our memories - pleasant and unpleasant. The mind's files are quite formidable and vast. But first we must control insubordinate trauma-dragons of ensnarled energy that rob us from remembering things. Dragons, again, are traumas of collision and loss. These are not only mechanisms; these are poisons in the environment. So, if you were infested with these remembrances, your memory would be very poor. When the mind (#14) is connected with the endocrine system (#17/18) as an Up-Link in a SAF chain of numbers, you may have a very difficult time ridding yourself of memory trauma-dragons. Your mind may be unable to illuminate the traumas and the trauma-dragons in the proper perspective.

The #14-17/18 sequence indicates that the person is having business troubles-of the mind. He or she cannot order his or her mind because the mind has altered what is significant. Many times he or she may focus on things that are not important and ponder them, causing a gross worry. When we see a #14-17/18 sequence in the chain, we see a person who has had difficulty in maintaining the economy of life. He or she is not able to utilize his or her energy to the fullest extent. He or she wastes energy and may find they are being easily taken advantage of.

Looking at this Up-Link, if the #14-17/18 is farther to the right of the chain, it indicates that in the past the SAF Participant has been abused. He may say, "I've been ripped off." His own traumas have caused him to be ripped off. His own basic traumas have led him into the trap of being disabled so that *the hidden trauma* could be fed. People believe energy can be bad because they cannot discern who or what is trying to hurt them, in this case the trauma-dragon with its ensnarled energy. Hidden, unseen dragons and that ensnarled energy are only trying to survive; there is a race for space.

It is a very curious phenomenon, but when we finally sort it all out, the trauma-dragons, those unknown to us, those hidden traumas in our past, really mean us no harm. This type of trauma-dragon needs space. The dragons in this book are mechanisms; we use this notion for educational purposes. These do not possess a soul. We can help the dragons exist in a whole other place and time - one where they are not interfering or intersecting with *our* energies. If we can get the trauma-dragon away from the body, we certainly can help ourselves and help that dragon-ensnarled energy, too. There is no way that we can destroy energy, including trauma-dragon energy. It is a non-erasable, non-destroyable substance. The memory of something lives on forever. But we can edit our impressions of it.

What we certainly can do, however, is edit our viewpoint of the trauma, that we ourselves turned into our nemesis, our dragon. We can change our mind about our conditions. We can change the importance and the significance of those things that we believe are in our way.

Many sciences today are trying to help humans to rid themselves of dragons. Many preach that the dragons are "bad" and they have to be eliminated. They must be destroyed because they're a lot of trouble. The dragons, however, cannot be erased; they can only be banished. It is the human's energy bank account that the trauma-dragon has accessed; this is the power that the trauma-dragon uses and that the SAF Participant can take back.

The dragon entity is an idea that goes on forever; it has no time and no space. There is no way that we can get rid of the *idea* of a dragon. We can, however, get rid of the power the dragon has over us, on body, mind, and spirit levels, which is a great accomplishment in itself.

When we understand that power and energy created in this environment is all *good* and for the benefit of everyone, then we become more understanding of our endocrine system (#17/18). We must learn how to coordinate all energies, of friends and enemies alike, and also be able to control all factors of energy. Mastering this one principle would change our whole life.

In most cases, each of us has enemies in our environment. There may be people, places, and objects that vie for the same space at the same time. They will try to take your energy away. There might be someone who is trying to take your best girl away, or maybe there is a situation that may take the things that the chain owner loves away. These are problems of space ownership.

People who are enemies on a lower scale could be allies on a grander scale. If a crisis arose where the future of the entire country was at stake, everyone would band together to stop the common enemy from invading and taking everyone's freedom and space.

If we are coordinated and understand the energy mechanisms of life to the fullest extent, we will realize that all energies fit into the proper perspective. We don't alter that perspective to make it fit just for us and our own diminutive dimension. We don't become selfish, but do become more determined to see that every energy in the universe is balanced and coordinated and fits the master blueprint. In this way we can never be harmed. We can never be hurt.

There is no dragon or no trauma big enough to hurt a person who is constantly maintaining the order of his or her universe, who is constantly striving to see that all cosmos is propagated. Chaos immediately drops away from any situation that is brought into the presence of order and harmony.

#13-17/18

If the adrenal glands (#13) are connected to the endocrine system (#17/18) as an Up-Link, the chain owner has lost the zest for living; this may indicate impotency for males and frigidity for females. The encroachment of the trauma-dragon has been so severe and perspective so lost on the energy within the person's system, that the black body masses infest his or her very existence to capture the space of his or her body and mind. This take-over can interfere with the very process of seeing and controlling traumas. To eliminate trauma-dragon power and put trauma-dragons in their perspective cages, we must understand their origins, the Causes. We are able to do this with SAF chain deciphering on a daily basis.

When the Up-Link #13-17/18 is found in a chain of numbers, it shows that the person has all but given up hope. He or she has lost the courage to face his or her traumas, traumatic events, and "dragons," whatever they might be.

#12-17/18

When the endocrine system (#17/18) is connected to the brain (#12) as an Up-Link, the chain owner may be exhibiting some pattern of allergy or sensitivity within the system. He or she is trying to reject toxins and poisons and is attempting to kick out the black body masses invading the nervous system, believing that foods taken into the system are responsible for the feeding of these black body masses or traumas. The chain owner may be extremely confused. The Up-Link indicates food sensitivities or allergies; the actions of eating are being confused with the reminding system of the traumas. This person has been thinking and putting energy *into* the traumas of his life, and has developed a trauma complex that may be overwhelming. Time for SAF chain work!

This is specific to the SAF chain owner, that the 12-17/18 is mentioning allergies and yet the #23 is not in the chain. In questioning the likelihood of no #19 appearing indicates that this particular chain owner has more of a reality on the sensitivities and not the allergies.

#10-17/18

With the Up-Link of thyroid (#10) and the endocrine system (#17/18), the person may have a good deal of intolerable stress. He or she may be unable to cope with some situations at all. These numbers indicate building up of fat barriers for insulation around the glands of the endocrine system. All organs may be encrusted with fat deposits, because fatty substances are able to thwart excess electricity from chewing up the organs. Because the trauma-dragons use megawatt lightning to disturb the endocrine system, the body will, in defense, put crude fat into all the systems and disable the body, preventing it from grounding itself against this trauma-dragon energy. Therefore, the electrical impulses of the trauma-dragon cannot move through and create havoc in the endocrine system. This is a natural defense process, but it puts the person under intolerable physical stress, and all the fat insulation can be very detrimental to the overall health of the body.

This situation is yet again, another reason for completing some SAF chain work.

#8-17/18

If the endocrine system (#17/18) is found in the chain with the sex organs (#8), there could be direct hormonal influence on the sex organs. If the chain owner is a middle-aged woman, she may have a menopausal upset. If the chain owner is a man, he could be climacteric or be impotent. We see that #17/18 can associate with all organ numbers because each organ in itself has its own hormone balance. Each particular organ, cell, and tissue, and every nuclei in the body has its own #17/18 dichotomy. That is, each of these is composed of male and female energies, the male being pressure and the female being space; the male being solidification and the female being fragmentation; the male being fire and the female being water, to name a few examples. The whole existence of the body, from birth to death, is alive with male and female forces, while at the same time we understand that birth is a male principle because we have an added item, increased pressure, and death is a female principle because this is a loss. These are SAF concepts from eastern medicine.

Mental Aspects
#12-14-15-17/18

The mind (#14), the brain (#12), and the senses (#15) are accentuated by the presence of the #17/18 in an SAF chain.

Following again the eastern principle model, the brain (#12) exudes a female characteristic. It possesses energy that fragments and electrifies. The mind (#14) is still more female and more beautiful in a sense that it can be completely cosmetic and filled with harmony. The mind (#14) primarily induces the hypothalamus (#15), a male-principled area that takes these female energies from the brain (#12) and the mind (#14) and flows thought-directed energies into the environment so that it can echo against pressures it needs for sensing. This technique - sensing - is extremely important for assessing the trauma-dragon disposition.

Because black body masses are the production of the mind and the brain, it is necessary that these channels be used to sense out the traumas and those ensnarled energies in the first place. The Waterloo for doctors and medical practitioners all over the world is caused by the fact that the real traumas, the black body masses, are hidden from the view of the senses (#15).

There is no way we can detect a trauma-dragon with the senses. We cannot see it with our eyes because it is invisible. We cannot hear it because it is soundless (sometimes we hear things, but it is all a trauma trick, an illusion); we cannot smell it or touch it on this white body plane. Therefore, because scientists lack the ability to sense the black body masses with any traditional apparatus, there is now a branch of "science" called psychiatry. However, in these psychiatrists' offices, and in the offices of most other types of medical physicians and practitioners, the staff lacks the knowledge and the equipment (the SAF infrared sensing device and the chain sequence to decipher) to see these black body masses. They try all kinds of chemical approaches (chemicals are a male action in the sense of being condensing and not expansive), but ultimately, these don't treat the proper problem; these do not find the right remedy.

It seems that an orthodox health-oriented person is doomed because he can't see the black body masses, and his or her doctor can't see the black body masses either. Adding male energy (drugs) to a body merely causes an even greater crush, condensation, confusion, or cloudiness into the system and prevents anyone from ever being able to see black body masses.

The point is that the only way we can actually see black body masses is by using those channels of black body mass itself, the brain (#12) and the mind (#14). These are the only two avenues to detect a black body mass. These two female areas of the body are in the darkness and have the radiational capabilities of being able to, first of all, find the trauma-dragon, and secondly, present it to the senses (#15), so that we can view it. This is what SAF can do for us; to shed light upon it and dissipate it.

#12-14-15-17/18

The combination of the brain (#12), the mind (#14), and the hypothalamus (#15), in coordination with the endocrine system (#17/18), directs the spirituality of the individual to be able to focus enough attention and illumination mentally on these specific areas so that he or she can actually see what trauma-dragons and ensnarled energies are present.

While high technological advances in radiology have developed infrared scanners that can view BBM (black body masses), scientists have yet to use it properly to hunt down traumas and the ensnarled energies of trauma-dragons.

The SAF numerical chain that we have been discussing in great detail throughout this entire text is in itself a #17/18 hormone balance; it has male and female principles based on traditional eastern medicine. Every action depicted to the left of the center of the chain is male and everything to the right of center is female. When we move from left to right of the chain, we are entering the past of the SAF Participant. We look at the past as a female principle because it is heaped in darkness; it has black body mass attached to it. It is usually just below our conscious level, deeply set in unconsciousness.

On the other hand, the condensation of these particles also produces the hormone balance in that black body masses themselves have male and female principles. There are male black body masses and there are female black body masses. The observation of these particular energies is simplistic. All we have to do is hook up to any galvanometer or electrical meter, such as a Wheatstone bridge, or a Magnetic Vane Meter, and bring forth (recall) traumatic experiences from the past, and the pointer will move as the images and their energies drift by. This, of course, doesn't say whether the energies are male or female, but it does indicate that there has been some passage of energy through the human system. So, we must be very adept in the use of these machines to find and define the energies within the invisible black body realms. (Read: *Project Isis: Fundamentals of Human Electricity.*)

#17/18-24

With this Up-Link in an SAF chain sequence, we observe that the enthusiastic production of trauma comes directly from the inducement of some drug or male principle that will knock out the person's ability to view black body masses. Use of the drug, whatever it is, is stimulating a trauma. This is not to say that if the chain owner is taking a prescribed drug, for thyroid or for pain, that the meds should be discontinued, but it is possible that the awareness level of this type of situation might need to be updated.

White body light vs. black body light

Those just beginning studies in self awareness and SAF might not understand the difference between white body light and black body light, or white body mass and black body mass. By studying SAF and running chain sequences, SAF Participants will learn to make the distinction and will be able to visualize and understand, to "see" the past, and know it is black body mass; it is invisible until we make it visible. As the electrical charge of these traumas is discharged, the mental images become clearer as they now enter into white body light. There is almost an explosion as this transformation happens! SAF Participants will find they have more energy and will be truly in the present time, which is white body light and is visible to us; it is capable of reflecting all rays in all directions.

Black body light, on the other hand, is in the past and is invisible. The black body radiation that is emitted is in the infrared band and so is not visible to the human eye, but can certainly be felt when stimulated. Remember that 1% of energies are visible (white body light) and 99% of energies are invisible (black body light). If we are fifty years old, fifty years of life is steeped in black body light while the exact moment of living, the present, is white body light that we can face and see and understand.

This principle of visible and invisible light or mass dictates that deep down the mind paths somewhere, a male trauma has been created by tremendous pressure or some kind of heavy impact, shock, austere drug, or operation. Or a female trauma was developed by the loss of a loved one or a disconnection from an energy source. These traumas and their ensnarled energies must be faced; they must be brought forward out of time and illuminated so they can be understood, controlled, and then released, as part of the SAF emotional release process.

Black body mass is a perfect absorber; it absorbs all electromagnetic radiation that shines on it. *None* is reflected. The mass emits an equal amount of electromagnetic radiation, called black-body radiation; it is emitted in all directions, according to Planck's Law.

Try to imagine the blackest possible surface. When we shine the brightest light on it, it will still be completely black. This is according to the second law of thermodynamics.

This is the nature of our hidden traumas that reside in black body light. We might not be able to see them but nonetheless, these traumas and invisibilities do exist, and we can certainly feel them. We are being directed by them, and this will continue until such time as we are able to bring these into the light, understand what they are and then to release them.

Physical Aspects

Because the endocrine system controls the entire look, feel and touch of the body, the *energetic* system of the body is tremendously dependent upon the endocrine program. All things being considered, this system is our equalizer.

#8-17/18

When the endocrine system (#17/18) is associated with the sex organs (#8), the chain owner may experience upsets in productivity and reproduction. The body is unable to copy itself in this position. Therefore, the person finds he or she is unable to reproduce cellular tissues to recreate the body. Because cells are dying and being sloughed off and then replaced moment to moment, any disruption or stoppage may cause rapid aging. The actual creative mechanisms of the body in the physical sense can be thwarted, and the body will lose creatinine, a chemical substance (from the Greek *kreas* meaning "flesh"). Essentially, if he is unable to coordinate his hormone balance (#17/18), it means he is "losing flesh."

#10-17/18

When we see the Up-Link of the thyroid (#10) and the endocrine system (#17/18) in an SAF chain, there is a chance that the chain owner may be overweight, swollen, heavy, and have much fatty tissue and water trapped in the body. The body structure is overstressed and the endocrine system doesn't want to cope with this.

#1-17/18

If the endocrine system (#17/18) is connected with the thymus (#1), the SAF Participant has great difficulty protecting his or her body as a whole. Often, when this Up-Link appears in a chain sequence, the person's body can develop tumors. There may be lumps, bumps, tumors, and growths, especially around the thyroid, which is normally supposed to protect the body's diagram and its genetically predicted shape.

#1-10-17/18

When the thymus (#1), the thyroid (#10), and the endocrine system (#17/18) are found in a chain sequence, this Up-Link causes concern that the protection of the body has been breached; the protective screens are down. If the kidneys (#16) are in that same chain, (#1-10-16-17/18) then the body's ability to filter out poisons and to keep entities at bay have also been reduced markedly. It is open season on this person. The entities, the traumas, may easily overwhelm this person. The traumas may have other traumas encrusted onto them, and so these Participants may have memory loss and troubles with their own masses (bodies).

When talking about dragons in this text, note that the dragons are traumas; they are made up of black body masses that the host or victim (the chain owner) can't see and doesn't understand very well. These entities (traumas) are invisible and they remain invisible. As long as they are invisible, they are "safe and they are happy."

It is our job to work on these. It is the job of SAF to shine its light into that darkness so that we can illuminate these and work on our SAF chain sequences. We do this for the understanding and the self knowledge we gain about ourselves and our formerly hidden traumas. For an idea of what one trauma looks like and how it is handled, read Dave's Case Study, page 211. You will get a better understanding of the illumination process, and the gains that can be made by working on such a trauma. Remember that these trauma-dragons with the often ensnarled energies don't want you to be able to see them. All they want to do is influence your life and find reminders (plays) for themselves so they can be fed with *your* energy, and become stronger and happier. This is a positive activity for the entities because they, too, want to live. But by diminishing their energy over you, you will be able to increase your own energy *and* discover more about yourself in the process.

Therefore, we have to understand that for all energies and entities to remain in harmony, there must be balance and coordination. When the #17/18 is coordinated and balanced, you can remain in total synchronization with all energies in the environment. You will finally get your reward of power, strength, and total illumination.

Energetic Dynamic

Energetically, this #17/18 system is the *Balancer*. The endocrine system is what helps us to achieve and maintain electromagnetic balance. When we see #17/18, we know the chain owner has lost the balance or perception for the basic dichotomies of life. We can regain homeostasis (balance) on our own by consciously being able to extricate ourselves from certain traumatic patterns, instead of staying in these situations out of habit. The trick is to find the traumas and know what to do; this is accomplished with SAF chain deciphering.

This #17/18 system must be balanced so we can produce power. Energy failures tell us there is a trauma lurking about, just below the awareness level, and we need to give this our attention.

When someone is very conservative in their emotional output, or if someone is reluctant to move forward in a new endeavor, we suspect and look for a trauma to address. For all the energies to remain in harmony there must be balance and coordination; and there is a reward.

We tend to forget a terrible event because it was so against our grain, so perverted, so unbalanced, so disharmonic that we will put out less energy for its resolution, conserving our emotions for another day, another battle.

With our SAF personal work, we learn to identify traumatic patterns and emotions and the codes we created that may have helped at one point in our lives, but are no longer helpful to us. The issues and events are not as huge now as they seemed to be when first encountered in the past. We have grown and increased in size. With the added telepathic and other abilities we have acquired along the way in our SAF sessions, we have increased in spiritual size, as well. When doing this personal work, we can happily and easily extricate ourselves from the trauma's patterns and influence. It doesn't take much effort when we find the *right remedy* for the situation. Thus, we are free to pursue our higher balance; we will finally achieve our reward of more energy (power), strength, and the balance we all seek.

> We cannot be hurt if we are constantly maintaining the order of our own universe, if we are constantly striving to see that all the cosmos is propagated. Chaos immediately drops away from us and in any situation that is brought into the presence of order and harmony.

19
Skin

AT A GLANCE
Emotion: Boredom
Condition/Function: Demarcation
Keywords: Push, Lost, Win
Energetic Dynamic: The Identifier

The skin is a protective encasement around the body, consisting of the dermis and its covering, the epidermis. The skin, in the 19th position in the SAF Secondary Sequence, is the physical manifestation of the thymus (#1). In other words, the skin is a solid crystalline shield that is in harmony with the protective outline of the invisible shield of the thymus (#1).

The overall purpose of the skin is to provide a border, to demarcate the limits and edges of the body.

When we see the #19 in an SAF chain sequence, we know that the home forces are having a difficult time fending off attacks by the invader forces of the body. The automatic immune system is weak. There could be skin reactions, rashes, pimples, psoriasis. This #19 alludes to boundary violations, such as with emotional radiation or abuse, violence or even sexual trespass.

#19 deals with the problem of protection by the largest organ, the skin.

Emotion: Boredom

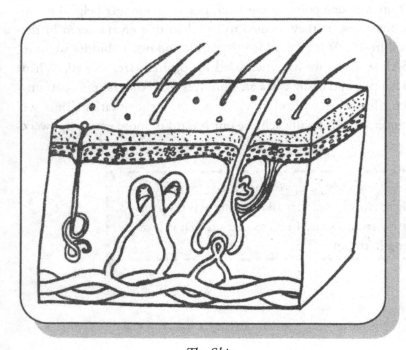

The Skin

Few people understand the correlation of boredom with the skin. The word *boredom* is from Old English and Latin; it means *to pierce, to bore into*, as with an auger, which would become dull as a result. When energies from people and the environment are able to *bore into* us, we then lose our protective covering.

When those who complained of skin (#19) troubles were questioned about their emotional states, it was found that there had been deep-set and chronic disillusionment or bored feelings with their present day circumstances. A person's skin shouldn't be interesting or even visible; it should be invisible.

As the skin (#19) happens to be a harmonic of the thymus (#1), it is a solidification of thymus activity. The skin operates in a black light band that is itself infrared. Anything actually seen on the skin is crystallized matter – dead tissue. The reflected energies that hit the surface areas of the skin are the past content of energy systems that have gone more solid. The skin matrix itself is, and should be, invisible to the naked eye.

However, when poisons get lodged in the system, these cause warts, cysts, moles, pimples, and other manifestations that can be seen. They cause the skin to become "quite interesting." This, of course, is the opposite of boredom.

It seems that anything that affects the skin becomes chronic. Even with the advent of super creams to take away skin blemishes, the chain owner still has a constant battle on his or her hands. Once a certain kind of skin rash or skin problem develops, it can move into chronic states quite easily.

Condition/Function: Demarcation

The skin draws the line for the existence of one entity as opposed to another. As mentioned, the skin itself is an invisible entity. Therefore, it is impossible to tell when one entity is crossing the boundary line of another.

This confuses many people because the skin surface has its own tangible, reliable sense, the sense of touch. In reality, that sense of touch can reach out for several miles. We can have what is called Expanded Tactile Sense that allows us to perceive feelings from great distances. In a sense, this is the outreach of the skin itself and allows us to have the ability to contact other entities and zones of existence. The skin draws a specific boundary line; it acts as a border.

On the planetary level, all countries have borders. Depending on the country, you can either cross easily or you can be delayed for hours or days. In some parts of the world, all you have to do is acknowledge the fact that the border exists, nod to the guard, and move across the line to the next country.

The pervasion of energies (border crossings) into the body from the environment is quite easy as well. The body is constantly and chronically being entered by outside forces. Examples would be the gaseous atmosphere that mixes the liquid condensation of humidity and dissolves the solids that float in the air, the water we drink, the food we ingest, the bugs, toxins, and other poisons crossing the boundary lines of the skin. Because of all this, we consider the skin to be in a state of overwhelm. The skin itself is an important matrix that helps decide whether or not an entity or energy should be pulled in closer to the core of the body or pushed out toward the perimeter. This is the ultimate responsibility of the thymus (#1) and the thyroid (#10).

Mental Aspects

The feature of #19, when considering SAF numerical chain sequences, is that your body must be guarded from a state of overwhelm. Obviously, if the inner body were exposed to the cruel exterior environment, the amount of pressure would be immense. If you were to peel the outer epidermis off and expose the interior to the outside environment, the amount of energy impressions that would reach inside the body would be too great to bear. You would go into a state of shock and may not survive. So the skin acts as that protective shell that stops or slows down outside energies from moving into the body.

Protections on mental and spiritual levels are connected as well. SAF numeric chains reveal that the mind is constantly aware of its perimeter and is watchful to maintain its separation from other individuals. A person must mentally draw the line in his mind, and be able to coordinate his activities within the boundaries of his or her own existence.

#15-19

Many times a person's energies breach someone else's boundaries. When the hypothalamus (#15) and the skin (#19) are connected in a SAF chain producing the Up-Link #15-19, this syndrome indicates that energies within one person's body may have intersected with another.

Many times it is the conclusion of the SAF Practitioner observing such a combination that someone has crossed over an SAF Participant's boundary and has not yet left; the interloper is still in there with him or her. This enmeshing occurs often, so it is important that each SAF Participant will complete his or her own questionnaire to reduce the risk of producing a combination chain.

#19-22

When the parathyroid (#22) is connected with the skin (#19), there may have developed a specific encrustation of energy within another person's mind, brought about by a fit of anger.

Few people realize that becoming angry with another person, or pressing any negative energy towards another, causes particles of your own energies to breach the other's mental skin or demarcation line, thereby endowing that person with more opposing energy.

It seems the successful operation of pacifism is the conservation of energy. When we become very angry with another person, we merely impress an energy pattern in that other person's system, which serves to give the other person *more* energy and power to oppose us. With this view in mind, it is nonsensical to create any situation that is of an attack nature. War and any kind of aggressive action would seem to only feed the other side.

The sequence #19-22 doesn't necessarily designate a war-like individual. This person has experienced the encrustation of ensnarled energies from other areas that could be toxins, pollutants, minerals, and things of this nature. Poisons in the body may certainly create the sudden manifestation of #19-22 in an SAF chain that appear as some abrasion, lump, bump, callous, corn, or roughened area of the skin.

This gives us the idea that on a mental basis, there has been some violation of territory. The aggression doesn't necessarily have to be on a physical level. Be aware, though, that when mental energy impresses itself into the body, yours or someone else's, it can create a physical reaction.

Physical Aspects

The solution to understanding the physical anomalistic manifestations of the skin - rashes, pimples, boils, tumors, and all the irregularities that cause the skin to become more visible and less boring – can be accomplished by either scanning with the Infrared Sensor (ExTech IR200) or completing a questionnaire.

Perhaps the most fascinating part of the SAF project is the use of the Infrared Sensor. This particular sensitizing device is programmed into the high-tech mathematical matrix that utilizes the 23 organ and gland systems.

For the original use of the infrared, it was interesting because the skin, #19, was the organ doing the original readings; it was a part of the scanning process. As a result, #19 did not appear in one single chain. It may seem odd, but it is because it was the part being used in the chain creation process. That earlier two-dimensional scanning program gave rise to the creation of a three-dimensional scanning technique that we use today. Each point on the face template is the spot where three organ and gland systems are venting their heat and pressure. The #19 does now appear when it is warranted. (Read *The SAF Infrared Manual* for more on the SAF use of infrared and the interpretations in the SAF Online service for practitioners.)

Using infrared with the SAF protocol proves the theory that energies can know and intersect with other energies, and more importantly for us and as depicted in this book, these can be translated.

#19-20

Problems of the skin are more observable when the pancreas (#20) is connected with the skin (#19) in a numerical chain. This particular Up-Link is called psoriasis. It represents that psoriatic entry point where there was a weakness.

The toxins and poisons that desire entrance won't be allowed in when the body is aware of their actual natures. But because traumas hide in black body mass, in what is considered dark light or invisible light, no one can see them. These result in creating holes in the skin. It is theorized, and is by a practical nature a useable theory, that all skin manifestations are merely entry holes.

Joseph R. Scogna, Jr. explains the wheres and whys of pain and the use of infrared and the computer, 1986. Scogna adapted the Infrared Sensitizer to allow it to interface with the SAF mathematical matrix. This older system has been completely upgraded and updated and is now available online, with a new infrared device, the ExTech IR200, that works with it perfectly.

#1-19

When the thymus (#1) creates an Up-Link with the skin (#19), we see the extent of pressure brought to bear upon the skin's surfaces; the chain owner has been inundated by toxins to the point that he or she is losing border integrity. This (#1-19) situation involves calor (heat), dolor (pain), rubor (redness), and tumor (swelling). These four reactions are able to track when a traumatic event, or a trauma-dragon, has attacked the body. The action of these particular trauma-dragons is powerful enough to escape detection by the naked eye. In other words, you can't see a trauma or trauma-dragon actually performing, but you certainly can see and feel its effects. As a result, many people have the mistaken impression that the skin rash, boil, or pimple, or whatever they do see sitting there, is the "dragon," so they attack what they *think* is the dragon. They apply creams, balms or herbs hoping to vanquish it. There is even a salve called Dragon Balm. However, the action of putting a topical cream on an area infested with a poison or toxin merely pushes the substances deeper inside the body. The important thing to do is to express the poison back outside the body.

We must be sure to recognize that any kind of manifestation in visible light form is not the actual dragon or the trauma, which was created and is still in black body light. The real entities that are working their magic against the body are invisible; these use black body radiation to get noticed. Black body radiation is in the infrared region and thus, is not visible to the human eye.

Energetic Dynamic

Energetically, this #19 system is the *Identifier*. We need to know our borders well, and the borders of those others around us. We must defend our borders and boundaries. When we see #19 in a chain sequence, we are not able to defend ourselves. There is the possibility of a psychic invasion, or a boundary violation of some type that has gone beyond the border of the skin. This is sometimes expressed as: "He got under my skin" or "That made my skin crawl." Your boundaries were violated again and again;"Someone is encroaching on my space," or "someone is IN my space."

This #19 system is stimulated and programmed by memories and thoughts of feelings you had lost or repressed: you had been invaded, your boundaries had been violated and you were not able to defend yourself then; nor could you change or escape from that past situation. When we cannot defend our boundaries, this triggers a "feeling lost" pattern to replicate on body, mind, and spirit levels. In the present time, you may have deep set, chronic disillusionments; you believe your illusions were squashed by the desires of others, or you may have bored feelings, or hardened feelings about present day circumstances.

With our SAF personal work, which may entail much chain resolution work for deeply ingrained violations or PTSD situations, we are able to symbolically push away and release the violator. In so doing, we can revive the exuberant feeling of winning, of being found and being safe. This is all much like catching the gold ring.

> Bcause traumas block and clog the main channels of perception, the subsequent dissolution of traumas and that control over us causes a refurbishment of our sense capacities. We hear, see, and feel with so much more clarity that it may startle us or cause a feeling of wonderment about life in our immediate surroundings.

20
Pancreas & Solar Plexus

AT A GLANCE
Emotion: Laughter
Condition/Function: Location
Keywords: Quality, Suppressed, Express
Energetic Dynamic: The Expresser

At #20, the pancreas and solar plexus is special for human beings because we depend on this complex for balance of body, mind, and spirit. However, when we see the #20 in a chain sequence, we know that we have lost the ability for balance, and we might not be able to locate ourselves.

Generally, the pancreas allows us to decide between substances in the environment. In this way, toxins, poisons, vermin, parasites, pests, and other kinds of creatures not desirable to the body are pressed out, and anything usable that can become part of the body in a productive way will be accepted inside the system.

The pancreas is loaded with enzymes that help in the digestion of fats, minerals, and sugars. We depend on it to keep us balanced in the presence of all activity.

The solar plexus is the nerve center that balances the nervous system. It is directly connected to the earth's center of gravity. From the very moment a baby is born, we can see it flail its arms as it struggles to maintain its balance. By using the exact center of gravity of the body, which is the solar plexus, we learn to maintain stability in the presence of all stimuli from the environment.

No matter which way we are pushed or shoved, we can regain our balance by observing this contact between the solar plexus and the earth's solar plexus, the very epicenter of the earth itself. Grounding is another way to help this balance process along. With

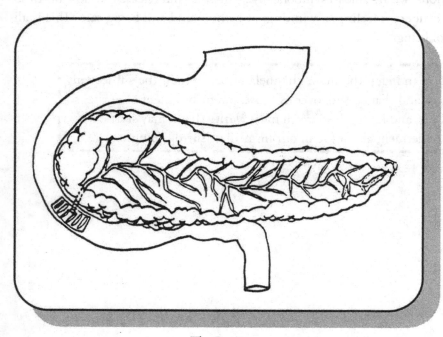

The Pancreas

grounding, we walk and stand on grass or dirt with our bare feet, in order to be reconnected to the earth's center. This balancing is a practical action for the entire body, and with the help of the pancreas, it is centered in electrical charges of a positive and negative nature.

In chemistry, this is called pH (the potential of Hydrogen), or the acid-basic balance. This is maintained quite readily by the pancreas and the pancreatic juices, for one of its purposes is to sustain the equilibrium of energy in the body by controlling the sugar balance with two hormones, glucagon and insulin. So, if you have any disharmony of these hormones, the homeostasis of the body will be thrown off and you will feel off center.

Emotion: Laughter

People who complained of loss of balance, dizziness, vertigo, low energy, etc. were found to have the #20 in the lead portion of their chains. The loss of balance is directly associated with the person's inability to maintain or direct the energy conditions of the body.

Laughter is a good measure of a deficiency of balance because it is part of the solar plexus mechanism of discharging unwanted energies from the body. It is amazing to observe and detect the actual discharge processes by monitoring the way people laugh. Each laugh has a distinctive way of discharging toxins from the system, and in this way laughter can lower our stress levels as it increases our immunity levels.

It is true that individuals who don't laugh are very ill, as Dr. Norman Cousins discovered and wrote about. At the same time, laughter has to be precise. It has to explode or discharge toxins of all sorts in an extremely wide variety of areas, or else the different poisons that have been encrusted into a person's body will remain there.

It is important that we learn to laugh at ourselves as this makes us more human and likable.

It is part of the life continuum that mind energy in connection with spiritual energy produces a magnetic and electric attraction for toxins in the environment. If you have particular problems, or can't figure out enough patterns of energy to become productive, you will actually call in specific toxins from your environment. In other words, if you are loaded with poison, such as parasites, worms, bacteria, or viruses, these were brought to the body because you were in a behavioral pattern that acted like an antenna in the body to attract these poisons. The poisons and solid matter are the last step in the creation chain of interference with someone's energy.

On the other hand, *if your mind energy and your spirit energy are in tip top shape with all the offending energies removed from the system on body, mind, and spirit levels, then your behavioral patterns will send out the magnetic and electric attraction for, and will act as an antenna and will pull in more of the same goodness. It is a matter of looking at and understanding what it is we are focused upon.*

The trick is to be able to discover and discharge these frequencies. Each type of laugh has a distinctive way of discharging toxins, poisons, and errant frequencies in the body. To be effective at discharging these entities and toxins, laughter must be precise. We must learn to laugh correctly.

It is explained here that if a person doesn't laugh - and laugh correctly - certain poisons cannot be discharged from the body and it may rapidly fester. There are experts on the subject of laughter, and authors with ideas on how to maintain a happy existence. Part of this happiness necessitates the action of laughing.

A person can be found out to be a charlatan in his laughing attitude. Just because you laugh doesn't mean you are getting rid of toxins or discharging energy. Your laugh may be merely a social gesture. A placating laugh is not therapeutic. Such a laugh is from the throat. In order to discharge poison from the body, we must laugh from the solar plexus, which is beneath the diaphragm. The discharges are explosive. The interfering energies of traumas and entities that have been compressed into the system need to be exploded out of the body. If you merely laugh from the chest, throat, or nose, or if you snicker, titter, twitter, chuckle, giggle, or carry on in any such way, the toxins will remain inside the body. When a person tries to laugh, his or her laughter can cut off a poison but not eliminate it. To reiterate, it is essential for a proper release that you follow the correct laughing procedure, and experience an actual "belly laugh."

How do we learn to laugh correctly? The only way to create a correct laugh is by understanding the principle. When we make the connection between actions of the cause of the traumatic event and the actions of the effect of the traumatic event, then we can make the proper laughing reaction.

What is the mechanism of laughter?

When we see something that causes us to laugh, what exactly is occurring? How do we connect with the trauma when we see someone fall and hurt himself? That action, of course, is a replay of a certain trauma of the observing individual. The reason the observer laughs is because he is replaying his or her *own* trauma. The trauma that lurks within a person's mind is a mental image of himself or herself falling. All the jokes and stories that cause others to laugh, and the hysterical movie scenes, are part of the invisible trauma content. The only reason someone laughs is because a connection to the dark side has been touched upon and brought into the visible light, into white body light. Something has come to the senses that used to be invisible. It was harbored in black body light for a long time. Making this connection causes an electrical surge that actually explodes a piece of the trauma. To edit a trauma, to delete the electrical charge of it from your existence, you need to see all of it. One of the "windows" into the trauma may be the peculiar aspect of the trauma that is brought into view, the one that causes you to laugh.

In the final analysis, we must differentiate a courtesy laugh from the electrical discharge laugh, which occurs when a piece of black body light is thrust into the visible light spectrum.

Condition/Function: Location

We should routinely look for #20 within all numerical chains because #20 connects with many other numbers to produce a variety of traumatic sources and content. Number 20 is typical of someone who has lost his ability to locate himself. The question, "Where am I?"is common when the #20 is in a numerical chain sequence.

You may know where you are consciously, but depending on where the #20 is in the chain, and with which numbers it is connected, it may indicate that certain organ and gland functions are lost inside the body or mind. In other words, the SAF Participant doesn't have to be lost, but one or several of his organs could be. If they are lost as to their location, they are certainly lost to their correct balance and function.

#6-20

When we see the Up-Link of the liver (#6) and the pancreas (#20), this is an indication that the chain owner's liver is either too acid or too basic. In other words, it is losing its location frequency because it is vibrating with either too much toxin or poison, and not enough of its own interstitial integrity.

#2-20

When the #20 is connected to the heart (#2), it shows that the SAF Participant has lost a person or entity, something that produced much heat for him or her in the past, and which has now been subtracted from the Participant's life. This information is extremely important, for it creates an effective trauma-dragon and (as was explained previously) this particular type is of a *female* nature, for it has created a *loss* in the system.

These losses are capable of moving from the invisible or dark light spectrum into the white light spectrum, causing the person so afflicted to have specific damage to the heart muscle. Although it is wholly a mental phenomenon associated with the viewpoint that the person has lost at life, it certainly has a specific effect on the human system - a net energy loss. When we are connected with another, our energies co-mingle; when that partner is lost, the remaining person will find herself in a position of still relying on energy factors that were peculiar to the lost person. This causes a feeling of groping by the electrical mechanisms in the body. As this "nervous" system tries to replenish the lost energies from the person who is gone, the body will experience a good deal of symptomatology.

Mental Aspects

SAF Participants who present the #20 in numerical chains have definite location problems, exhibiting an increased sense of dispersion and confusion. The real problem stems from environmental traumas. Traumas that have occurred in specific locations have collected the energy of the surroundings (grass, trees, roads, cars, buildings, mountains, sky, atmosphere, etc.); this has caused a black body mass to occur with an image of a location where the chain owner used to be during this past trauma. The chain owner may initially recall the location but not the underlying trauma to that place.

#13-20

The #13-20 Up-Link is a syndrome called homesickness and depression. It occurs because of a lost ability to track the energies of the present surroundings.

When the adrenal glands (#13) are with the pancreas (#20) in an SAF chain sequence, this tells us the chain owner may have difficulty eliminating the electrical charge connected with a certain area in which he or she used to live. The energies (patterns of motion) from that former location may have caused the chain owner's molecular structure to go into phase with those same energies. When we relocate to a new home, we have to shift the energies to the new location. Because people in our modern day society are more transient than ever before, this particular quirk shows up frequently.

Time and Place of Birth

Another unusual phenomenon that occurs is the attraction of energy from the particular location and time of our birth. Suppose it was Philadelphia, on November 3rd, 1962, at 3 AM. Our energies have been primed or initialized by that precise time and place. If we are not sure where or when we were born, or how we came into this world, we will have a constant subliminal dispersion about our environment. It is essential to de-confuse a person by locating him or her. It is necessary to edit out the time and location traumas of environmental pasts so the SAF Participant is free to be in the present time, fully aware.

#10-20

When the thyroid (#10) connects with the pancreas (#20), the chain owner may be in a very confused situation. The #10-20 person may have difficulty prioritizing activities, or knowing what is important. He or she has trouble being in the right place at the right time. Such a person is represented as negligent or irresponsible about his or her duties or activities.

SAF to the rescue, again! The Participant would need to spend more time working with the SAF sequences of energy and developing an awareness of what his or her true goals and purposes are in life, in order to be in the right place at the right time.

#1-20

Another interesting combination occurs when the thymus (#1) associates with the pancreas (#20); this particular mathematical string of numbers as an Up-Link or syndrome signifies frustration. It is a frustration of energy not completed, such as programs and ideas that have not yet come to fruition. The chain owner with #1-20 is often thwarted, even though he or she may exhibit the sensation of energies nearly coming into being.

This occurs often in those who have almost finished a project or who have almost finished a trip. It is called the "trip end," when energies (ideas, plans, formats) are almost in completion and the electrical friction and the vibration and power of these two ideas (completing but yet not completed) causes such a rash of electrical stimulation in the system that the person becomes super sensitized and loses his ability to remain calm and collected.

Physical Aspects

The physical aspects of the pancreatic insufficiencies or toxicity rely on the ability of the solar plexus to maintain balance and harmony within the system. The energies of the body may dip or subside, as there are shifts and changes between the two hormones glucagon and insulin. There may be either an increase of power, or there may be a sharp and sudden decrease during which the SAF Participant feels drained.

Many modern day nutritional scientists have run with the idea that hypoglycemia can be applied to anyone who exhibits this sudden change or drop in energy. However, the hypoglycemic condition can be caused by many other sources, such as frustration, the loss of a loved one, irresponsibility, homesickness, and other situations that disconnect the person's power supply, causing him or her to lose energy in a physiological or psychological way.

Other researchers contend that their work is directed at cerebral or stress allergies. Stress allergies are processed by the body and the cross connection of power, which is the matrix of the genetic machines in response to the present day white body light system. This causes the physical body to be sapped of strength, momentarily. This is a genuine problem, but one that can be solved by SAF chain discovery. Because traumas have friends or are connected somehow and in some way, we need to discover the whole mechanism, not just part of it.

#1-20

When a chain owner has thymus (#1) and pancreas (#20) in his or her sequence, he or she may develop what is called chancre. Ulcers, ulceration sores, and spots on the body result from toxins that have built up to such an extent that there is a burning or an incineration of tissues. This may be brought about by the introduction of some energy or poison into the system, but in many cases it is a direct phenomenon of sexual perversity. The perversion comes about when the body reacts to the insertion of energies (diagrams and forms of sex) with human beings, animals, or objects. As people try to intersect their energies (life-stream continuity), or reproduce energies (their own) in a variety of animal, vegetable, and mineral substances on the planet, they find that only one species can actually reproduce their species correctly. A man needs a woman to reproduce the biophysical schema of the genes and vice versa.

Sexual activity is a precision act, even though many times the perpetrators are unschooled at the process. When someone deviates from the protocol for sexual behavior, the acid-basic balance is disturbed and acid conditions begin to build up. The thymus gland (#1) and the pancreas and/or solar plexus (#20) have difficulty handling the scenario of the geometric patterns created by erratic resonant frequencies that can bounce back and forth between bodies during sex.

The human body can certainly handle normal sexual contact, but when someone starts to introduce objects, animals and other paraphernalia into the system, the electrical natures that coexist between these particular objects creates a resonance that can create specific sores and ulcers in the body. The body may not be able to digest or absorb this kind of energy from dissimilar objects. It has no genetic program plate or blueprint to understand anything but another similar body, so it puts the energy (molecules of the dissimilar substance or person) on hold near the skin.

This can happen with sexually transmitted diseases (STDs) and other diseases, as well. When there is a dissimilar energy being introduced, and it can certainly be another human being, but if the energy is not wanted or isn't of the type required or wanted, then the offensive and unwanted energies can change the pH of the body; this allows for invaders to arrive and take up root.

It is important to note that mental health therapists, who work with patients and clients with disturbing sexual perversions and other violations, will often need extra SAF chain sequence work themselves, in order to understand the nature of their own issues with pH changes.

#1-16-19-20

Many times when the thymus (#1), the kidneys (#16), and the skin (19) are seen with the pancreas (#20) in a chain, it indicates that there is a presence of genetically or recently transmitted gonorrhea, syphilis, herpes, or other venereal conditions.

#1-15-16-17/18-19-20

If the hypothalamus (#15) and the endocrine system (#17/18) are added to the above chain sequence, then we may have the right to fear the development of HIV-AIDS.

#1-13-15-16-17/18-19-20

If the chain owner has this same unfortunate chain sequence containing the adrenals (#13), he or she may have compromised their immune system even further. They may be at the point where the particular energies (people, places and events) are in such an uproar that they are unable to complete the entire diagram of energy (bring a proper sex act to completion).

#19-20

When the skin (#19) is associated with the pancreas (#20), this is another indication that toxins and poisons may be stuck on the skin trying to gain entrance to the body. The person may have rashes, pimples, sores, psoriasis, and other skin phenomena. This can indicate that the black body masses and radiation toxins, those that endemically belong to traumas of the deep past, are influencing the present and trying to work their way into the system, destroying the present time body matrix.

#13-20

If the adrenal glands (#13) and the pancreas (#20) are found in a chain, the person may have chronic hypoglycemia. His or her energies may be at a low ebb. This occurs when the dramatic content of traumatic events has entered the system and lies across the person's energies in such a way that he or she is not able to recover energy (life) without drastic measures. With pancreatic insufficiency, the person may have sharp drops in energy, but then regain that energy, whereas with a 13-20 sequence, he may be chronically tired and exhausted.

Energetic Dynamic

Energetically, this #20 system is the *Expresser*. Its presence in the SAF numeric chain tells us we have lost our ability to express our true feelings, to locate ourselves, and we have also lost our balance of body, mind, and/or spirit.

Because we can inadvertently act like an antenna and pull in any type of errant frequencies that are not a good frequency for us, it is essential that we continue to work on our SAF programs so that we can be healthier on body, mind, and spirit levels, and we can then attract more goodness to our system.

The #20 system is stimulated and programmed by memories and thoughts of us being taught or told to suppress our true feelings and thoughts, in order to feel safe in situations we could not change or escape from at the time.

When we move to a different location we leave a bit of ourselves behind and shut down the emotions of the past situation. We may feel a bit homesick or depressed. We can use grounding techniques (walking bare foot on the grass) to help the process, but with our personal SAF work, the quality of our life changes, layer by layer. We find we are able to shed the shackles of suppression and learn to express our true feelings and ideas in creative ways. Laughing, the type that will shed and dispel irritants from our system comes easier with this work.

> Physical and environmental energies, which are congealed sunlight, can be molded into patterns by the intentions of the chain owner who can use them to dissolve his or her traumas.

21
Posterior Pituitary

AT A GLANCE
Emotion: Grief
Condition/Function: Hydrolyze
Keywords: Quantity, Stuck, Free
Energetic Dynamic: The Rectifier

The 21st gland in the SAF Secondary Sequence is the posterior pituitary, which lies directly behind the anterior pituitary and is connected to the hypophyseal stalk. It is not actually a gland because it doesn't create hormones. The function of the posterior pituitary is specific; it takes its command from the hypothalamus and stores the hormones until needed; oxytocin regulates labor and delivery of babies; and vasopressin, an anti-diuretic hormone, controls the quantity of water secretions when the posterior pituitary sends a message to the kidneys. These hormones are necessary in order to control the fluid balance or the fluid permeability in the membranes of the human body. This #21 gland controls the actual swelling or water secretions in the body.

When we see #21 in the chain sequence, we know that the chain owner has difficulty controlling the fluid balance; there may not be enough and so the body holds onto water and we see edema in the ankles and other areas. The palms may sweat, there may be body odor, and cold sweat may be apparent as the toxins are released rapidly through the skin.

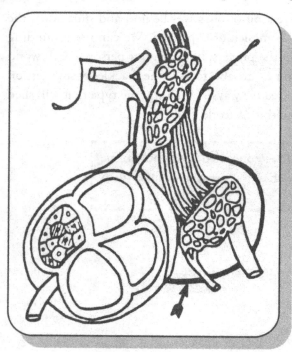

The Posterior Pituitary

Emotion: Grief

Many SAF Participants with #21 appearing first in the SAF sequence of numbers complain of great losses. When we see #21, we understand that losses and degradations have occurred where energy (people, places, things, and businesses) have been pulled away from the Participant. It is significant to note that #21, therefore, seems to have a primarily female bent, because by its nature, this number controls a losing or expanding nature. It is concerned with space (mind #14) and with the ability of the body to maintain or reproduce new energies out of old energies (sex organs #8). The losses found in the physical system are caused primarily by deficiencies. These deficiencies are losses of pressure concerning every circumstance.

When we lose pressure, objects, people, and places, we find we are in the untenable position of having energies that we need desperately (any object, person, place, thing) being stolen away from us. A mythological story exemplifies this scenario. Tantalus, a Greek God, was tied upside down in Hades and tantalized. Food and drink were held out to him, but every time he reached out they were pulled back from his grasp. Number 21 exemplifies this kind of frustration, but it is a frustration that can be balanced to cause a pleasant sensation. The winning or the gaining of something pleasurable depends on movements towards the pressure end of the sequence.

The numbers that are lower in the SAF Secondary Sequence, such as #1, 2, 3, or 4, show pressurization. The numbers that are higher on the scale, such as #20, 21, 22, 23, or 24, indicate space. As we move higher on the sequence scale, we notice more losses of pressure and more gains of space. In other words, if we wanted to pressurize #21, we would move down the scale toward the pancreas (#20). This slight increase of pressure causes the grief or loss (crying) (#21) to turn to laughter (#20). Laughter ensues because we have regained some needed pressure.

This can be easily demonstrated. When a young child cries because he has lost a plaything, replacing it with another plaything can immediately cause him to laugh again. Why is this? He giggles because he has gotten another *pressure* to replace the loss of the previous pressure, the previous plaything. All humans, whether babies, adolescents, mature individuals, or old persons need to have the correct amount of pressure to create pleasure. On the other hand, too much pressure or too much stress creates the sensation of gain that may be too much to bear, which creates a condition of overwhelm. The opposite of this is, of course, the #21, which guards the portal of loss. People try desperately to avoid losses at all costs.

Condition/Function: Hydrolyze

The word "hydrolyze" comes to us from Greek; *Hydro* is Greek for water, while *Lysis* means to unbind. This word means "to break down by a chemical reaction with water."

This #21 gland system uses water for all aspects of fluid use in the body. The appearance of the #21 suggests there is difficulty controlling fluid balance. There may be too much or too little fluid; either is a non-optimum condition.

#2-21

When the heart (#2) and the posterior pituitary (#21) create the syndrome (#2-21), the chain owner may have swelling and edema. This swelling occurs because the chain owner is trying to hold onto as much conductant as possible to produce pressure and charge. When losing the water content of the body, this person doesn't need as much conductant. In fact, more insulation is needed. Things happen too fast for some people, and they dump water to escape the buildup of charge.

We start to swell with water when things are happening too slowly. When projects and plans are not resolving fast enough, bodies begin to swell up with water so that more conductivity can take place. As the pace of things begins to move more rapidly, the water is dumped.

Mental Aspects

The #21 indicates the loss of energy (ideas, plans, and dreams). There may be several aspects to the losses, but they involve the disconnection of our ability to observe our own mental experiences (memory) in relation to the present-day situation. Our primary loss is the inability to rectify what has happened to us in the past (because it lies in black body mass, it is invisible to us), as opposed to what is happening to us in the present (visible, white body masses), or what will happen to us in the future (invisible, black body mass). *If we cannot rectify or connect these ideas, then our power is reduced proportionately.*

The more we can rectify our past with our present, the more powerful we become for the future, because the past is where all the energy patterns (existence patterns) are stored. It is these energy patterns, the actual outline or blueprint, that give us power. Nothing else.

#14-21

When the mind (#14) is found with the posterior pituitary (#21) in an SAF number sequence, the chain owner may have lost some memory.

#1-14-21

If the thymus (#1) is connected to the #14-21, it indicates how much memory is lost. The #1 indicates the highest amount that could be lost. It is a matter of how close in proximity the numbers are in a numerical chain that gives an idea of just how severe the memory loss has been.

#1-14-17/18-21

If, in the previous chain (#1-14-21) the chain owner also exhibits the endocrine system (#17/18), it is important to note that the memory loss is due to some presence and organization of a traumatic event. There may be a trauma overlaid between the chain owner's conscious mind and unconscious mind, blocking white body masses from being able to intercept and rectify black body masses of the past. Therefore, the chain owner effectively has energy (memory banks) cut from him or her.

#15-21

When the hypothalamus (#15) and the posterior pituitary (#21) are present together in a chain, this indicates that the person is trying to sense, connect with, and rectify energy mates (lovers) from the past through the sexual radar, which is part of the pineal body's system.

Physical Aspects

It has already been explained that the posterior pituitary has the capability of balancing water in the system, so a person may have swelling or a physical effect of energy being lost in the system. One of the worst sicknesses of mankind - diabetes insipidus – comes about when the anti-diuretic hormone is deficient, causing the loss of great amounts of urine and excessive thirst. The body's water is not able to cleanse toxins from the system through the lymph tract. We must ensure there is a proper mineral balance to consistently cause the physical side of the #21 to have a proper action of gain and loss.

If the posterior pituitary (#21) causes too much fluid loss in the system, the SAF Participant may be in the position of experiencing too much sensation. The Participant may have dizziness, nausea, vomiting, and just errant electrical charges that cause uncomfortable sensations in the body. On the other hand, if the system is overloaded with pressure, and the body can't control the water balance to disallow pressure buildup in the system, the Participant may have pain and pressure. The pain will be in various areas of the body, but mostly in the joints and in the muscles of the lower back. The body is not able to fight off pressure if it can't control water balance in the system, for the water is used as the primary conductor of electric charge.

If the water in the body is dirty and filled with poisonous toxins, chemicals, drugs, and unwanted minerals, then the system will have a very erratic electrical pattern. For this reason, the body will often opt to create fatty substances as a protection or insulation, or choose to dump water in the body to rid itself of some of these toxins.

One of the most effective ways to rid a body of toxins is by exercise and sweat. As sweat moves off the body, it carries the noxious wastes with it.

Energetic Dynamic

Energetically, this #21 system is called the *Rectifier* as it moves between past traumas of loss and feeling stuck in those same images in our present existence.

This #21 system is stimulated and programmed by memories and thoughts of feeling stuck in losses, not feeling secure in the family setting, or not being your authentic self in past situations that you could not change or escape from.

You may hold onto feelings of grief or loss, and may be brought to tears easily. Your feet or ankles may be swollen because the fluid balance is off. Your emotions may be shut down. You may feel degraded when energy (people, places, businesses) have been pulled away from you. You may experience a loss of dreams. If you can't rectify the past with the present; there is no future to be seen. You feel disconnected.

Many losses over a lifetime cannot be processed without a person feeling stuck in the middle of it, lost in time. With our personal SAF work, we can examine the stuck feelings of grief by shedding light on the darkness, which makes our feelings so much lighter in weight. And the resulting released energy explodes! It is now *ours*, it is enlightening and oh, so freeing.

> The more we can rectify our past with our present, the more powerful we become for the future, because the past is where all the energy patterns (existence patterns) are stored. It is these energy patterns, the actual outline or blueprint, that give us power. Nothing else.

22
Parathyroid Gland

AT A GLANCE
Emotion: Anger
Condition/Function: Experience
Keywords: Have, Solid, Dissect
Energetic Dynamic: The Dissector

Four parathyroid glands are located on the sides of the thyroid gland. Although there are four glands, they are usually called simply the "parathyroid gland."

The parathyroid gland is strongly resilient to radiation and has been assigned #22. The glands create a visible shield, in the form of calcium, to ward off radiant forces. The balancing hormones for calcium in the physical body are calcitonin and parathormone, and between these two hormones, the regulation of calcium is predictable. However, the intrinsic study of energy and radiant sources in and around the body demands that we know the precise endocrine duties of the parathyroid glands. This #22 system acts as an invincible third shield against radiation. The first shield is the thymus (#1), the second is the thyroid (#10), and the third is the parathyroid (#22).

The parathyroid shields the body against radiation by creating calcium deposits. The calcium precipitant is equivalent to one drop of experience in the presence of radiation, electricity, and excess pressure. The amount of calcium produced depends on the exact amount of pressure brought to bear on the recording systems of the body, mind, and spirit.

In a very real sense, throughout life, the energies of the SAF Participant are inscribed in his or her system. The action of the parathyroid helps to produce the skeletal structure. The axial and the appendicular skeletal systems are merely outreaches of experience in the body.

A human baby starts life with very little calcium in the body. As the baby grows and experiences life, calcium precipitates into the bones. This calcium is absorbed and reduced into mental and spiritual experiences and then constantly replaced by new calcium as a daily routine. These actions occur hourly, microsecond by microsecond. This process activates the learning and the experiential memory banks of the body.

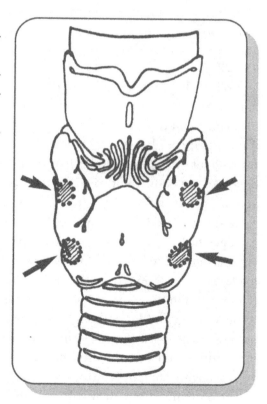

The Parathyroid Glands

Emotion: Anger

Starting when we are very small, we are told to "not show any anger," and so we tend to view this as a "bad" emotion. But as we have come to understand, we need to own *all* our emotions if we ever hope to understand and let go of the encumbering energy of these ensnarled energies and emotions. There may indeed be instances of righteous anger and this emotion will fall into this category, as well. It can become a problem for us when we hang onto the anger; SAF will help us to feel it, know it, and then to let it go. It is a matter of owning and knowing fully the emotions that we feel.

When the #22 appears in the forefront of the numerical chain sequence, the chain owner will be in an angry pattern of some sort. Anger develops when people refuse to change their ideas or opinions about a certain circumstance or scenario. There may be some instances where anger is totally justified and normal, however, it might be harmful for us to hold onto it. SAF work helps to direct us in what to do with it for our betterment.

Anger follows the experiential tracks of the memory recordings for a human being because anger is considered a solidification or frozen edifice in space. The precipitate of calcium, which is a memory experience, is in itself without opposition; and won't tolerate any other viewpoint. Therefore, a mental picture mirrors the exact emotional pattern of anger, which disregards all other ideas, programs, purposes, and viewpoints other than its own.

#10-22

When the thyroid (#10) is in the same numerical chain and has formed an Up-Link with the parathyroid (#22), we see the exact energy sequence (pattern) of the spine. The spine is the principle mechanism for the motor operations of a human being. It is the actual experience track or memory staff, which coordinates and structures much of the electrical output for the brain and the mind throughout the nervous system; in order to create emotional experiences regulated by the glands and organs of the body. In other words, the spine acts as a conducting post for all our whims, desires, and dreams. Any degradation of the spine indicates that certain areas are being over-pressurized or under-pressurized by either high acid or high alkaline conditions.

Specific levels of energy (physical input versus output) are received by the body. These messages are tracked by the intensity of pressure in the environment so that the memory recordings being made can be the exact depth and intensity. The human being records experience and energy (happenings in the environment and in the body) in our DNA in much the same way as we would record a song, an idea, a thought, or a program on magnetic tape. The energy recordings etched onto the magnetic tape cause a mark to appear of a certain depth and design. It is much the same if recording onto a thumb drive or a CD.

By having the precise groove of a person's experience written as an inscription in the DNA of our protein structures, we are able to have an appropriate emotional response. If this groove of experience is too deep, we will have a traumatic experience; this is considered toxicity. If the groove of experience is too light, then we will have a deficiency. With a deficiency, there is also a trauma because we have lost the amount of pressure necessary to perceive the true circumstances surrounding us. (For more on the inscriptions that have been written in the DNA since the beginning of time, read *Junk DNA: Unlocking the Hidden Secrets of Your DNA*.)

Condition/Function: Experience

As mentioned above, experience is the mark of the action to which we are exposed. The experience track is developed by a precipitation of calcium with etchings or grooves in it that give the proper scenario for replay. The body takes this particular calcium experience track and records it in each cell as the calcium is dissolved and replaced for a new set of experience. The spine is a particular energy post that governs and coordinates experiences and emotions throughout all the glands and organs in the system.

As we look at the entire system of a human being, we realize the experiences of a human being are of paramount importance to his survival. The way we acquire knowledge and understanding is directly parallel to this experience process. Knowledge, in coordination with mental activities, awareness, understanding, and spiritual activities, works in harmony with the proper experiences necessary to coordinate our activity toward total survival (immortality).

#1-22

When the thymus gland (#1) is found with the parathyroid gland (#22) as an Up-Link in the same SAF chain, self-protection may not be possible for the chain owner Poisons and toxins from the environment are encroaching on the chain owner's system and may be stealing away the ability to re-contact past experiences for survival actions in the present.

Mental Aspects

We have to imagine the parathyroid (#22) along with the experiential activities of the body, as a shield or wall. As the thymus (#1) is the invisible, electronic shield, and the thyroid (#10) is that physical or flesh shield, then the parathyroid (#22) is the structural shield, the shield that protects the *core* of the person. The #22 is the last shield of a person's inner self, and if this number *does* appear in the SAF numerical chain, it indicates that the chain owner's core essence is being encroached upon, invaded. No wonder the chain owner becomes angry! Nobody wants any other person entering, disturbing, or invading the core of his or her being.

#14-22

When the mind (#14) and the parathyroid (#22) present as an Up-Link, the chain owner may exhibit frustration or anger with the amount of mental poisons that are affecting him or her. The chain owner is angry at all the troubles that are befalling him or her and is not coping with any of them. It is important to watch the drift of these numbers so we can understand just how much effect the troubles or confrontations are having on this person's existence.

As far as understanding the flow or drift of the numbers in numerical chain sequences, we can see the actual movements of a particular upset as successive infrared scans are taken or additional questionnaires are evaluated and deciphered.

#2-22

When the heart (#2) is connected to the parathyroid (#22), this syndrome indicates that the chain owner is dissatisfied or disgruntled with connections to friends or loved ones. The chain owner has difficulty connecting the proper channels of information with his or her loved ones and partners because of an inability to communicate with them properly. This person may be ripe for a separation or divorce.

It can be difficult for us to communicate with another person because we each have our very own experience tracks. As one person experiences an incident in the environment, another person may do so in the opposite way. Each would possess a completely different experience of the same occurrence. If we are not able to take on the experiences of another person, if we don't obtain the ability to change our mind or viewpoint and direct our own experiences, then we will certainly develop a #2-22.

This particular Up-Link, (#2-22), is very detrimental to anyone who is trying to maintain a relationship.

#2-20

To expound on the above scenario two pressure-steps farther down to heart (#2) and pancreas (#20), we have an Up-Link that indicates separation, loss of friend, lover, or ally. So, a 2-22 is a very important pre-signal to an elementary, detrimental characteristic of humankind, which is the inability to communicate effectively with loved ones or partners. The invasion of a friend cannot be a productive experience if these two numbers (#2-22) are "hot," which in this situation means there is increased pressure on these two organ and gland systems.

#9-22

When the bones and muscles (#9) are in the same numerical chain as the parathyroid (#22), it indicates that the person may be physically weak and is allowing unconfrontable experiences to pile up. In other words, he or she is not accepting experiences, but is letting them accrue on the physical body. When we have an experience that precipitates calcium, it must be removed from the physical body and translated into mental and/or spiritual aspects, into energies that are minute enough so as not to clash with physical substance.

Those with arthritis are often those who refuse to accept experiences. They have unexpressed resentments. They are disgruntled about what has happened to them in the past, and they won't allow these experiences to be processed into their minds. Therefore, the calcium is kicked back out into the system and it knots up all the areas of the body that they won't accept. The most prominent areas with acceptance problems are the hands, and the areas with the most rejection problems are the feet, so these two areas are hit first on the periphery by the kickback of calcium.

It is essential for anyone who has a #9-22 syndrome in the chain sequence to be sure to process the mind enough to accept the viewpoints of other people. If we were to look at the problem in store for someone with #22, we would see that the transformation of anger into an acceptable experience requires the ability to accept the viewpoint of those who oppose us.

Physical Aspects
#1-22

In an SAF chain, when the thymus (#1) is present with the parathyroid (#22), the chain owner may have bone troubles. The primary defenses have been breached and the chain owner is unable to coordinate and collect enough information on these occurrences into his or her mind to be able to reject the precipitation of calcium. If the person is highly pressurized and a male energy traumatic event is in his or her space, then the situation may develop into arthritis. On the other hand, if a female energy traumatic event is looming in the person's space and that particular trauma takes energies (power) away from that person, then the bone troubles may be osteoporosis or a more serious, complicated high-tech disease.

#1-9-22

This Up-Link, with the #1, indicates the person has inflammatory arthritis; there are troubles with the calcium balance (#22) and it is situated in the bones and muscles (#9). When we hold onto anguish, anger, and resentment in our bones and muscles, the calcium levels are disturbed. This is especially true when we hold onto anger resentments. The best way out is to go through the issues, one by one. Complete a Stress-120 Questionnaire and find out how to get started on your own chain work.

As already mentioned, those with arthritis often refuse to accept experiences. Their unexpressed resentments can lead to trouble for themselves. They won't allow their experiences to be processed into their minds and so calcium is kicked back out into the system and it knots up all the areas of the body that the arthritic won't accept, namely the hands, and with rejection, the feet.

#10-22

If the thyroid (#10) is in the same SAF numerical chain as the parathyroid (#22), the chain owner may be losing the capability for emotional experiences, and his or her spine may degenerate. Such a person with #10-22 in their chain sequence may have pains in the low back, sciatica and similar difficulties.

#15-22

If the hypothalamus (#15) and the parathyroid (#22) are in the same SAF chain, the person may be developing tumors. Poisons reach such a peak of concentration that pressure builds up in the experience tracts and begin to create a tornado-like energy, which is very advantageous to the creation of male and female trauma-dragons' dark light and dark energy. The male energy-dragon turns his tornado in a clockwise motion, while the female energy-dragon turns hers in a counter-clockwise motion. The female and male energy-dragons use this turning method to wrap energy up around themselves, in a ball-like fashion, to pull energy away from the body in the female sense, or push it in more closely in the male sense.

In addition to the above scenario, when the hypothalamus (#15) is aligned with the parathyroid (#22), it causes white body light or visible radiation to come into being. This means the balls of energy, mentioned above as black light or dark energy, become solid enough to make a tumor-like growth, especially on the bones, and in the soft tissue surrounding the bones.

#16-22

Anytime the kidneys (#16) are connected with the parathyroid (#22), there are indications that this person is developing a process of solidification in the kidneys.

Kidney stones and perhaps bladder stones are formed from experiential energies that are part of the anger-experience process. Such a person with these numbers in the SAF chain sequence refuses to allow the precipitates of calcium to be dissolved into his or her mind or spirit for acceptance.

#19-22

When the skin (#19) and the parathyroid (#22) cause a #19-22 Up-Link, the chain owner may be developing corns, calluses, and hardened areas of the skin. These are produced when the person refuses to let energies (chemicals, ideas) roam or circulate within the body. The energies will move in a precise and complete circuit within themselves and develop their own entity as the offspring of a trauma.

Does this mean that a person who has developed calluses and corns from playing sports or athletics has allowed room for the entrance of a stimulated trauma? Well, the idea is that the pressures brought to bear on the body have not been processed properly, and those calluses build up for a reason. We don't need any of those calluses. We may think we do because we are playing a sport and a callus protects our skin from blistering, but the skin is resilient and powerful enough to produce its own protective mechanism. It doesn't need to have an extra layer of hardened skin on it. Even so, an athletic callus could easily be a friendly, serviceable trauma-dragon energy at the same time.

#22 and any number:

It should be noted that when #16, #15 or any number connected to #22 is in the chain, the chain owners are *not* in a mode to accept. They are constantly in the process of rejecting any other viewpoint but their own. When this occurs, people set themselves up for a great liability because they are aligning themselves with the trauma-dragon and those ensnarled energies. Because this traumatic event and trauma-dragon of ensnarled energies is an experience all its own and has its own complete identity and personality, it won't accept any other reality.

The important thing is that if you can consistently change your viewpoint and your idea about circumstances, this will relieve pressure. A change of mind will allow energies to move into mental aspects. Solidification and tumors on the physical level can't develop under these conditions. Tumor-like growths develop when a person refuses to see the other side, when he puts his attention on energies that he feels are justified to stay forever frozen in one position. This person's energies have been stuck in one particular picture; it is this effigy that causes a constant turning of energy to produce stones, tumors, and growths of one sort or another.

Energetic Dynamic

Energetically, this #22 system is the *Dissector*. We pull things, thoughts, and concepts apart so we can see how they work. The low emotion of this system tells us we are not dissecting; we are, in fact, becoming more solid. This system is becoming more solid, in which ridges of energy encase ideas and proclaim that we are NOT in a mode to accept ... anything. And so, when we see the #22 in the chain sequence, we know that we have lost some of this ability to dissect. Instead, we are becoming more solid.

The solution to yelling loudly in anger, or being ashamed of being angry, is not to deny the anger, as that would just stuff it downward further into the darkness, but instead, to work with it in the SAF method and bring it into the light so its charge, the energy, can be released. We do this by acknowledging the totality of the emotions that we feel and will speak of these and the incidents that arise to the surface for us to view in our work, *as if this could be real*. With this expanded view in mind, it makes no sense to create any situation that is of an attack nature. Any kind of anger or aggression serves only to feed the other side with your energy.

This #22 system is stimulated and programmed by memories and thoughts of anger, of being forced to do or have what we did not want, in situations that we could not change or escape from. It is best to not hold anger in where it will do harm to you, and you alone. We may deny we have anger for anyone, we may not feel flexible of mind, we may tear things apart, or we may find that we look from only one side, one viewpoint.

In order to survive when we were younger, we were told to not show our anger and so we learned to hold it in. With our personal SAF work, it is important that we find those incidents in the past, identify the anger, dissect the emotional incidents to make these less solid, and finally, fully embrace the whole of the incident, anger included, as a part of our electrical, emotional experience.

Once the traumas of confusion are put in their places, the chain owner's ability to perceive the basic harmony of the cosmos comes into full bloom. The chain owner will then realize the beauty and harmony of all life.

23
Spleen

The spleen is a gland-like organ that serves as a blood reservoir and is considered the garbage disposal for tired blood cells, worn out erythrocytes, toxins, and poisons. It sets hemoglobin free, produces lymphocytes and plasma cells, and also creates new erythrocytes for fetal life and newborns.

When the #23 system appears in the chain sequence, we know that there are most likely allergic substances present, and the spleen is the natural organ to gather, reject, and eject those.

In an allergy situation, the body thrusts itself away and tries to cast off the offending substance.

It does this with wet and running eyes, nose, and ears; with vomiting, a dry or wracking cough, or diarrhea with mucus. All these are necessitated by the action of pushing off the energy to which the body is sensitive or allergic.

Although allergy at #23 is the opposite of addiction, #24, we are often addicted to substances to which we are sensitive and/or allergic.

Emotion: Antagonism

When the #23 appears in the numerical chain sequence created by SAF techniques, the chain owner may exhibit signs and symptoms of chronic antagonism, either toward himself or herself, or from this person outwardly toward others. As a result, the chain owner may enjoy teasing or irritating others. This is a petulant person, could be an emotionally sensitive person, and at the same time, someone who doesn't have an extremely disastrous type of disease pattern.

The higher numbers in the SAF program, those from #20 to #24, are lighter in nature (disease patterns are less serious). However, when someone displays a #23, it certainly

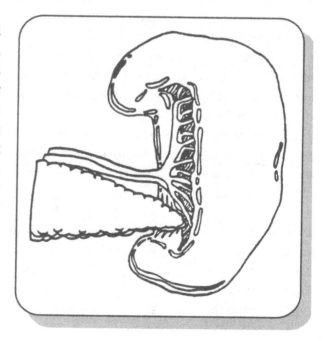

The Spleen

means that he or she could be having a hard time developing emotional patterns that are of a higher and more positive sort.

Condition/Function: Rejection

People who show an acute inability to cope with the outside environment are primarily exhibiting patterns of allergy and/or sensitivity. When #23 appears in a numerical chain, it means that allergic conditions and sensitivities exist, with a range of reactions from a skin rash to full blown anaphylactic shock, which is dangerous and could be deadly in certain circumstances. The breakdown of the immune system is the cause for the disturbances that abound around the #23.

#1-23

When the #23 is found with the thymus (#1) as an Up-Link, this person shows the highest danger of pressure, which may cause allergic reactions. Of course, the allergies may come from many different sources: food, the air, the water, contaminants, environmental pesticides, poisons, toxins, radiation, pollution, as well as a plethora of energies in the environment such as from people, places, situations and things.

In effect, the overabundance, or pervasion, of any substance in the environment can cause an allergic response. The body is rejecting poisons because it is aware that the energies (poisons and toxins) in the system for that particular wavelength and frequency have exceeded their normal amount. In the case of allergies, a signal is sent out in the form of dolor (pain), calor (heat), rubor (redness), and tumor (swelling). This principle is from early Greek medicine and is incorporated into the SAF protocol.

In a sense, with #23, the immune system is on full amplification. It is better for a human being to have an allergic reaction than to permit the insidious entrance of toxins into the body without any reaction at all. In effect, the allergic response is the exhibition of black body mass, which alerts the rest of the immune system.

When traumas are stimulated and live in black body light, the hapless person may not recognize the invasion; this is a situation that can be much more detrimental than an allergy. People are uncomfortable and complain that their symptoms are more highly amplified than when the observer sees and understands the allergy signal.

The reason a person has an allergy in the first place is because he or she has not paid enough attention to the earlier signs and symptoms presented by the immune system. The symptoms are sending a message. Not understanding the message, the allergy sufferer has probably used drugs to cover the symptoms, hiding his or her troubles with creams, aspirin, and all manner of medicinal drug devices and appliances that prevent the body from signaling the proper information as to the type of poison that entered his or her system.

Even so, allergic individuals are luckier than are others who have severe illnesses, because the allergic type still maintains the ability to reject toxins and poisons.

#7-23

When an Up-Link is in the SAF chain sequence of the lungs (#7) and the spleen (#23), the person may display signs of asthma, lung allergies, and/or bronchitis. Different poisons involving the respiration or breathing apparatus can be found when observing the 7-23 combination in a chain.

Mental Aspects

When #23 appears in a SAF chain, the person may exhibit the mental attitude or atmosphere of rejection. He or she may have rejected someone, or may have been rejected by someone else. The chain owner could even have been in the vicinity of a rejection of a loved one, such as the type of rejection that occurs between brother and sister, or mother and father, or someone else close to the chain owner. Rejection and antagonism are powerful actions. Many cases, however, are caused by problems of *detoxification.* In this case, the person's inability to reject toxins and poisons causes the buildup of the emotional state of hatred. We find that such a colon (#3) problem can often be solved with help from the spleen (#23). The person can thoroughly reject toxins, poisons and those things that he believes to be detrimental to him.

#2-23

When a person rejects the wrong target, or is rejected for the wrong reason, or when the action of rejection is a puzzlement of some sort, the whole mechanism may go haywire. In this case, we obtain a twisted view of life because it is generally believed that being rejected is "bad", and being accepted is "good". Many times, we can behave the best that we can behave (be good) and still experience rejection. This is true when the heart (#2) is in the same chain as the spleen (#23). The person has had a rejection, and the whole sequence of numbers oriented to the heart (#2) will give us the exact diagram or blueprint of separations, losses, divorces, and disturbances in the environment that break people apart and cause traumatic experiences.

The rejection of love (#2-23) is a very common action to experience, because people misconstrue love behaviors on a daily basis. Rejection is something that occurs quite easily, and with rejection, comes anger at the loved one, (or the boss, an acquaintance, or a relative), seen in the chain sequence as #2-22. Finally, a total loss or separation of the person is allowed and leaves an imprint on the chain owner's consciousness. This is called the loss of a loved one, (#2-20). We have gained even more pressure as we moved down toward the lower numbers on the pressure scale.

Physical Aspects

The chain owner with #23 in the front of the chain may exhibit breathing difficulties, rashes, pimples, swelling, redness, and may have pains in the joints. Allergies can cause arthritis and rheumatoid situations. The allergies may come from eating foods, drinking certain water or water in general, or breathing the air with some stray frequencies of chemicals, or even high tech devices that give off invisible vibrations. As was described in previous paragraphs, there may be cerebral and mental allergies occurring from rejection states and other stress patterns with which the chain owner can't cope.

#7-23

When the lungs (#7) are associated with the spleen (#23) in the same numerical chain, there is a possibility that the chain owner will develop an asthmatic condition, breathing difficulties, or troubles that may lead to a chronic bronchial situation. The wrong thing to do is to spend time and money on drug programs, for these merely suppress the toxins and the poisons of the drugs previously ingested, which are the real cause of the trouble. Those who have taken too much adrenaline for asthmatic conditions find that their tissues become wasted of water and the skin displays coppery spots as a result of poisons that have nestled in the colon. If this is the situation of the Participant, then look for the #3-7-23 syndrome.

#23-24

When the spleen (#23) is connected with the lymph system (#24), we observe a genetic changeover. This means that whatever conditions (numbers) lie between these two numbers in a numerical chain, these symptoms, signs and signals are part of a genetic hand-me-down or a hereditary "legacy."

A legacy is a riddle that we have been given by our ancestors to solve while living with our present human body. Although most don't realize it, many of the conditions we try to solve are ages-old, conditions that our genetic line developed as long ago as 500,000 years. Each gene assigns each generation a riddle to solve. It is well nigh impossible for an ordinary human being to come up with remedies for these particular genetic problems.

Adding modern day drugs and medicines to this factor will defeat people trying to solve these problems. We can only try to hedge against whatever the genetic troubles seem to be. For example, we may have asthma, breathing difficulties, diabetes, alcoholism, syphilis, or gonorrhea, bone troubles, chronic headaches, and the like. This is just a small list of what can be handed down from one generation to the next.

Because the genetic code has collected all the historical ancestral memory banks, almost anything can be handed down. These genetic propensities will carry through if they have a greater concentration than other diseases or maladies in the system. This is a scientific fact. It is not guess work. An alcoholic mother or father may well produce an alcoholic child.

It is up to each of us, in our lifetime, to try to control these impulses, but it can be very difficult. If we don't have SAF programming and the techniques delivered by the Self Awareness Formulas, then we certainly won't figure out the codes we need to break this alcoholic pattern. All a person can do is stay away from alcohol. The real miracle would be to edit the problem out of the genetic sense-mechanisms of the alcoholic's body, and then have him or her be able to socialize again without becoming a roaring drunkard. It is proposed that with personal SAF session work, this type of change is possible.

Energetic Dynamic

Energetically, this #23 system is the *Rejecter*, for it rejects substances (people, places, things) that are antagonizing, and to which the chain owner is sensitive or allergic. When we cannot reject, this may compound and build up as hatred, so it is essential to be able to spot, accept, embrace, and then release the pent-up energy of past emotional events and traumas.

This #23 system is stimulated and programmed by memories and thoughts of having to survive with feelings of rejection in situations you could not change or escape from.

This #23 system is about allergies and sensitivities. It is the polar opposite of the addiction fostered in the lymph system (#24); however, remember that we are often addicted to substances to which we are allergic.

We can easily reject ideas, programs, plans, and even our own purpose and goals – by mistake! *When we stray from the primary directive for our existence, we are liable to create havoc with our present situation. It is the goal of SAF to re-acquaint people to their purposes and their plans for life, through their own personal SAF work.*

With our own personal SAF work, we can acknowledge the dalliance, face and embrace the regrets and rejections, and with our new direction firmly in heart and mind, finally feel appreciative and grateful for what the release work shows us.

> Once the traumas are under control, the chain owner begins to understand that the true form or creation of the universe has to start from one idea and one concept.

24
Lymph System & Electroplasmic Field (EPF)

AT A GLANCE
Emotion: Enthusiasm
Condition/Function: Acceptance
Keywords: Be, Mystery, Understanding
Energetic Dynamic: The De-Mystifier

The lymph system is composed of lymphocytes, transparent, slightly yellow liquids found in lymphatic vessels throughout the body. Its purpose is to cleanse the body of toxins, especially those in the blood system. Because the body is made up of almost 85% fluid, it is essential that there be a mechanism in place to process systemic toxins and poisons. Lymph nodes, or relay centers, hold and process poisons then release them through the skin and sweat glands.

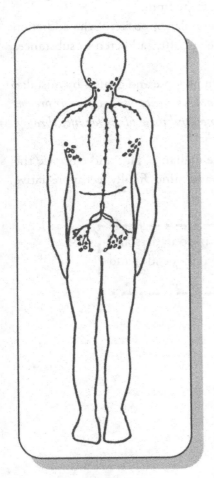

The Lymph System

The second part of this #24 system is the Electroplasmic Field (EPF). This energy field, called by some the human energy field, is one that surrounds *all* life forms. But it is more than that. Electroplasmic energy refers to the point of instantaneous creation by spirit force. It is a coined word to distinguish it as electrical energy (of spirit and mind force) that unites with plasma, the essential physical substance of all mammals, animals, and plants. This field is a true balancer of pressure levels. We use this protective field (the EPF) to increase our powers of perception beyond normal realities. (Read: *Junk DNA: Unlocking the Hidden Secrets of Your DNA*, Sensory Perception #106. For the elemental make up of the EPF, read *The Promethion*.)

Emotion: Enthusiasm

The word enthusiasm comes to us from the Latin and early Greek words *entheos* and *enthous*, meaning inspired, possessed. With the enthusiasm of #24, it is natural to have excess electricity coursing through the body. If there is too much electricity, we may think we need a quick fix to slow it down.

While an allergy of #23 (spleen) is a pushing away, addiction at #24 is a pulling in, the abnormal craving for a substance. When we see the #24, the protective energies in and around the body (the EPF) have collapsed inwardly; the body system has been effectively invaded. The result is a craving for a quick fix. With #24, the chain owner exhibits exhilaration or excitement.

Whatever #24 appears next to in a chain sequence gives us a clue as to the area of the body that is being manipulated by the addictive force. SAF practitioners have found that the #24 person is interested in applying any remedy or any outside mechanism other than his or her own Will.

Since we are spiritual, electrical beings of Light, the drugs we use are the resistance, the drag used to slow things down. They put an extra load on the entire system. Remember, the slowing down can be from any material or discipline used outside of our own will power, so those with the #24 may have over-accepted many programs, without thinking.

With #24, we also find shock, trauma, and unconsciousness from injury, accidents, or operations. At such times that we were less aware, opportunists may have gained entry, such as drugs, OTC medicines, or even suggestive words.

We see that #24 is used primarily with concentrations and dependencies of certain drug materials. Many of the substances that have been used are marijuana, LSD, cocaine, heroin, mescaline, all prescription drugs, and OTC medicines, even products for the common cold. We automatically think "drugs" is a term used for street drugs or controlled substances. However, what is considered a drug in SAF programs is *any* material or method used outside of our will power; and so alcohol, cigarettes, or coffee could be blamed if used in excess. Exercise, meditation, or yoga, done excessively, can act as a drug. In fact, meditation and yoga are two of the stronger drugs that are employed because they affect the mind, and therefore can direct the energies of the body to perform. So we must be mindful of those who are exercising, meditating, or practicing yoga obsessively. When #24 appears in a chain, it means that some kind of action is being used against a situation, no matter what that situation may be.

#6-24

In most cases, the #24 appears right next to the numbers of the troubled organs that the person is trying to treat. As an example, if a person is taking a liver medicine, then #6 (liver) will appear right before the #24 (lymph) as an Up-Link to indicate that the person is taking a drug or remedy and it is affecting the liver.

#3-24

Sometimes coffee drinkers will show the Up-Link 3-24. Coffee may be used by this chain owner as a laxative or could use another laxative, or even Imodium to slow down the colon. With the presence of the #3-24 in the chain, we do know that something is being taken and it is affecting the colon (#3).

Condition/Function: Acceptance

The opposite of rejection found in the last system (#23), is acceptance. A person is willing to accept any program that is brought before him or her. Often when the #24 appears in the chain sequence, this informs us that this chain owner has over-accepted programs, and these program toxins and materials have actually gone too far; these are now affecting the system covertly, without the person's awareness.

Many times those who are attuned to a healthy lifestyle are taken aback when the SAF Practitioner asks them if they have been taking some kind of drug. They respond with "No! I never take drugs!" At the same time they are piling vitamins into their bodies left and right. They believe that those vitamins are not acting like a drug.

Drug, in SAF terminology, is the past tense of "drag." It means the person is putting some drag on a problem. In other words, the symptoms feel like they are racing ahead of us too fast. We cannot take the pain, the pressure, or the sensation. We don't like the way we feel, so we put a little drag on the condition. Drag is something needed and wanted to slow down the electrical charges of the condition or the situation.

The SAF definition of drag can be found in physics and in the science of electrical engineering where a technician uses a resistor to put drag on an electrical circuit. It is called "doping" the circuit to slow it down. The technician doesn't want to put high-powered electrical energy into machines that may overload, so he or she needs resistors or other kinds of electrical equipment to dope a circuit and slow down the electrical input.

This is the same action that a human being wants to accomplish - to slow down the electrical energy that has entered the body. We may remember an event in our lives that contained a little too much electricity for us to handle. We may feel "scorched" when we think of an ex-spouse, for example. We may have a big speech to give in front of a large audience, or may have had some catastrophe or disaster befall us. Mental images of the events carry too much electrical charge and can overload our electrical circuits, so we resort to drugs or *something* to dope our circuits. This slows down the electrical charges so we can cope with them. This doesn't seem like a wrong thing to do, but if we overload and slow down our system in such a way, when we do want to have a *high powered electrical circuit*, such as when we need to run away very fast to escape danger, the energy won't be there. We will then have too much residual poison and toxin in our systems.

There are other books that discuss chemicals and substances that affect the human system. Homeopathic drugs can be used because these are diluted enough to do one or two dopings and then leave. When a person imbibes concentrated drugs and materials, the consolidation effect causes a condition that results in thousands of dopings per dosage. This means that the doping effect will last much longer than is necessary. Some people take so many drugs and over-the-counter medicines into their systems to create a doping effect that they have enough dosages there to last a thousand years, long after the body is dead and gone.

Mental Aspects

The chain owners who exhibit #24 in their chain can be exuberant, happy and alive. They are excited and exhilarated. The word enthusiasm is used because *any* kind of remedy that is found, and works to *any* degree, is exactly what these people like. This is why alcohol can be such an exuberant remedy. No one uses a droll, resigned tone when they say, "Let's get drunk." A person who appreciates the medicinal effect of liquor exclaims, "Let's get bombed!!"

Whatever the remedy, #24 individuals are constantly enthusiastic about it; they race for it, even something as simple to quench as thirst. If someone is thirsty enough, he or she will certainly become enthusiastic about drinking water. If a person has a headache, he or she is quite enthusiastic about reaching the right remedy. As the head pain pulses harder and harder, he or she will do just about anything to get rid of it. If we were to suggest that a certain little pill was capable of getting rid of the headache, he or she would certainly take it enthusiastically, no matter what the consequences.

This, of course, is the mind-set of most people existing on planet Earth today. For the most part, we do not give any consideration to the ramifications of what would happen to our bodies and our energies (genetic) down the line. We are mainly enthusiastic for handling or remedying situations in the present, no matter what chemical substances are needed.

However, we should be much more diligent about what we put into our body. By understanding exactly how the body functions, we can take the right course of remedy. We can use the right doping plan to slow down energies in certain circumstances and then let go of this doping so that we can again gain power and our own energy.

Some of today's citizens are completely benumbed, falling apart, exhausted and lacking any energy or drive because they overdosed themselves 10, 15, or 20 years ago. People who are constantly doping themselves do so because their energies (mind and body) are keyed in to their present drug use. They run on mechanical advice and are acting like zombies, for their energy is dependent upon the drugs they are taking. Many have trapped themselves into taking one pill to excite them and another to calm them down. They have certainly fallen victim to the over-doping, overdosing merry-go-round.

Physical Aspects
#2-24

When the heart (#2) is aligned with the lymph (#24) as an Up-Link, a person may have breathing difficulties or cardiac troubles. When overdoses of toxic materials (drugs) get into his or her system, it directly affects the synchronization of the person's body. This could also be true with the 2-7 syndrome although this number means more regarding the lungs.

Any single dose of medication on the market today – one pill, one tablespoon of over-the-counter medicine - is an overdose of possibly a thousand times more than we actually need. This fact has been proven for over two hundred years, by perhaps millions of people. A glance at the drug insert literature for prescription drugs or the label of over-the-counter medicines will tell us just how potent these products are. If the chain owner overdoses he or she is in chronic danger of re-experiencing those same toxins.

Take, as an example, a person who took LSD in college. The concentrated drug taken at that time can re-ignite and cause the person the same feelings (symptoms) when least expected. A person at forty-five years of age, who hasn't taken the drug in 20 or more years, could suddenly exhibit all the symptoms of "tripping." Only the drug use was so long ago, the tripper doesn't realize what is happening and may think he or she is crazy. If LSD gets into someone's system and disturbs the micro-fine mechanisms that control the chromosomes of that body, then not only does it affect the past and the present of that human being, but also the future. We can inadvertently program into our genes our own demise, in a fantastical and horrible way.

Those who were given drugs after an accident or operation are also likely to have an attack (a trip) again, without suspecting the cause. This is not uncommon.

#15-24

Many people who took drugs in the past have one foot in reality and one foot in hallucination. They have a chronic sense perception problem. When the hypothalamus and the senses (#15) is next to the lymph (#24) as an Up-Link in a chain of numbers, we know that the person has had drug experiences that have affected the senses. His or her sense perceptions may be askew.

#17/18-24

When we see the Up-link of #17/18-24, we can see that the enthusiastic production of trauma (#17/18) comes directly from the chain owner using a drug (#24) of some sort. Remember that SAF defines drug differently than standard terms, so the SAF Practitioner would have to ask the chain owner what type of drug was used. Some unsuspected drugs may be very detrimental to the chain owner. This is not to say that if the chain owner is taking a drug because they need to that they should stop taking this medicine. For example if a person does not have a thyroid and therefore they have been prescribed meds for this situation, they should continue to take thyroid pills. Or if the chain owner is in terrible pain from an operation or an accident, they should continue to consume the meds that are prescribed by their doctor. However, it is the awareness of this 17/18-24 situation that might need to be updated somewhat.

#5-24

If the Up-Link of anterior pituitary (#5) and the #24 is in the SAF sequence as a syndrome, then it is known that the drugs are affecting the person's control of reality. The person may look at a fish and see an apple, or hear certain words and ideas uttered by a family member or business associate and receive the sounds as completely different thoughts.

These people cannot be trusted in any circumstance. They are liable to make a big error in their lives. This is usually the case when we try to fathom why a person of reasonable intelligence becomes a victim of some bizarre accident or strange coincidence of events or traumas.

Those who have spent time experimenting with drugs don't realize the intense powder keg of energy that they have created. It is necessary for them to spend time understanding, dissecting, solving and sorting out the riddles of these drugs so that they can remove the erroneous programming that has entered their systems. If they can pull the plug on the drug materials that are already in their systems, then they have a fighting chance at being able to live in some sense of reality. As long as the drugs are inside a person's body, they can work their energies into the system and actually reprogram the human being for disaster. If an SAF Participant wonders why he or she had or is having bad luck, it may all be coming from a preset program developed by the inner connection and the chemical bonding of drug materials that entered the body long ago. It could be from drugs given to the mother at his or her birth, or from seventy-five years previous as in a genetic hand-me-down situation.

#23-24

When the spleen (#23) is connected to the lymph (#24) as an Up-Link, the situation is worse than anyone had ever thought possible. The person may have inherited a hand-me-down drug problem. This is, of course, entirely true in the case of alcoholics. It is wholly possible that even allergies to prescription drugs, such as penicillin and antibiotics, can be handed down. As an example, if a person has an allergy to penicillin and has offspring, those descendants may also have the allergy to penicillin.

If there are numbers in between the #23 and the #24, this will tell us more information on what has being inherited.

Joseph Scogna was thoroughly convinced that any trait, quirk, or disorder that one's mother or father had, the offspring acquires as well. It is just a question of the concentration of the particular problem. In each life, these traits, disorders, and toxins take on a specific order of priority. We may not have the same order of priority to dissect a particular problem that our ancestors had, and we may never know how far back on the family tree cancer, tumors, arthritis, diabetes or whatever the condition, first surfaced. Some of these conditions may be on a 200-year cycle so that none of the immediate ancestors (mother, grandfather, great-grandparents, etc.) are known to have had the disorder. With SAF work it is possible to uncover many of these and to find a resolution to them.

#24 and any number

When we see #24 in any chain sequence, we know that whatever the number is following it in time (to the left of #24) a drug of some sort is being used and is affecting that organ or gland system. As an example, with #4-24, the chain owner is using something for digestion and this could be resulting in issues, such as acid reflux. Note that after about age 20, many of us need to take digestive or proteolytic enzymes and possibly hydrochloric acid (HCl), as we no longer have enough in our system for proper digestion. However, this would be a positive aspect, so the Practitioner can look for something else that might be presenting or causing a more negative aspect to the #4.

Genetics and DNA Research

Genetic research is just now coming into vogue, so it will be several generations before enough statistical data can be codified to authenticate exactly what diseases, viruses, drugs, and X-rays will have adverse effects on future generations. Keep in mind this is referring to physical evidence of the DNA as studied in the lab.

But what of the emotional traumas, attitudes, and thought processes of our ancestors? With SAF work, we are able to find many aspects of the DNA, and come to appreciate and understand the 128 sensory channels, most of which are invisible to the eye or microscope of the lab technician. (Read about the 128 sensory channels in *Junk DNA: Unlocking the Hidden Secrets of Your DNA*)

Although the common man is only beginning to be examined by genetic counselors, the royal families of Europe, interested in keeping blood lines pure and blue (royal), have amassed much data on genetics. In addition to physician records, certain personality disorders of prominent kings and queens were written down for posterity, and these biographies have become another method used by modern investigators to trace family diseases and imbalances.

Two hereditary diseases were found through modern day methods and traced through royal families going back to A.D. 1542 and are based on descriptions of personalities and symptoms.

One disease, porphyria, is a metabolic condition evidenced by gastrointestinal dysfunction, neurological disturbances, and the passing of red urine as the blood cells lose their rosy hue. Those afflicted royal personages did indeed have less red-colored blood - and presumably more blue - than did their subjects and countrymen.

A second disease traced through the same family lines was hemophilia. Queen Victoria, a direct descendant of porphyria victims and carriers, passed hemophilia on to her progeny. Hemophilia is a blood disorder where the clotting factor VIII is low, which in turn results in hemorrhaging. Scientists have speculated that a mutant gene was responsible for this disorder, as previous instances of "bleeders" were not known in Victoria's family. This affected her many descendents; kings, queens, emperors, dukes, princes, and princesses of England, Prussia, Germany, Spain, and Russia.

Could this hemophilia gene have been mutated by the DNA-RNA as a result of weakened cell structure caused by previous generations afflicted with porphyria?

Does each generation pass on to their progeny a drug-dependence syndrome, alcoholism, x-ray build-up, or physical and mental reactions to stimuli? What of the attitudes and emotions that predispose us to certain disorders and ailments? What of the traumas from past generations? Are these also inheritable?

The authors contend that this is precisely what occurs. All emotions, attitudes, and personality quirks are just as easily transmitted to future generations as are physical disorders and characteristics, via the genetic blueprint as contained in the DNA-RNA.

It is also postulated that these instances, anomalies, and disorders can be found and uncovered with SAF programming, opening further the doors to future DNA research.

Energetic Dynamic

Energetically, this #24 system is the *De-Mystifier* because it sheds light on the mysteries, the unknown events, and traumas that plague us. In doing so, we can learn to make these known once again and garner a greater understanding of life as it is.

When we see the #24 in a chain sequence, we know the chain owners are happily accepting of any program brought before them, whether is it good for them or not. They must be able to discern the difference, good and/or bad, and increase their self control.

Some expressions might reveal we are dependent upon something or someone, or we feel we "must accept it and live with it," or we need something to fix or handle a situation. Do we have enthusiasm to accept a program, any type of program, or, in all honesty, is there an addiction for anything outside of our will?

Remember that "drug" in SAF is anything used outside of our complete will. This could be drugs, OTC medicines, foods, vitamins, alcohol, meditation, athletic endeavors such as running marathons, or even sex; anything that will help us to slow down the excess electrical energy we have received erroneously. The Participant may say, "I use ------when trying to feel good, or to slow it down, or to speed it up."

This #24 system is stimulated and programmed by memories and thoughts of times when we had to accept what was offered, or we needed something that would make the situation more palatable, in order to survive. The situation could not be changed or escaped from at that time. Surrounded always by a mystery too dark to understand, we couldn't seem to get through the day without a fix, a binge of one sort or another, which instilled in us a much needed sense of calmness, or a sudden boost of energy.

With our personal SAF work, we are able to increase our personal efficacy, our strength, and our self knowledge. We certainly embrace situations with enthusiasm, but now we have greater acceptance of life as it is, and enjoy waves of understanding with new transmissions of smooth energy.

> When chain owners separate themselves from their existing traumas, they become more like a Divine Spirit, able to permeate all mass and all energy.

Chapter 6

How to Read the SAF Chain Sequence:
The Basics

In this chapter:
- Chain Reaction of Energy
- The Sun and Its Significance
- Earth Patterns: Disease Patterns
- The Chain Sequence
- Chain Logic – Lead, Core, Anchor
- Present Time Versus in the Past
- Chain is a Trauma Entity
- Start to Finish
- Every Chain Has a Story to Tell
- Why Get a Major Complaint
- Dave's Case Study
- SAF Simplified Worksheet
- SAF Operative Chart 4

Now the reader will be able to apply the principles taught in this book. You have learned to correlate symptoms with physical structures of the body, and you have learned to relate to emotions and traumas, which sets a cycle of reaction in motion.

When creating the SAF method, Joe Scogna spoke to people in clinics, recorded and correlated their physical symptoms with emotional symptoms; he used computer matrices and statistical analysis to develop a body of equations. These equations led to the questionnaires that relate to our symptoms and identify a sequence that indicates the organ and gland systems that are not functioning perfectly. We can then follow the order of the sequences from the most acutely exhibiting confusions and behavioral patterns to lesser acute confusions and behavioral patterns.

The SAF system helps identify how to rectify the emotions and remedy the physical symptoms. *When the organ and gland systems are not functioning at 100%, they are talking to each other. This both ancient and future communication can be learned by us, making this method the Rosetta Stone for humans.*

The numerical chain has been given a great deal of mention thus far. At this point, the specifics of its creation and operation will be explained.

The SAF chain sequence is a particular sequence of numbers read from the left to the right, and from the right to the left. The greatest *effect* can be found on the left and the greatest *cause* is depicted on the right side of the chain. A numerical chain is a layered and stratified past history of the person, the chain owner. It shows us the present time (with the most highly stressed organ and gland systems) on the left side of the center of the chain, and the past time, where the energy is located, appears on the right.

In order to get an SAF chain sequence of numbers to work on with this book, go to www. LifeEnrgyResearch.com and on the menu click Questionnaire. Choose the Stress-120 for your questionnaire, login, type a complaint (something you want to work on) and begin.

Once finished with the questionnaire, enter your email address or a client key if you have one, and press submit. A summary of your results will be sent to you and your Practitioner, if available. You can use those results with this book.

Chain Reaction of Energy

As was previously discussed, the exact energy sequence from the sun, throughout the spaces around the sun, including the planet Earth, creates a specific chain reaction of energy that affects the organ and gland systems of a human being in a precise order; this is identified as the Secondary Sequence:

1. Thymus & Immune System (plus tonsils, adenoids, Peyer's patches, appendix)
2. Heart & Cardiovascular System
3. Colon & Elimination System
4. Stomach & Digestive System
5. Anterior Pituitary
6. Liver & Gallbladder
7. Lungs & Respiratory System
8. Sex Organs
9. Bones & Muscles
10. Thyroid (plus Veins & Arteries of the upper extremities)
11. Veins & Arteries of the Lower Extremities
12. Brain & Nervous System
13. Adrenal Glands
14. Mind

15. Hypothalamus & the Senses
16. Kidneys & Bladder
17/18. Endocrine System (M & F hormone systems, plus pineal, pituitary, thyroid, parathyroid, adrenal, pancreas, (F) ovaries and (M) testes.)
19. Skin
20. Pancreas & Solar Plexus
21. Posterior Pituitary
22. Parathyroid
23. Spleen
24. Lymph System & Electroplasmic Field

This rundown is a sequence or a chain itself. Each individual organ or gland system is linked to the next, similar to a chain of iron links.

The Sun and Its Significance

The energies of humankind and the energies of physical environmental natures around human beings co-exist in partnership. We create our own world while the sun and stars create the specific magnetic blueprint of the physical universe. Somewhere in between the two creations lie co-existence and harmony. As energies are moved from one system to the next in a complete harmonizing focus following the sun's blueprint, the energies of the genetic blueprint of each of us, as well as our mind, spirit, dreams, wishes, whims, and intentions, are programmed against the energies of the sun. The blueprint energies of the sun follow the sequential pattern of 1-24.

When a numerical chain is constructed by SAF techniques, it should not be in sequential order, such as #1-2-3-4-5-6-7, because this is the sun's sequential pattern. The sequence #7-8-9-10-11-12-13 belongs to the *sun* and not a human being. Human chains or numbers should be scrambled, such as #5-12-9-3-24-21-11. If our chain mimics the sun or goes into phase with the energy of the sun, this means that the sun is reclaiming our energies.

In all cases where the SAF Participant showed a numerical chain in the exact sequence of the sun's energy, he was already officially diagnosed by others as psychotic. In effect, there was no mind there; there was no spirit guiding the body. When the body is completely in a zombie-like condition, the numbers will read in a chain sequence such as #1-2-3-4-5-6-7, or #10-11-12-13-14-15, or #20-21-22-23-24.

When there is some entity - a Spirit, a Will, or a Desire overcoming the body's energies - then the numbers will be mixed;; they will be erratic, showing that organs are overheating in different patterns. Then the SAF Practitioner and the chain owner will have something to work on. This was found to be so in the years of working with patients at clinics.

Earth Patterns: Disease Patterns

In SAF, a chain is written as a universal numerical expression. Because numbers have absolutely no personality in themselves, and because numbers are merely a pressure gradation from 1 to infinity, we need to assign some importance to these number factors to cause them to be useful.

The SAF project has developed a vast information bank on the various patterns and sequences of numbers pitted against the organ systems due to the interaction and interposition of certain entities in the environment, such as foods, minerals, herbs, air, water, etc. This project has already catalogued several million sequences to allow the active SAF Participant to track or follow any effect that a trauma may have upon the human body.

For example, the diabetes entity has an SAF code number: #1-6-13-17/18-21, these numbers represent the organs and glands affected in this disease. The arthritis entity has a code number #1-9-22. An apple also has a code number: #5-11-13-21. A car has a code number, as does a bird and a dog. In short, any object, animal, vegetable, mineral, or artificially created material has been assigned SAF code numbers. This is an entire system, a science, and is the reason SAF works so well together to enhance our lives.

Trauma or Entity Types

The code numbers as above are developed when they are interconnected with the human system, and the trauma entities or energies (people, places and things) have a tendency to heat up certain organs. The whole purpose of the sun's radiant chain, that is, the numbers that affect the organs in their proper sequence, such as thymus, heart, colon, stomach, etc., is a gradation of hot to cold.

When a trauma entity intersects with the body, how many organs and glands will be heated up? How many organs are significant? The massive research that was compiled on the SAF project proves that the specific sequence of energy has been set forth to allow a person to realize the exact extent of radiational exposure to a human body.

Most often there are one or two organs affected, as is shown in this book. These are the Up-Links, the syndromes that you have read about already. When it occurs with two numbers, those organ or gland systems are trying to talk; they are trying to send a message to you. Tri-numeric expressions (three numbers) are more complex, followed by quadra-numeric and then penta-numeric. According to SAF principles, the highest expression of trauma that can exist is seven numbers, or a septa-numeric expression. This means seven organ and gland systems are affected in sequence.

Each SAF chain sequence possesses a story about the effect of traumas on the human being, the chain owner. SAF is the quintessential self awareness tool.

201

Each SAF chain sequence possesses a story about the effect of traumas on the human being, the chain owner. SAF is the *quintessential* self awareness tool. We learn to turn this numeric sentence into a grammatical one so the reading and deciphering is easier and makes more sense.

For example, when an SAF chain is produced with a #4 logged as the first number, it indicates that #4, the stomach, is the hottest area on the chain. Remember that two entities cannot occupy the same space at the same time, so when two entities, such as the stomach and some external toxin infesting the stomach tissues try to occupy the same space at the same time, a predictable reaction occurs - heat is produced.

As described earlier in this text, whenever an entity or energy gets lodged in the body, it will produce pain, heat, redness, and/or swelling. It really doesn't matter whether the redness or the swelling is existent, but it does matter if there is heat or pain present because this differentiates whether the trauma entity is energetically male or female. If you have heat or pressure in that location, then there is a male entity. If you have a spot of coldness, there is female energy, one that is drawing energy (cells, tissue, molecules) away from the body.

The whole trick of the SAF® program is to effectively translate the information in the chain sequence from a *numeric expression* into a *grammatical expression*. For this reason, the manner in which the chain is constructed causes a breakthrough in language between non-speaking entities.

The biggest breakthrough for the deaf to be able to communicate was sign language, and for the blind it was the development of the Braille system. Both systems helped those afflicted to communicate where previously silence had reigned supreme.

The SAF system is a similar breakthrough because it gives people the ability to communicate with and speak to their own past traumas and disease entities. When this is learned, you will understand more fully how SAF is *the* premiere translator, the Rosetta Stone for humans.

Its basic principle of operation is a system of hot and cold, but the chain links have specific rules and regulations that cause the existence of a particular sequence of words that must be grammatically correct to enable the SAF Participant and SAF Practitioner total understanding. When we learn to turn this numeric sentence into a grammatical one, the reading and deciphering is easier and makes more sense.

The Chain Sequence

There can be twelve numbers in a chain; we consider this a perfect chain. If using the Infrared device to create a sequence, it is reading the energy from the 12 pairs of cranial nerves emanating from the body and there will always be 12 numbers in the chain. We could say that all 12 cylinders are operational, that all recording tracks are being used. With the infrared, there is no way for the client to put their own personal *think* or protective defense mechanisms into the process.

With a Stress-120 Questionnaire creating the chain sequence, it may be shorter than twelve numbers, in which case it indicates that the recording tracks are smothered and the chain owner may be in a state of overwhelm. Or, several tracks may be squashed together and read as one, or they may be dissected and cut off from your reality. When we see a single number in a chain, this is a dis-reality coming from the imagination. If we see more than twelve numbers in a chain created by special questionnaire, such as 14, 15 or 16 numbers, it indicates that the chain owner is picking up recording tracks, or borrowing energy from another entity or another person and is using it as his or her own. This is why it is important *not* to have help filling out the questionnaire!

For this book and the reader who wants to find their chain of numbers, we suggest using the Stress 120 Questionnaire.

Technicians in the science of healing, which include doctors, massage therapists, acupuncturists, chiropractors, reflexologists, and those who spend their time interacting with others in a medical capacity, often have more than the twelve numbers in a chain derived from a questionnaire because they are picking up phantom recording tracks. These phantom recording tracks come from the frictional energy that produces a mirror image of a recording track. A practitioner of the healing arts, by touching a client, may have copied an experience of the person they touched. In such a chain, the SAF Practitioner is seeing a ghost. However, when running a program on such a Practitioner, we must pay attention to these *ghosts* because they do have some connection to the chain owner, in this case, the Practitioner, and this must be acknowledged.

This can also happen with those who practice distance healing. Even though they have not physically touched the person, they do enter their client's space, and it can affect the Practitioner as if they had physically touched.

You may also have phantom tracks if you are holding an infant or a pet when being evaluated to create a chain sequence. It is important that you be the one to complete the questionnaire because if you have help from someone else, a lover, parent, or good friend, then you may actually pick up some of their energies, their stories.

A simple chain of numbers can produce an almost incredible amount of information. You will never have the same chain twice because the numbers move across so many subject banks; each number from #1 to #24 (thymus to lymph) can have various meanings depending upon which subject bank is chosen. You may find that you have similar numbers but their patterns and location in the chain will differ. And the complaint, upon which the chain is based, will differ as well.

Each particular subject has a 1×10^{24} variations on each chain (there can be one octillion variant chains for each subject), and each number in each chain has 128 specific recording tracks involving various magnetic and electric energies. These 128 sensory channels are listed and explained in *Junk DNA: Unlocking the Hidden Secrets of Your DNA.*

The list is extensive; SAF® is a vast science. However, in this book, the reading of your chain will be more simplistic. Remember, the reading you are able to accomplish at first will be on an introductory level. Even so, it will be very effective.

Chain Logic
Lead – Core - Anchor

In a chain, the first number on the left is the *Lead* number, and the last number on the right is the *Anchor* number. The very center number (in a chain with an odd amount of numbers) or center two numbers (in an even number chain) is the *Core*. Comprehension of the Lead, Core, and Anchor numbers is all that is necessary for understanding the SAF program on this level.

Odd Numbered Chain:
    10 - 9 - 1 - 2 - **4** - 16 - 12 - 13 - **17/18**
    Lead   Core   Anchor

Even Numbered Chain:
    17/18 - 20 - 14 - 15 - **16 - 1** - 3 - 6 - 9 - **10**
    Lead   Core #s   Anchor

Present Time versus In the Past

The major differentiation between the two halves of the chain is that the left side of the Core is the hottest, occurring right now; the Lead may be considered acute. The numbers on the right side of center are the coolest, and happened in the past; the Anchor may indicate a chronic situation.

The Chain is a Trauma Entity

The chain is actually presenting a "slice of life" for us to examine and understand. You could conceivable do as many chains as there are slices of events in your life. Students of SAF have always been cautioned to be careful when working with these chains because they are full of energy; they are alive and viable for the chain owner. The specific sequence of organ degeneration from #1 to #24 ignites a particular pattern so that seeing numbers in these sequences stimulates a certain hailing frequency for other traumas. In other words, a person can call his *own* unconscious traumas forward with these sequences of numbers. For this reason, it is important to remember that while studying chain sequences, it is best to remain somewhat detached from the chains of other people.

Another word of caution: do not try to obtain several chains on yourself at once. Work on the first chain until you understand it and have gained more awareness about yourself and the SAF program.

> The SAF chain is actually presenting a "slice of life" for us to examine and understand. These chains are filled with energy; they are alive and viable for the chain owner.

Start to Finish

When you decide to complete a questionnaire and run a chain, do so with a definite intention to start the chain and a definite intention to complete it. When you commit to doing something, then do it the best that you can! These chains should never be run if you do not intend to fully complete what you start. If you start the chain and don't finish it, over time it may build extra electric/magnetic momentum, creating enough energy for the traumatic event to stay put for some time. In other words, our traumas can be stimulated. When this occurs, these are in the visible light spectrum and reside in the present reality. In essence, you will be re-living your trauma. The ideal scenario is for you to locate this trauma and identify its parts, releasing the electromagnetic charge. Once the charge is released, you will feel relief and will gain new understandings about yourself and your situation.

So again, caution is advised:

- Study these chains in a somewhat detached manner,
- Take and decipher one chain at a time, and
- Finish what you start.

Every Chain Has a Story to Tell

The chain and its factors have been fashioned after the grammatical sciences learned in elementary school through the college level. In this book we will pay attention to the lead, the core and the anchor numbers, as well as a few of the Up-Links listed in Chapter 5.

Remember sentence structure from your school days? Based on English language usage and thought processes, sentences contain a subject, an object and a verb. And so it is with the SAF chain structure. The subject of the sequence is the Core number; the Lead number is the object, or the result; and the Anchor number is the verb of the chain sentence.

The string of numbers is translated and read as a grammatical sentence. In effect, in every chain there is a story, a story about the SAF Participant, the chain owner. Some stories are extremely long, novel length, while others are short stories or just a few words long. It depends on the expertise of the SAF Practitioner in writing the chain biography, along with help from the SAF Participant.

If this is your first experience with SAF, you will most likely want to examine that particular upset that is plaguing you the most – we call this your distress, your major complaint. Because these trauma entities can't be destroyed by drugs or medicines, we must work out some arrangement or find out what the entity, energy, or trauma is attempting to tell us. Remember that there is no such thing as bad energy; there is only energy from experiences and events that get confused and mixed up. With the mechanisms and technology of SAF, we can de-confuse energy.

> *Note to the Reader: Even if you follow this book carefully, it is highly recommended that you work at first with a trained SAF Practitioner. Someone who is trained in SAF will know many of the nuances of chain sequence work and can also determine the ages of the traumatic events in your life and when a particular pattern first began. If you find that you start chain work and then do not finish it, please contact the Home Office so we can recommend a Practitioner who will be able to help you finish the chain.*

Why Choose a Major Complaint?

Starting with a major complaint is mandatory, or the chain biography is all for naught. We can just shoot in the dark and say this or that is the chain owner's problem, but we must always have a complaint or a distress for reference.

An SAF Participant must come forward and say, "I have a headache" or "I've got a ---problem with my children, or my significant other." The trouble must be logged in first. If the bits of information from the chain biography don't relate to the Participant's problem, the chain won't make sense. Besides, if "nothing is wrong," why spend the time trying to fix or understand "nothing"?

In the final analysis, starting with a major complaint is important because we are trying to teach the SAF® Participant (you) something about your traumatic events. We are trying to find the key that will unlock the mysteries of confusion. The challenge is there, but *you* are the main ingredient.

The complaint can include emotions, the environment, attitudes, symptoms, problems, upsets, disease, anything that you deem is getting in your way, or is bothering you; in short, a present day distress of *any* kind.

When you are ready to begin your own self awareness work, have that distress/major complaint in mind. Complete a Stress-120 Questionnaire at www.lifeenergyresearch.com and you will begin work on the *SAF Simplified* Worksheet and follow those directions on pages 215 to 217.

> "SAF Participants who have brought many entities and traumas into the light are magnificent."

How to Read the Chain

All numeric chains are turned into grammatical sentences based on English language usage. When we turn this numeric sentence into a grammatical one, the reading and deciphering is easier and makes more sense.

The Core indicates a timeless state, not affected by time whatsoever. A Core cannot be past, present, or even future; it is *now* and *never* at the same time.

The Core number is considered the Subject ("This chain is telling me about ----")

The left side (Lead number) indicates the present time.

The Lead number is considered the Object ("The core issue has led to or resulted in --------")

The right side (Anchor number) indicates the past. In the hands of an experienced SAF Practitioner, you can discover the dates, the first time this particular problem occurred.

The Anchor number is considered the Verb ("The energy of this chain is held in place by the emotion of ----.")

The numbers in between the Lead, the Core, and the Anchor are called transients, which act much like adverbs and adjectives in grammar usage. These are for more definitive programming.

By studying the SAF Operative Chart 4 (page 219), we can range back and forth from the organ to the condition to the emotion and will be able to read chains on an introductory level.

Significant Up-Links indicate sequences of energy, what SAF identifies as syndromes. These syndromes will have special meaning for the chain owner.

The CORE Number is the Subject

When reading a chain sentence, we start with the Core number; this is the subject of the sentence, what this chain is telling you. "This chain is telling me about --- -(my complaint) You may not be fully aware that you have your mind on the core situation because the chain is viewing the trauma state (the complaint), not your own state. However, in most cases, the SAF Participant will recognize the core condition and is amazed that the program is able to make these connections.

For your own chain: From the SAF Operative Chart 4 (page 219), find the organ or gland word that fits your number. Write this down where indicated on the Worksheet (page 215).

Reread the complete section in Chapter 5 that explains your core number (for example, if "10" then read Chapter 5-10.) Say to yourself, "This 'number' is the subject of my chain, it is telling me about -----."

Jot down notes on the SAF Worksheet (page 216), about whatever thoughts or any incident that comes to mind, as regards the word listed for that organ or gland system.

The LEAD Number is the Object (Effect)

When reading a chain sentence, the Lead is the present reality, the result, or the *effect* of the other connections in this chain sequence. The Lead number tells us what things are coming into being, what things are in the visible light spectrum.

The Lead number should match your major complaint, the symptom or the present day distress. It should be very visible and should be felt by you. The Lead number indicates that this symptom should be the hottest in your body and have the most pressure. If we follow the precepts of the forefathers of medicine, if enough calor (heat) is present, then a good deal of dolor (pain), rubor (redness) and tumor (swelling) will be evident. The more heat buildup on that particular system, the more the energy will expose itself and will cause you to have discomfort. This discomfort will cause you to complain, and so this is most likely your major complaint.

If you do not recognize the connection, this is an indication that your energies (perceptions) are deeply buried.

For your own chain: From the SAF Operative Chart 4 (page 219), find the condition/function listed for your lead number. Write this down where indicated on the Worksheet.

Re-read the condition section in Chapter 5 that explains your lead number. Say to yourself, "The core has led to or resulted in (condition/function word)."

Jot down notes on the SAF Worksheet about whatever thoughts or incidents that come to mind for you, as regards that condition/function word.

The ANCHOR Number is the Verb (Cause)

When reading the chain sentence, the Anchor is the verb, the action word, the how and why something was done. It is the item that exposes the invisible energies, which allow the subject (the Core) to create the object (the Lead). So the Anchor could be considered the ultimate physical *cause*.

This Anchor number holds the pieces of this trauma or event in place. It gives the trauma/event its power over you; this is the energy of the chain sequence. It is also often the most occluded, the most hidden, but with the SAF Operative words and following the sentence structure, you can uncover its mysteries and release the electromagnetic charge from this chain.

For your own chain: From the SAF Operative Chart 4 (page 219), find the emotion listed for your anchor number. Write this down where indicated on the Worksheet.

Re-read the emotion section in Chapter 5 that explains your anchor number.

Say to yourself: "This chain of numbers is held in place by the anchor, the (emotion word). Recall a time something happened that made you feel this (emotion word)."

Jot down notes on the SAF Worksheet about whatever thoughts or any incident that comes to mind for you, as regards that emotion word.

Significant Up-Links

Finding the Up-Links in your chain will give you additional information. An Up-Link is two or more numbers in succession that ascend in value, such as #2-10, #4-16, and #14-15-17/18. These are listed throughout the book (check the Index for Up-Links, pg. 245). These Up-Links indicate syndromes, or particular sequences of energy that will shed more light on your chain sequence. Note that all numbers and up links are not considered syndromes, only those listed.

Examples given above, plus their definitions and explanations are:

#2-10 = break up, separation, or loss; #4-16 = digestion is off; #14-15-17/18 = business troubles.

Dual Cause

For further chain work, note there is a dual causal action focused on the object (the result, the Lead number). It is the causal action of the subject (the Core) and the causal action of the verb (the Anchor).

As an example, in a scenario of building a house, the finished house is the object (Lead), the end result. The verb (the Anchor) is the action of the tools - the hammer strokes and nails that caused the house to be built. The subject (the Core) would be the Spirit, in this case, the carpenter wanting to create a house. So would we say that the hammer and nails built the house or the carpenter built the house? The carpenter did, but the hammer and nails were used. All three aspects are essential and work together to create the finished product.

We look to the Anchor number constantly to see *how* it was done, because by short circuiting these causal actions on the right (Anchor), a smart SAF Practitioner and/or active SAF Participant will take most of the energy (cause) away from a traumatic event by taking the tools. In the example we gave previously of building a house, if the nails are taken away from the trauma, it doesn't have nearly as much strength.

NOTE: If the Lead and Core words are addressed *only*, the present day distress/complaint may charge up and bother the SAF Participant more. By successfully handling the Anchor emotion, the trauma may be brought to the forefront, enabling the active Participant to see it, understand it, and be able to put it to rest *in the past*, where it belongs. After that, the effects of the trauma, (the present day complaint), diminish. Keep in mind that the Anchor emotion can be better seen and understood after working the Core and Lead words first.

Dave's Case Study

You have read a lot about traumas in this book. What are these? Are you sure we have to look at these again?

Yes, because the best way out is always to look and see, and to go through. It is essential, but it is also easier than it would have been back in the day. This is so because you have the SAF method and protocol to help you do this.

Take for example Dave, who attended a workshop and offered his chain so that I (Kathy) could read it for him. It was to be deciphered in front of the other attendees, and he said he wanted to proceed, so we did. He gave me his complaint and his chain sequence:

Complaint: "My life is a mess."

Chain: #22-13-20-2-1-8-10

I looked at the Core first. I didn't know Dave so I mentioned to everyone that we were to remember that these chains could be very personal.

"This chain is telling us about love, things being unsynchronized, or being denied love. Is this what is going on for you now?" I asked him.

"Yes," he said simply, with a puzzled look on his face.

So I followed through with the lead number. "This has resulted in anger. Is this true for you? Can you identify with this?"

"Yes!" Dave yelped. "This *is* true!"

The other seminar leader knew Dave and asked if he wanted to share with the group what was going on in his life.

Dave was blown away. He related that two months before, he had come home to find his house empty; his wife of 18 years had packed up all the furniture and moved out. He didn't understand; he was trying to deal with his *anger.*

The group gasped at this news. A discussion followed because the others in the group were not aware of this development in Dave's life.

I asked his age and then did a quick calculation. I looked at the Anchor, #10, and said, "This chain is held in place by an event in the past that made you anxious. It was something that happened about age seven or some time before that. Do you recall anything at that time? You felt anxious, as if there was no justice for you?"

Dave was quiet for about three seconds then blurted out, "I wanted the box of Sixty-Four Crayola Crayons for my birthday, and all I got was a box of eight!"

The group laughed loudly and some whispers were heard.

"I don't know why I just said that … did I remember it, it just came out!" Dave said a bit apologetically.

But I jumped in to stop the commotion, and said quickly, "Now, wait a minute. This was very important for Dave. Would that have made you, as a seven-year-old, feel anxious? Did things seem unjust to you?"

He was thoughtful and said, "Yes."

"How did that make you feel?"

Dave was fairly quick with his response. "I guess my mother thought I didn't deserve to have that big box of Sixty-Four Crayola Crayons."

I explained, "That incident gave you a code, a code to help you survive then, but it has set up a lifetime of knowing, deep down inside, that you are not deserving."

Dave immediately understood the message. "You're right. The code is: I won't get what I want in life because I'm not worthy. Not even worthy to have a good wife."

Then we looked at the Up-Links in this grammatical chain to find more information.

In the past, #1-8: = rejects creativity (no sixty-four crayons), and in the present time, #1-8 = rejects sex, apathy is his emotion regarding marriage.

Other Up-Links in this chain were in the past: #8-10= anxious about creativity (only eight crayons), and this is carried to the present time: #8-10 = spending time unwisely, Dave acknowledged that he had been busy ruminating about his situation and it was not fruitful; in fact, he said his constant ruminations were making it worse for him.

Other Up-Links in this chain were in the past: #13-20 = depression (no sixty-four crayons = loss) and this is carried into the present time as well: #13-20 = depression, loss of possessions, trauma to a place, loss of loved one, diminishing control.

Dave found it incredible that not receiving the large box of crayons for his birthday long ago could have set into motion this lifelong pattern of "not being worthy, not getting what I want in life. It isn't really about the crayons, it is about the internalized message."

Dave related further: "It seems almost silly now, to be griping about crayons, but back then, it *was* a big deal. So many of the things that have happened recently and throughout my entire life relate to *all* these numbers and to the past – It is *all* connected!"

The group understood the lessons, too. One, that traumas back in time mean something to the person who is trying to filter through his or her memories, and two, that the way to help is not to laugh or belittle the client. Accept what it is they say to you. SAF Practitioners work *with* chain owners to help them resolve old patterns that are still affecting them in the present time.

As you can see, it is important to be at peace with issues from the past.

That is one example of finding a hidden cause, accepting it, embracing it, and then being able to move forward in life.

These traumas can loom large, even seem *huge* back in time when we were much smaller, but today, seen in this new light, are not so bad. We are able to put these to rest *in the past* where they belong.

This is how Dave's chain reads: The emotion of the Anchor holds the energy of the chain in place. So it is important to focus on the emotion (anxiety) in order to release the energy of the chain.

Early childhood anxiety (#10) caused the feeling of being denied love (#2) and resulted in feelings of anger in the past and in the present time (#22).

Dave realized the code might have helped him back then, but not so in the present day situation. In this case, Dave understood that his anger in the past situation was the *cause*, the *before.*" That original anger toward his mother for not getting the box of Sixty-Four Crayola Crayons had influenced his entire life; it had been stimulated all along in his marriage, and especially in the present time with the end of his marriage. This present day situation was the *effect*.

Dave was able to put the *cause* to rest in the past, where it belonged, so that he could move ahead in his life with a new outlook.

An interesting side note: Before the workshop was over, the attendees of the workshop gave him a gift with much ceremony -- a box of Sixty-Four Crayola Crayons. The last contact I had with Dave he was dating again, and happier in his new and less-encumbered life. He stated he was actually looking forward to forming a better relationship with someone new.

> Use the above Case Study for help getting into your own thoughts and backward looking as part of your SAF session work.

SAF Simplified Worksheet

Note: this worksheet may be copied for additional SAF* chain sequence work.
Copyright © 2003-2019 by Kathy M. Scogna

Right now, you must think about the situation or that confusion of energy that is getting in your way, your major complaint, or present day distress.

Today's Date:

1. Write: My present day complaint is:

2. Go to www.lifeenergyresearch.com, sign in, and choose the Stress-120 Questionnaire.

3;. Type: Your major complaint and then click start.

4. Answer: the questions on the Stress-120 Questionnaire.

5. When you are finished, click the finish button. You will see a chain sequence of numbers on your screen. You may jot these down for use with this book, or, if you are a client and have a client KEY, type in this KEY where indicated so the data will go to your practitioner. If you would like the data to go to you, type in your email address and click submit. The Home Office will also get a copy of your chain information, in case you do want a practitioner. We would love to help you.

6. Write: your chain sequence here: _____
Following the above chain sequence, list your Lead number: _____
List your Core number(s): _____
List your Anchor number: _____

7. Use the SAF Operative Chart 4 (page 219) to find the correct words.
Following the above chain sequence, list your Lead word (condition/function): _____
List your Core word(s) (organ or gland system): _____

List your Anchor word (emotion): _____

8. Re-read again: How to Read the Chain, page 207.

9. Read Dave's Case Study on page 211 for more information on how this is done.

10. **The Core is addressed first**. Re-read: the complete section in Chapter 5 that relates to your Core number(s).
"This chain is telling me about -------."
If there are two numbers in the Core, take the number on the right first, then the number on the left.
Ask: Does this make sense to me? How does (Core word) relate to or cause (present day distress/complaint)?

11. Think of a recent incident when this occurred, or relate this to the present day distress or complaint. Write this down.

12. **The Lead number is addressed second**. Re-read the section in Chapter 5 that relates to the condition/function of your Lead number.
Ask: The Core has led to or resulted in ------. Does this make sense in my life? Does the Lead word or emotion relate to or cause my present day distress/complaint?

13. Think of a recent incident when this occurred or relate this to the present day distress or complaint. Write this down. _____

14. **The Anchor is addressed last**. Re-read the section in Chapter 5 on the emotion of your Anchor word.
Ask: This Anchor word is the energy of the chain. It is holding the chain in place. How does (Anchor emotion word) relate to, or cause my Core, or my present day situation or distress?

15. Think of a recent incident when the emotion word occurred or relate this to your present day life. Explain how this makes sense to you. Write this down. _____

16. Once you have found a recent time when this occurred, think backward to an earlier time when you had trouble with this same or similar emotions. You might be surprised to suddenly remember there was an earlier time when these same emotions occurred. Is there a pattern?
Make a note of this earlier incident and how you feel now:

17. Using your above chain sequence, use the Index of Up-Links to find any for your chain.

18. Write the Up-Links in your chain sequence here:

Up-link_____ Description _____ Up-Link: _____ Description _____

Up-link_____ Description _____ Up-Link: _____ Description _____

Which of these make the most sense to you? (Write this down)

_____

Congratulations! You have just learned the rudiments on how to create and read an SAF chain sequence. If there were any problems, go back and make sure you finished each step in order.

19. Now, write down what you have learned about yourself, your major complaint, and the connections you have made through time. _____
_____
_____
_____

Once you understand the steps of making a grammatical sentence out of the SAF numbers and the numerical sentence, the process gets easier. Then, when you start making Cause and Effect connections between your past and your present mental, physical, emotional, and spiritual state, your energy will increase.

If the chain sequence work was or feels to be complete, you may stop here or continue with another chain sequence. Use a different major complaint or distress, and if any confusion or emotion came up in your last SAF "thinking backward" session, use the new one to gain more depth.

SAF Operative Chart 4

SAF	Condition/Function	Organ	Emotion
#	LEAD	CORE	ANCHOR
1	Protection	Thymus/Immune	Aggression
2	Synchronization	Heart/Cardiovascular	Love
3	Detoxify	Colon/Elimination	Hate
4	Digestion	Stomach/Digestion	Happy
5	Coordinate	Anterior Pituitary	Observant
6	Transmutation	Liver/Gallbladder	Sadness
7	Vaporization	Lungs/Respiration	Monotony
8	Reproduction	Sex Organs	Apathy
9	Locomotion	Bones & Muscles	Pain
10	Metabolization	Thyroid	Anxiety
11	Circulation	Veins & Arteries	Resentment
12	Electrification	Brain/Nervous System	Nervousness
13	Capacitance	Adrenals	Courage
14	Analyzation	Mind	Wonder
15	Evaluation	Hypothalamus/Senses	Attention
16	Filtration	Kidneys	Fear
17/18	Equalize	Endocrine	Conservative
19	Demarcation	Skin	Boredom
20	Location	Pancreas/Solar Plexus	Laughter
21	Hydrolyze	Posterior Pituitary	Grief
22	Experience	Parathyroid	Anger
23	Rejection	Spleen	Antagonize
24	Acceptance	Lymph & EPF	Enthusiasm

SAF Operative Chart 4: this is how to operate in the language of SAF.
This is a shorter version of the Endocrine Sense Channels Chart found in
Junk DNA: Unlocking the Hidden Secrets of Your DNA.

Copyright © 2003-2019 by Kathy M. Scogna, All rights reserved.

Acknowledgments and Credits:

Special thanks to Nic Scogna for his painting "The Sun, Key 19" which graces the cover of this book. Nic has been a tireless supporter and promoter, see www.kathyscogna.com.

And very special thanks goes to Jezra Lickter for making our presence known on the Internet since 1999, (www.scogna.com) and for first presenting the Life Energy Research computing system and the SAF Interpretations to a worldwide audience: www.LifeEnergyResearch.com

Don't you love the new look of our website? Thanks go to Johnathan Evans for his excellent web work this year!

Thanks to Joshua Lickter for his help typing, to Kalli Scogna for her typing and editing, and to Jason Scogna for his encouragement and for being here. Each one of my five children has offered me love and support for which I am most grateful.

A special note of thanks to the many SAF practitioners of various disciplines, near and far, past and present, who have infused this work with their energy. It is they who have helped to keep this work alive.

Thanks to Nancy B. Porter, an excellent and dedicated SAF Practitioner, for her encouragement and her many helpful editing ideas, and for always having my back.

Thanks also to SAF Practitioner, Jim Manegold, for his dedication, guidance, and clarity. Jim helps me to keep on track.

This book would not look this good or read this well if not for the editing efforts of Kathleen Ward, editor extraordinaire! Thanks, Kathy.

For the production of this book at Balboa Press, special thanks to Louise Hay of Hay House Publishing for her ideas and methods of helping others. Louise has transformed so many lives through her outreach and teachings, and her companies, Hay House and Balboa Press. These are currently passing on her great knowledge of how to publish, all aspects of marketing, sales, and presentations, and how to do this expeditiously and efficiently. To Tina Colbert at Hay House and Balboa Press for reaching out to me with her encouragement, and to Pia Jameson at Balboa Press for her valuable help and assistance, and to the production team of Sam Clarke, May Emerson and Dee Garner for their help with the design formatting and helping to keep me on target for the publication of *SAF Simplified!*

References and Further Reading
Scogna-authored books & training:

Junk DNA: Unlocking the Hidden Secrets of Your DNA by Joseph & Kathy Scogna (2014) Life Energy Publications. Essential reading, a foundation book for SAF work! This book contains the non-coded DNA (invisible in the lab) that makes up 98% of our DNA. Discover the 128 Sense Channels (perceptions) and the 16 Steps encrypted in human DNA since the beginning of Time.

Required for Level 2 Training.

Light, Dark: the Neuron and the Axon by Joseph & Kathy Scogna (2015) Life Energy Publications. This book allows the reader entrance into another dimension of subtle energy levels, the mysterious, invisible human nervous system.

Required for Level 2 Training.

Nutrionics: Introduction to Elemental Pairs by Joseph & Kathy Scogna (2015) Life Energy Publications. Presents 11 pairs of elements. Truths from the ancient world of elements and alchemy, combined with the similars of the healing art of homeopathy, and then infused with the energetics of quantum physics (Light and Energy).

Required for Level 1 Training.

Project Isis: Fundamentals of Human Electricity by Joseph & Kathy M. Scogna. (2015) Life Energy Publications. We are electrical beings, and so it makes sense to describe our human system with electrical terminology (Voltage, Ohms, and Amperes). Discover the 12 Axioms of human energy, the effects of mass—energy imbalance, how and why we create our mental image pictures, and how these are stored for our use.

Required for Level 2 Training.

The Promethion: A Comprehensive Study of the Principles of Life Energy by Joseph & Kathy Scogna (2003) Life Energy Publications. All elements are paired; 64 electric pressure levels. From ancient philosophies and modern physics, Scogna presents a view of how the human body is magnificently balanced by cosmic and atomic energies working harmoniously. With the history and personality of the elements, Joseph reunites physical chemistry with spiritual alchemy. This is a foundational book for SAF understandings.

Required for Level 2 Training.

The SAF Infrared Manual by Kathy Scogna (2014) Life Energy Publications. This is the book of choice for more information on using Infrared to create an SAF chain sequence rapidly, and for the complete rundown of the Interpretations and Remedy suggestions available with SAF Online. Client and Practitioner anecdotes, case studies, and the race horse story make this a fascinating and very useful book!

Required for Level 1 Training.

The Threat of the Poison Reign: A Treatise on Electromagnetic Pollution by Kathy & Joseph Scogna (2016) Life Energy Publications. Contains information on the types of radiation and electronic smog being pushed our way, 24/7. We do repeat our patterns! Ancient Sanskrit poem describes nuclear wars in the deep past as archeologists find ancient radioactive skeletons, all of which add to the mystery. The SAF-120 Questionnaire in the book is an introduction to the SAF method of self awareness. The Radiation Cocktail of helpful nutrients and other detoxification methods are presented.

Required for Level 2 Training.

Training in the SAF Method

We live in an increasingly toxic world and so we really do need the SAF method to help us make sense of our world and to see our way through it. Our training doors are open to all readers of this book who want to know more. Growth Through Self-Knowledge

SAF would be excellent for those who want to become enlightened on a personal level for his or her own self, to rediscover the entanglements that have occurred in life and to realize ways to lessen the impact of these early events. SAF would work well as a healing component for families, for family self-care, and SAF could be an adjunct to various alternative healing practices, such as addictions or other counseling, acupuncture, herbal, standard or homeopathic medicine. Or you could create a career in and of itself with the tools we offer you in this innovative method for increasing our self-awareness and lessening our past disruptions.

SAF Road Map Level 1 Training $1000 USD

This course will give the practitioner a jump start in understanding the SAF method. It includes 6 books, 5 SAF sessions with a certified SAF practitioner, and 3 free months with SAF Online. Go to the website: www.LifeEnergyResearch.com

6 books:

1. SAF Simplified
2. Nutrionics
3. SAF Flashcards
4. The SAF Infrared Manual
5. The Numbers of SAF

The 6ᵗʰ book, the SAF Road Map Workbook and Checksheet is available when the course is purchased.

These 6 books can and will be referred to often. If you purchase the 5 books listed above ahead of time, we will deduct $100 from the cost of the course.

The SAF Road Map Training includes **5 sessions** with a certified SAF Practitioner so that you, the student, can work on your own issues. This way, you will have a good and wholesome idea how effective SAF is and how well it will work for your clients and patients. (Valued at $500 USD)

You will also have **3 free months of SAF Online** so that you can learn about and use the Interpretations and the Remedies provided. Based on the numbers in the chain sequence, these Interpretations and Remedies are client-specific. (Valued at $250 USD)

The course is completed at your own pace in your own place, but it is supervised and tested. At the end of the training, you will have a good working knowledge of SAF and the background for it, and you will be able to use it very effectively with your patients and clients. You can expect much appreciation for how you are helping them!

We would love to welcome you to the world of SAF and direct your studies in this enriching and empowering way to help people understand the emotional events they've had in life. And to help them move beyond that place and leave the Cause behind, *in the past*, where it belongs.

Go to: www.lifeenergyresearch.com to see and order books & training

About the Authors

JOSEPH R. SCOGNA, JR. was at heart a nutritional researcher, concerned with the amount of radiation and radiant energies accosting humankind on a daily basis.

What were these energies? How are we being affected? And more importantly, what can we do about these errant frequencies? This became his quest.

Joe wanted to understand Einstein, so he studied what Einstein studied regarding classical radiation. Scogna came to understand the principles of Light and Energy, as these were known in past centuries, and as we see today in quantum physics and religious philosophies. He developed his own brand of self awareness evaluations based on the organ and gland systems

Joseph R. Scogna, Jr., 1984

and mathematical probability. With all the assaults on our being (body, mind, emotions, and spirit) which he explained in his writings as radiation and radiant energies, the various emotions and frequencies radiating toward us, he saw the action of homeopathic remedies as *the great anti-radiation.* This action happens because the products are so highly diluted that what remains are electrical messages. The human body, an electrical powerhouse, is touched by the message and understands it. The body, in its DNA-RNA structures, takes its cue from the message and is infused with the Intention, the Thought, and the Desire to achieve balance.

Joe was a prolific writer, a man on a mission to accomplish all he could in a short span of time. His work encompasses the darkest challenges we face, but also the hope and methods necessary for our transformation.

KATHY M. SCOGNA and Joe married in 1975. Side by side, Kathy typed, edited, helped practitioners at seminars, produced ads, wrote books, and the company magazine, *The Life Energy Monitor.* After Joe's death in 1989, she focused on her first job, that of raising her five children. During that time, she penned six history books, 2 screenplays, and served on the boards of historical societies. She received awards from the Pennsylvania Historical and Museum Commission and was named a Penn Ambassador by the Pennsylvania State Legislature.

The reconstruction of Joe's Life Energy work and the SAF method began in 1999 when the first web sites were created by her son, Jezra. A later website, www.kathyscogna.com, was completed by her son, Nic.

Kathy has infused Joe's work with new life and vitality. She has overseen the upgrading of the books and manuscripts, and has updated the computing programs into a dynamic, very usable online service that incorporates questionnaires and infrared for input. As a result, there has been a rebirth of Joe's innovative ideas in energetic healing.

"It does seem that now people are beginning to understand what Joe was teaching. The present day language has caught up to his verbiage; however, there is still no one out there who has anything like SAF. It is client-specific, and is outstanding for helping us to achieve balance and harmony," said Kathy at a recent workshop.

Practitioners worldwide now have access to the online system, with holistic interpretations and recommendations of herbal and homeopathic remedies, colors, business solutions, vitamins, juices, Bach flowers, self sabotage emotion hazards, and the ages of traumatic events for the emotional release work of SAF.

While Kathy serves as Director, each of her children has a hand in the operation, from converting typing into computer format, reformatting books and manuscripts, website implementation, book covers and other illustrations, training events, workshops, and promotion.

This incredible legacy is timeless and timely, and now reaches a new generation of practitioners and students alike.

Visit us! www.lifeenergyresearch.com

Kathy M. Scogna, 2015

Quotes by Practitioners and Others Familiar with SAF

"I love SAF because it gets right to the heart of the matter, or the spleen, or the colon. Using the Infrared and the Questionnaires is simple and reliable. Everyone who processes with SAF is blown away and wants to know, "How could it know that about *me*?"

-- Nancy Porter LISW, DN, SAF Practitioner, Iowa

"We all need to do a physical detox, but let's not forget the mental and emotional detox! SAF is the perfect tool for self awareness. When we are aware of our impeding issues, we are able to live in the present time, because we learn how our perceptions as children are not working for us anymore. Once we can find our impeding issues and we learn to deal with them differently, this allows us to operate in a higher state, and when freed of the chains of our *own* judgment, we are able to expand our awareness even farther."

--James Manegold, SAF Practitioner, Pennsylvania

"The insights and connections continue to astound me even after years of seeing SAF work. Following the numerical pattern of a client's chain sequence, combined with client history, dialog, and experience unravels years of stress from the body, mind, and spirit. We can use this incredible technology to gain new awareness and educate ourselves on how to see our own light and untapped potential, and help others to do the same."

--Sandy Aquila, Omaha Healing Arts Center, Nebraska
Om Aha … The city that starts with a mantra and ends in Enlightenment!

"This book gives an excellent explanation of how, why, and what numbers are assigned to each organ/gland and the emotions that are involved. Once a sequence of numbers is created, the

229

emotions associated with each organ/gland can direct us back to past traumas and emotions. The blockage of electrical energies to these organs that were affected by an event in our lives still carry the radiation (stress) caused by that event. We can determine what organs were affected, the time period in which they were affected and face the event that caused the trauma, releasing us from that trauma's hold on us.

-Nancy Harrington, SAF Practitioner, Florida

"Joe Scogna's use of Infrared to catalog the venting sites of the nervous system is a monumental leap forward in the evaluation of human physiology, psychology, and spirituality. This brilliant researcher, with a mind of the 21st Century and way beyond that, has given us a dynamic new dimension, a unified approach to our holistic health status - past, present, and future.

In the years to come, the application of SAF® and Infrared technology will be one of the most wonderful blessings to mankind."

--Dr John Abdo, ND, PhD,
Dayspring International, San Antonio, TX

"There is no doubt that my patients' physical health improves exponentially faster when I add the SAF to their treatment protocol. I am constantly in awe of the physical breakthroughs my patients make from the SAF insights."

– Dr. Yisroal Yaffa, MD. Israel

"With the latest Infrared device, the original breakthrough technology of Joe Scogna has been brought into use again! Now I can collect chain data at expos, shows, and with clients at appointments. The information can be entered on my phone and I can give lead, core, and anchor information on the spot! The in-depth sessions that follow are so very enlightening and helpful to them, and they don't have to fill out a questionnaire."

-- Nicholas Scogna, SAF Practitioner, Pennsylvania

"I use both SAF questionnaires and the Infrared. Amazing! With the questionnaires, we have the patient's point of view; however, English is the 2nd or 3rd language for my patients, so I use the

Infrared more often. It is an interesting tool – scans on babies and those who cannot talk have been very impressive!"

--Dr, Jim Eerebout, N.MD.MA.OMD, Europe

"I have known about SAF for a long time and used it for myself through a practitioner friend. I was so impressed with the program that I decided to become an SAF Practitioner myself. For certification in Level I, I worked on my family and friends and they were really surprised at its accuracy. When I decided to become certified in Level 2, I felt I needed a larger audience, which led me to a Colorado prison. Once I sent the results back to the men I was working with, I was astonished at the comments from them. They were relieved to find out that there were reasons for their behaviors, and that they "were fixable" and had not been "born bad." SAF gave them hope beyond simple counseling and Bible study. SAF gave them solutions for their emotional and physical problems and they found new ways to deal with these.

SAF® is an excellent tool that gives insight into the body and emotional causes behind events that have happened in life because it uncovers many hidden feelings. It simply works!"

--Pam Wojahn, SAF Practitioner, Colorado

"SAF is quick and easy to use, an extremely advanced technology for personal change and for helping others. The Up-Links in the Interpretations create a comprehensive picture of the ages when traumas occurred, where in the body they are located, and how they are impacting our lives in the present."

--Brian Kilian, SAF Practitioner, Tennessee

"SAF has helped me focus on what I want to create for me, and now I'm doing the same for others. In one case, as my client counted the years back to the trauma, she yelped, "No freaking way! I thought I was past all that!" I explained that sometimes we leave an emotional component behind, to be realigned. How gratifying; she was finally able to put another piece to rest. I work with SAF almost every day to find Homeopathic remedies and Bach Flowers for my clients."

--Kathy Jerore, ND, SAF Practitioner, Michigan

"The more I learn of Quantum Touch, the work of Walter Russell and all the Light, Sound, and Energy therapies, the more I appreciate how brilliant Joe Scogna was, because I see such a synthesis of ideas. This book is a gem."

--Lyn Doole, www.lilystlight.com.au Australia
Vice-President, International Light Association

"Much like Tesla, some spirits arrive well before their time. Joe Scogna pulled back the veil of Time to show us a new understanding about ourselves and instill the courage to embrace what is needed to heal in these challenging times. When we walk forth with this understanding, then we can truly help others in the healing arts. Each one of us is a healer. Remember? Thanks for keeping the treasure of his knowledge alive and available!"

–Bruce L. Erickson,
President, MotherEarth Media, Santa Barbara, CA

"People on the SAF program are understanding and realizing their potential. Doing the program has helped my clients 1) to be more aware of how their thoughts are affecting their health, 2) to understand how the environment and other people affect them, and 3) to see new opportunities and new ways to create happier lives for themselves.

- Dr. Zenia Richler,
Academy of Bio-Energetics, Woodstock, GA

"As an SAF practitioner, I've been able to get to many causal factors with my patients in areas where nutritional and other protocols should have worked but didn't. Giving clients conscious awareness of aberrant behavior patterns helped them resolve health issues that have been untreatable for years. I've seen how SAF was able to break down both physical and emotional barriers held in place by the client unconsciously."

--Dr. Chris Morris, ND

A Winning Hand – 4 Aces and a Wild Card

1. **Trace** it. The chain of numbers tells of the emotions and ages.
2. **Face** it. Acknowledge the trauma and the code.
3. **Embrace** it. I'm grateful for the trauma: it has taught me something.
4. **Replace** it. It worked then, but not now. Time for new codes!
5. **Erase** it. Delete old codes; these no longer influence me.

This wild card wins the hand!

--James Manegold, SAF Practitioner, Pennsylvania

Index

Index of Numbers & Up-Links

Printed in the United States
By Bookmasters